SELLING

C000257078

R   ore
radio in its social and political context. In doing so, he challenges
many of the myths which have grown up around the phenomenon. The particular story is framed within an examination
of   developments in Br   America: the BBC's
initial   to embrace pop culture and the Corporation's
eve   of pirate programming into its own pop
se

Selling   also meticulously unearths evidence from
the   uding   interviews with those
d   radio material from the period.
T   relationship between the illicit   ed
b   world of pop culture   will appeal not
o   communications, mass media and cultural
st   of those working in   broadc   ory,
p

Robert   ars   broadcasting experience includes BBC local
r   and Northampton. He has also   ted
a   currently
L   Performing Arts
a

Author	Shelf Number
CHAPMAN, Robert	306.4

E.58.

Selling the Sixties

THE PIRATES AND POP MUSIC RADIO

ROBERT CHAPMAN

London and New York

First published 1992
by Routledge
11 New Fetter Lane, London EC4P 4EE

Simultaneously published in the USA and Canada
by Routledge
a division of Routledge, Chapman and Hall, Inc.
29 West 35th Street, New York, NY 10001

© 1992 Robert Chapman

Typeset in 10 on 12 point Palatino by
Falcon Typographic Art Ltd, Edinburgh
Printed in Great Britain by
Redwood Press Ltd, Melksham, Wiltshire

British Library Cataloguing in Publication Data
Chapman, Robert
Selling the sixties: The pirates and pop music radio.
I. Title
306.4

Library of Congress Cataloging in Publication Data
Also available.

ISBN 0–415–07817–2
ISBN 0–415–07970–5 (pbk)

For Caroline

Contents

Acknowledgements

As *Selling the Sixties* began life in January 1987 as a Master's degree thesis it seems appropriate firstly to express gratitude to Graham Murdock, at that time Research Fellow at the University of Leicester's Centre for Mass Communications Research, for acting as my tutor, for introducing me to much useful research material, tempering a little (just a little) my obsessive hostility towards the existing literature on pirate radio, and helping fashion a readable thesis out of a typically unwieldy first draft. Simon Frith, as external assessor, offered both empathy and constructive criticism, and commissioned the abridged earlier draft of Chapter 3, which first appeared in *Popular Music* (vol. 9, no. 2) in April 1990. Claire L'Enfant set into motion the initial publishing interest while at Unwin Hyman. Sarah Dann brought the project to fruition with HarperCollins and contributed much appreciated editing to early drafts. Dr Richard Barbrook of the Centre for Communication and Information Studies at the Polytechnic of Central London, also made a detailed analysis of early drafts and a valuable contribution to the book's overall structure and emphasis.

I wish to thank all those who consented to be interviewed, several of whom had never spoken publicly on the subject of pirate radio before. Fewer still had ever previously had their comments framed in such an analytical context. Interviews were carried out with the following between February 1987 and November 1990:

In alphabetical order: Mike Ahern (disc jockey, Radio Caroline, BBC Radio One); Ted Allbeury (Managing Director, Radio 390, Radio 355); David Allan (disc jockey, Radio 390, Radio 355, BBC Radio Two); Andy Archer (disc jockey, Radio City, Radio Caroline, BBC Radio One); Tim Blackmore (production assistant, BBC Light Programme; producer, BBC Radio One); Edward Cole (disc jockey, Radio 390); Tim Davis (music publisher); Simon Dee (disc jockey, Radio Caroline, BBC Light

Programme and Radio One); Tom Edwards (disc jockey, Radio City, Radio Caroline, BBC Radio One and Two); Tony Hall (disc jockey, Radio Luxembourg and BBC Light Programme; Head of Artists and Repertoire (A & R), Decca Records); Tom Lodge (disc jockey, Radio Caroline, BBC Radio One); Steve Merike (disc jockey, Radio Scotland, Radio Caroline, BBC Radio One); Richard Palmer (disc jockey, Radio Essex, BBMS); Michael Parkin (Advertising Manager, Radio Caroline); John Peel (disc jockey, Radio London, BBC Radio One); John Ridley (disc jockey and Sales Director, Radio Atlanta; Advertising Manager, Radio 390); Keith Skues (disc jockey, British Forces Broadcasting Service (BFBS), Radio Caroline, Radio London, BBC Radio One); David Symonds (disc jockey, BBC Light Programme and Radio One); Johnnie Walker (disc jockey, Radio England, Radio Caroline, BBC Radio One); John Walters (producer, BBC Radio One); Teddy Warrick (producer and programme organizer, BBC Light Programme and Radio One); Alan West (disc jockey, Radio London, Radio 355, Radio 390, Radio 270).

Given the subject matter of this study, clandestine and unauthorized broadcasting, it is not surprising that occasionally interviewees requested anonymity. Where necessary comments offered 'off the record' have been incorporated unattributed into the text. Similarly it is a reflection on the continued sensitivity of much of this book's content that four interviewees – a disc jockey, a producer, a record plugger, and an employee of one pirate station's administrative staff – requested complete anonymity. This request has been honoured.

Interviews ranged in length from 30 to 45 minute 'one offs' to in-depth discussions lasting several hours, and follow-ups spanning several months. I found the majority of interviewees only too glad to be of further assistance when needed and would like formally to thank everyone contacted for their time and patience. Additional thanks go to Tim Blackmore, Edward Cole, Kevin Howlett, Michael Parkin, and Teddy Warrick for donating press cuttings, an abundance of memoranda, and various other valuable documentation relevant to the period. I am particularly grateful to those who took the time to go beyond the well-worn anecdotes and into more considered evaluation of the offshore radio phenomenon.

There are inevitably themes which remain underdeveloped

here, in particular the technological argument in its broadest sense, and also the BBC's relationship with the various factions of the entertainments industry. Even the conclusion of this analysis was to some extent dictated by quantitive considerations brought about by the sheer weight of material amassed in dealing with the 1960s. I had originally rather naïvely envisaged being able to cover offshore radio's second generation of activity off the Dutch coast (1970–4), the origins of Independent Local Radio in Britain, and even a case-study of Radio Caroline; this was celebrating 25 years of uneasy existence while I was writing this book, aware of its probable demise by the time of publication. These themes will be covered in a second volume. Richard Palmer (Radio Caroline), Andy Archer (Radio Northsea International, Radio Caroline), Alan West (Radio Northsea International), and Steve Merike (Radio Northsea International), all provided valuable information in addition to that acknowledged in the main text, based on their continued involvement with offshore radio during the 1970s, as did Norman Barrington (Radio Caroline), Dave Rogers (Radio Northsea International, Radio Atlantis), and Ian Anderson (Radio Geronimo, Radio Caroline, Radio Northsea International). Interviews with several others on the above list also went beyond the scope and chronology of the original study and provided much usable material for further analysis.

The central question of what the pirate stations actually sounded like was addressed by recourse to my own archive of pop radio broadcasts – comprising some 1,000 recordings, of over 10,000 hours of material, ranging in length from 5 minute extracts to entire 12 to 14 hour segments of uninterrupted station output. This, I learned as I researched, is far more extensive than anything either the National Sound Archive or the BBC possesses in the area of pop music and pop culture, and proved invaluable in providing much of the factual detail of this analysis. A people's history sub-text runs constantly though unobtrusively throughout *Selling the Sixties*, and I would suggest that these hitherto unexamined primary sources are of immense significance. Existing literature on the period is pitifully scant, and fresh insight on the offshore era even rarer.

With this in mind I would like to thank Jean Knight for making available to me the personal tape archive, diaries, telephone transcripts, videos, and collected interviews of the late Roland C. Pearson, former editor of *Monitor* magazine. Chris Elliot of PAMS UK and Hans Knot of *Freewave* magazine in Holland loaned assorted Radio London files, memos, and interviews. Monni Aldous made available nearly 40 hours' worth of rare tape recordings of John Peel's 'Perfumed Garden' programme. Additional thanks to Graham Bunce, Paul Coates, Andrew Emmerson, Peter Lenton, and Andy Pell who all provided valuable tape material, and other related documentation. Tommy Rivers, who was able to complete his own Master's degree on American pop radio for the University of Minnesota, while in the employ of the 1980s pop pirate Laser 558, loaned much useful material concerning the development of format radio in the USA.

I spent far more of the third summer of love in front of a green screen than I would have wished and would therefore like to conclude by thanking Caroline Julyan for being a soul mate, for tolerance when I rambled on about ships and forts long into the night, and for endless instant *karma*.

Robert Chapman

CHAPTER 1

Selling the ether

It is a long way from the docile charm of 'How much is that doggy in the window?' to the moody intensity of 'Heartbreak Hotel'; while BBC Radio in the mid-1950s might have been able to accommodate the polite sentimentality of the former on its light music service it was just not prepared for the apparent quantum leap made possible by the emergence of rock and roll. Rock and roll's evolution may have been a gradual one, a slowly fermenting fusion of white country and hill-billy music and black rhythm and blues which brewed up during the postwar years, but to the BBC this raucous cultural hybrid came from nowhere. The institutional responses which greeted it ranged from bemused indifference to outright hostility. BBC policy makers continued to go about their cultural missionary work much as they always had done, selectively retrieving a folk tradition here, acting as a kindly public service benefactor there, bestowing sponsorship upon those deemed worthy of official approval. As a youth club of the airwaves the Light Programme could embrace trad jazz and skiffle readily enough, as these satisfied existing cultural criteria, while on the Home Service or the Third Programme the music could be transformed into a series of genre options, classified, made respectable, appreciated rather than enjoyed. Such outlets were also a convenient refuge for all the carefully vetted risqué and contentious songs to which the BBC permitted only restricted airplay.[1] The trad versus modernist debate could be academically indulged, while skiffle, by self-consciously alluding to its do-it-yourself ethic (as if modern folk forms were an extension of some sort of Duke of Edinburgh award scheme) could be accorded limited patronage.

The BBC approached the youth phenomenon anthropologically, as species. The newly located adolescent subculture was

1

meticulously combed for traces of a moral malaise, scorned for its tribal wants and needs, and decried, especially in the case of the Teddy boy, for its anti-social behaviour (in or out of national service captivity). Its totems were denigrated, its icons mocked, youth's postwar existence and identity were solemnly conceded but never celebrated. Rock and roll, with its racially mixed parentage, patented sneer, dumb insolence, rapid turnover of product, and built-in obsolescence was deemed to be inappropriate to the public service pursuit of the great and the good. When the first rock and roll records began to arrive at the BBC the common consensus within the gramophone department was that while these cultural artefacts might be aired occasionally there would surely never be entire programmes devoted to them.

Rock and roll, although not wholeheartedly embraced, was at least played on Radio Luxembourg, certainly more regularly than on the BBC. Here Elvis Presley, Little Richard, and Bill Haley coexisted in the schedules alongside the Al Martinos, Harry Belafontes, and Mario Lanzas, all equal under the auspices of commerce. But by the late 1950s the major record companies (EMI, Pye, Decca, and Philips) were dictating the station's programming policy, buying up all existing airtime in slots ranging in duration from 15 minutes to one hour. By playing only tantalizing extracts it was possible to cram as many as 14 records into one quarter-hour programme. Luxembourg's overriding purpose was to serve as a promotional vehicle for the top record companies. In this capacity Luxembourg was fulfilling its function perfectly adequately, but its role was limited to just that: a shop window for the industry's goods.

In order to see how the state and commercial sectors came to develop the particular strategies that they did when attempting to administer and distribute one of the major cultural phenomena of the twentieth century – one which specifically relied on the channels of mass communication for its sustenance – it is necessary to sketch a route back to the beginning of sound broadcasting, and briefly examine radio's complex variety of technological, organizational, cultural, and political imperatives.

2

The BBC model of promotion

The first committee inquiry into the workings of the BBC included the statement, 'We attach great importance to the maintenance of a high standard of broadcast programmes, with continuous efforts to secure improvement, and we think that advertisements would lower the standard';[2] a situation was already developing where commercial radio funded by advertising, and public service broadcasting funded by the licence fee, were being presented as incompatible competing interests. The concept of advertising became synonymous with 'slot' promotions for products, thus obscuring all other forms of selling. As well as establishing the licence fee system as the major method by which the state monopoly could be self-supporting the Sykes Committee actually recommended some form of limited sponsorship for the BBC. Even though this was never developed beyond a few temporary initiatives[3] the concept of 'promotion' was. It took the form of a specific type of benevolence which the BBC was able to incorporate into its general philosophy, allowing public service broadcasting to be an institutionally favoured form of prestigious patronage, encouraging the preservation of high culture. This interpretation received encouragement from the London cultural establishment and helped create a virtual monopoly on what were considered legitimate models of promotion. The tenuous demarcation between cultural promotion and commercial selling had a crucial bearing on programme and policy makers' attitudes, as certain types of cultural promotion were prioritized at the expense of others. This emphasis on cultural promotion was what the BBC under John Reith took on board when its own public broadcasting archetype shunned the American commercial model – a model for which Reith and many of his colleagues nurtured particular distrust.

Reith saw the American radio system as the apotheosis of vulgarity, its apparent deification of entertainment a chilling prophecy of what would happen to the British system if commerce was allowed to run rampant. However, although American commercial radio developed into something very different from the BBC model its evolution was no less restricted; both systems encountered conflicts specific to sound broadcasting's formative period. Similar fears were voiced about standards; education and entertainment were seen as incompatible, and the same ethical disdain was expressed from official quarters over product promotion. Herbert Hoover, Republican Secretary of Commerce, made a similar distinction to that developed by the Sykes Committee between direct advertising and prestigious sponsorship. Advertising was so distasteful to some early American stations that they called sponsors 'chaperones'.[4] Time-selling stations were still a minority during this period and legislators were so wary of advertising that even prices of goods and store locations could not be mentioned.[5] When advertising was recognized as a potentially lucrative source of income its development owed much to the large networks which concentrated primarily on urban areas. Even recorded music, eventually the staple diet of light entertainment radio, was held in reserve. In 1922 the Department of Commerce 'prohibited the playing of phonograph records . . . except in emergencies or to fill in between programme periods'.[6]

By 1927 the US Congress had nationalized the ether. The setting up of the Federal Communications Commission (FCC), to counteract unregulated expansionism and frequency chaos, had the immediate effect of marginalizing the small independent stations and turning over the airwaves to the growing networks. In the reorganization there was a systematic dismantling of low-power stations serving small regions in favour of their formidable large competitors.[7] By the 1930s most programming on US network radio was sponsored, and ad-libbed unscripted output was kept to a minimum. The strong link between sponsored programming and scripted output was apposite, because sponsors not only controlled the flow of revenue, but also helped to shape the form in which popular entertainment was broadcast.

As with so many other constitutional ideals the cherished principle of free expression gave way to an argument about property rights; 'freedom of expression' was effectively reduced to 'freedom to own the means of expression'. The aim of the system was to encourage investment and asset accumulation and maximize corporate profit. The radio industry itself was dominated by a few large companies, the majority of which were founded on maritime military interests and were in existence before radio became a medium of mass communication. The RCA–NBC conglomerate, for instance, ensured that radio-set manufacture and radio broadcasting developed along parallel paths.[8] Actual set manufacture had such a high priority during the early development of the medium that advertising was not even entertained as a possible source of revenue by the manufacturing interests. At the first Washington Radio Conference of 1922 it was suggested that the high cost of maintaining a radio station was essentially a loss-making investment, necessary to sustain the new expanding market of radio production.[9]

The technological entrepreneurs who made up the BBC's first consortium of shareholders also desired effectiveness, efficiency, and profit. And, as in America, these objectives predated the existence of public broadcasting, harking back to the origins of wireless telegraphy itself. One major difference between the two systems was in programme content. New forms of mass entertainment soon began to emanate from US airwaves, while in Britain the main course was a 'pre-mass' notion of culture. Also peculiar to the British system was the way the public service ethos reflected civil service traditions. By embodying this bureaucratic legacy of correct behaviour, duty, and integrity, and offering conditions of service and expecting allegiance comparable to those found in the civil service, the major financial institutions, the Post Office, and the armed forces, BBC defined for its employees its notions of responsibility and professionalism at a very early stage.

Despite some initial flexibility (the kind of role autonomy peculiar to any new organization) the BBC's own work practices were soon organized along rigidly departmentalized lines. In the early 1930s, in line with much of the industrialized world's move towards the principles of scientific management (role specialization, the demarcation of planners and producers, separation of job conception and work execution, etc.), separate departments for administration and output were developed, effectively transferring all creative decision making from programme makers to bureaucrats. By 1935, as in the USA, most programme output was scripted. Another noticeable consequence of this process of rationalization within the BBC was the formation of separate live music and gramophone departments.

These were not mere bureaucratic conveniences, they embodied crucial ethical assumptions about the relative merits of live and recorded performance. The former's authenticity was deemed to be superior to the mass-manufactured and reproducible nature of the latter, and the BBC ensured that appropriate departments were set up to accommodate and valorize such thinking.

The commercial model of promotion

Somebody clearly not burdened by the highbrow concerns of the BBC in its formative years was Leonard Plugge, a former consulting engineer on the London Underground, and later Conservative MP for the Medway towns. In 1931 he had arranged a sponsorship deal with the Dutch company Philips, which was developing Philco car radios, and Essex Motors (part of the General Motors group), in which he was to give practical demonstrations of car radio efficiency while driving round Europe. At Fécamp in Normandy he initiated an English service on one of the small commercial radio stations which had just started broadcasting in France. Among the first advertisers, not surprisingly, were Dunlop and Philco. Leonard Plugge was a shrewd entrepreneur, who saw in the new facility of radio the potential for profit maximization. What began with a reciprocal deal to sell new technology to a new market rapidly prospered, with the setting up of the International Broadcasters' Club (IBC), a commercial cartel responsible for the buying and selling of sponsorship time on Radio Normandie, and on the other newly emerging commercial stations, such as Poste Parisien, Lyon, and Toulouse. The IBC's virtual monopoly of sales was considerably strengthened in 1934 when it became responsible for selling advertising space on the newly formed Radio Luxembourg too.[10]

Early criticism of Luxembourg and Normandie focused on their amateurism, (relative of course to the BBC's notion of professionalism), and the irregularity of their broadcasts, while takers of the moral high ground indicated that there was something distasteful, if not about advertising on the wireless *per se*, then about the kind of shoddy palliatives being promoted.

By 1934, 90 companies were advertising their goods on the commercial stations; Luxembourg accounted for 71 per cent of all advertisements, Normandie 17 per cent.[11] In 1936 Philco, who held a significantly high profile in the development of both European and American commercial radio, began providing Radio Luxembourg with the Philips–Miller system of recording sound on to film. This system, the forerunner of magnetic tape recording, was far more advanced than anything the BBC was using at the time. It was also being utilized by J. Walter Thompson, the largest advertising agency in the world, and a pioneer of radio sponsorship. Luxembourg thus achieved compatibility of technological systems with its commercial allies within three years of coming on air.

By 1936 Leonard Plugge's cavalier approach was out of favour and with the potential looming for more powerful broadcasting facilities Luxembourg embarked upon a little expansionism of its own. After winning a costly court case, instigated by Plugge for breach of contract, Luxembourg's directors successfully severed all connection with the IBC. By 1937 companies were actually instructing their agencies to advertise on Radio Luxembourg, threatening to take their lucrative accounts elsewhere if the agencies did not comply.[12] Both Cadbury and Reckitts adopted this flexing of promotional muscle through their British outlet, the London Press Exchange. Other lucrative contracts from the USA soon followed, with Ford Motors, Colgate, and Palmolive helping to shape both radio entertainment and mass market consumerism with American capital. British firms such as Rowntree, Stork, and McDougall also became familiar names on Luxembourg and Normandie.

As well as experiencing pressures from advertisers during the 1930s the commercial stations found the Newspaper Proprietors' Association was no kinder to them than it had been to the BBC. The Sykes Committee of 1923 had included representation from the NPA (Chairman Viscount Burnham) and not surprisingly condemned the use of advertising to finance the BBC, fearing that such a method of funding would mean competition with the newspapers for advertising revenue. With the advent of the new foreign competitors the NPA refused to distribute any paper which promoted or published the programme schedules of the commercial stations. Smaller publications who were sympathetic to the commercial cause, such as the *Sunday Referee*, were effectively squeezed out of existence by such power wielding. While it had enjoyed good relations with Radios Paris, Normandie, and Luxembourg, even offering its own advertisers space on the commercial stations,[13] the *Sunday Referee* had trebled its circulation, but within two years of the NPA ultimatum it had been merged into the larger *Sunday Chronicle*.

Direct political and economic intervention played a major part in shaping the development of the commercial sector. In the 1930s neither Radio Toulouse nor Radio Lyon was able to match the comparative success of Normandie and Luxembourg. Both were hampered by a failure to negotiate daytime transmitting hours to Britain for their popular music services. Even with the strength of a commercial cartel the other IBC affiliate Poste Parisien found that a long wave frequency, a powerful 60 kw transmitter, and unlimited daytime broadcasting were not enough to survive because of a legislated prior commitment to its home audience. Parisien was taken over by the French government in April 1933, and sponsored programmes were ended in November.[14] The Dutch had already banned sponsorship in 1930; Belgium followed in 1932. Elsewhere in Europe, Austria, Denmark, Hungary, and Yugoslavia permitted no advertising on their radio networks. There was a limited amount on Spanish radio and on Athlone (later Radio Eireann) but by the spring of 1939 only Luxembourg and a few French stations were broadcasting advertisements.[15] Listeners, it seems, could enjoy occasional respite from the BBC's preached litany of high culture, but these examples underline the extent to which strict legislation and regulation determined the evolution of commercial radio in Europe.

In addition to generating revenue the commercial sector, like the state sector, had to generate its own notions of prestige. It did so by nurturing an image of populist underdog. While the BBC promoted the Reithian triumvirate of 'Educate, Inform, Entertain' the commercial stations interpreted listeners' desires in quite a different way, acknowledging public taste, and constructing their audience around the promotion of consumer populism. While courting such appeal in the prewar years Radios Luxembourg and Normandie ran regional talent shows and soap operas, aspects of popular culture largely shunned by the BBC. Luxembourg had also indicated in its original broadcasting manifesto that time would be allocated to 'interludes' of speech-based programming.[16] These interludes were to have featured debates and discussions in a far less instructive and formal manner than that adopted by the BBC, but as there was not a sufficient response from advertisers to justify programmes of this kind the idea never came to fruition, and instead listeners were offered canned laughter on band shows,[17] accompanied by a heavily scripted gushing *bonhomie*, already familiar to American audiences, and similar to the approach which the BBC was later to adopt as part of its genuflection towards populism.

Programming

Before the outbreak of the Second World War Radios Luxembourg and Normandie accounted for anywhere between 50 and 80 per cent of peak time listening in the UK on Sundays.[18] In 1938, despite the fact that light entertainment was given over a third of its programming time, dance music, variety, and revue provided a mere 10 per cent of the BBC's output, and among this meagre ration only the most innocuous forms of music were played, the BBC favouring continental styles over dance band music. Jazz was often treated with barely concealed racist contempt by the BBC.[19] In 1935 the term 'hot jazz' was forbidden; the BBC decided it should be called 'bright' or 'swing' jazz instead. 'Scat' singing was banned outright. In 1938 the BBC broadcast its first ever dance band concert on a Sunday, and the moment Reith's cultural curfew on the sabbath was lifted Radio Luxembourg reported that its own audiences dropped significantly.

The sober and formal broadcasting style which developed during the years when John Reith was Director-General of the BBC, with its dinner-jacket-wearing announcers, sermons and Shakespeare on Sundays, and 'giving the people a little more than what they want', reflected a powerful heritage, a cultural inheritance which is crucial to a wider understanding of the functioning of the Corporation and the way it initially approached light entertainment provision. The sobriety and moral leadership which characterized the early years of the BBC were not merely the whim of one man who had experienced a strict Presbyterian upbringing and now just happened to be in charge of a public broadcasting system. These traits were enshrined in the values which permeated most of the dominant educative institutions of society. Concerning its attitude towards popular culture, for instance, much has been made of the BBC's initial antipathy towards 'dance music' (which in the 1920s and 1930s was synonymous with jazz), as if such disdain was particular to the BBC alone. But the Corporation was not setting a precedent when many of its leading figures condemned 'wisecrack, song, and the blare of the jazz band'[20] as next to worthless. It was merely at the forefront of a campaign which could also call upon prominent symphony orchestra conductors, military bandleaders, and other like-minded purists and aesthetes for support. The issue was also tainted with colonialism and carried underlying assumptions about the relative merits of the European and Afro-Caribbean traditions. Even Reith's legendary loathing of 'Americanization' was only a reflection of wider concern within the cultural establishment about the predicted erosion of refined European culture by vulgar commercialism.

The promotion of a cultural hierarchy with its accompanying notions of critical evaluation, was apparent in the BBC's broadcasting style, and up until the Second World War programme controllers steadfastly refused to embrace the populism of their commercial competitors. Being the first line of contact between audience and Corporation, announcers were ambassadors, public servants for the BBC, and were strictly forbidden to develop on-air personalities of their own. Their style was formal, programmes were scripted and heavily edited, and output was often censored. Improvisation was simply inadmissible; according to BBC doctrine spontaneity was synonymous with frivolity and irresponsibility. Meanwhile on the commercial stations locations were fantasized, radio orchestras 'invented'. Announcers developed 'persona', and were chatty and informal. They also linked records, thus giving programmes some semblance of continuity. Such contrivances were shunned during the early days of the BBC; even the idea of 'slotting' programmes into daily or even weekly 'series' form was rigorously discouraged at first. Listening was a refined art according to the BBC's decision makers, and each item was supposed to stand on its own merits regardless of what preceded or followed it.

The thumbnail sketch of the formal procedures of programming style outlined above suggest that the commercial stations were more in tune with the listening audience than the BBC was. In fact the context in which the commercial stations' programme ethos developed was no less duty bound. The broadcasting style was certainly more risqué, but its contrived use of the vernacular and the commonplace was as artificial in its way as the BBC's Received Pronunciation. Nor were the commercial stations free of plummy accents and the well-rounded vowel. Radio Luxembourg's most famous prewar advertising campaign, for Ovaltine, featured sketches performed by a group of impeccably spoken upper-middle-class child actors, and a presenter whose clipped tones were indistinguishable from those aired on the BBC.

Commercial radio announcers, although undeniably amiable and chummy in style, were, unless they displayed creative initiatives above and beyond the call of duty, basically administrators, subordinate to the dictates of commerce. As in the USA, advertisers initially tended to sponsor whole shows rather than single slots; these ranged from 15 minutes to one hour in length, and the consumer items endorsed were advertised at times of day deemed most likely to maximize sales. The sponsor of Radio Normandie's early morning programme, for example, was a manufacturer of breakfast cereal. Although, unlike his BBC counterpart, the announcer as salesman was allowed to develop a personality, the sense of fraternity he cultivated was firmly contextualized by the sponsor whose products he was giving airtime to. The repertory acting and sales backgrounds of many who went into commercial broadcasting would have prepared them for the formality of speaking well-rehearsed lines scripted by others. Many were jobbing actors, 'resting' between parts, and were ideally suited to the 'jack of all trades' aspect of their promotional role. Most announcers willingly complied with the constraints that were applied to them. Indeed collective obedience and self-regulation became hallmarks of commercial radio's normative procedures very early on, and the majority willingly adopted notions of responsibility every bit as restrictive and duty bound as those codes of behaviour nurtured by state regulation. It was merely BBC bureaucracy that was anathema to the more maverick element among announcers on the commercial stations.

During 1940–1 the BBC began to appropriate the techniques and expertise of commercial radio, modelling its Forces Programme upon Radio Normandie's successor, Radio Internationale, which had continued broadcasting after the outbreak of war to entertain the British Expeditionary Force in northern France. This service, financed by the British government, ran many programmes produced by the J. Walter Thompson agency, previously noted for its involvement with the commercial sector. For the first time staff with previous experience in commercial radio and advertising agencies were recruited and a noticeable Americanization briefly crept into BBC programmes.

Format radio

US radio underwent an extensive regeneration programme after the Second World War, but despite the number of stations on AM, rising from 1,045 to 2,403 between 1946 and 1952[21] the radio industry in America couldn't keep pace with the lucrative salaries being offered to big stars and bandleaders by television and the Hollywood film industry. Recognizing that American radio's golden age of growth was over, the major networks concentrated their profit-maximizing efforts on television. The result of this was that the proportion of stations unaffiliated to a major network increased from 18 per cent in 1946 to 47 per cent by 1952.[22] From the end of the war until 1951, when the FCC ended its temporary freeze on the expansion of the television industry it seemed that radio was literally living on borrowed time. Not being able to afford either the luxury of live broadcasts or syndicated recorded programmes by famous bandleaders the smaller stations found themselves having to rely increasingly on improvisation, small-scale talent shows, and phonograph records – those forbidden items formerly reserved by the Department of Commerce for emergencies. Out of these circumstances came the first urban 'race music' stations, rural hill-billy and country stations, jazz stations, and the cultural hybrid which became rock and roll. Small independent record labels, like Chess, Atlantic, Sun, Dot, and Duke, also appeared around this time and were to enjoy an almost symbiotic relationship with these developing musical styles and their subsequent exposure on non-network stations.[23] American radio, no longer able to rely on the large media conglomorates, became increasingly dependent upon smaller markets and localized advertising for revenue. The AM band filled with small stations serving small localities, financed by backwoods investment. Most of the 'race music' stations were white owned, as indeed were most of the independent record labels. They were also predominantly white staffed and quickly attracted white listeners as well, although not in sufficient numbers to satisfy the networks, for whenever they made tentative forays into race music the initiative usually died through lack of sponsors.

The pioneers of non-network US commercial radio tended to treat the facility like any other neighbourhood commodity; prospectors bought up unprofitable stations and sold them on at a profit as they would the local hardware store or gas station. What became American Top 40 radio was built in a similar climate of accumulation, most station licences by this time having been acquired by purchase rather than by application to the FCC.[24] George Burns, who was national programme director of the Pacific and Southern radio chain during the rise of Top 40 radio, described the pop radio innovators Don Burden, Todd Storz, and Gordon McLendon as 'the three little rich boys whose fathers bought them radio stations'.[25] McLendon, for example, was a Harvard Law School drop-out who quickly built up a media empire. Commercial radio could be sold as an entrepreneurial expression of the frontier spirit, as ripe for exploitation as any other aspect of the American merchandiser's dream.

The primitive 'hit parades' of the 1930s–40s were calculated by radio performance, sheet sales, record sales, requests to orchestra leaders, and 'coin machine performances'.[26] Coin machines were first mass-produced in 1934; by 1939 there were 350,000 operating in the United States.[27] The juke-box, as well as being essential to the distribution and sustenance of both country music and rhythm and blues, was from a very early stage used as a measure of a record's popularity, a tacit acknowledgement of what people were actually listening to. It was a public utility, functional at street level in the places where people actively indulged their leisure, the bars and diners. It was also a reliable barometer of cultural preferences, measuring both consistency and durability. Recognizing the wider business implications of such recurring patterns of automated obsolescence the marketing men began to take readings and started to plan what came to be known by the mid-1950s as format radio.

The original format idea was to give a high programming profile to the top 10 juke-box hits. These were featured in flexible rotation throughout a typical day's programming. This format was soon expanded to take into account the typical duration of American music radio programmes, which invariably came in three or four hour 'strips'. As it was not thought desirable to repeat any of the top 10 during one show the play-list was extended to 40 'high profile' records, and so the Top 40 format was born.[28] Format had various degrees of interpretation and application, but depended upon one essential formula: a programming continuum. Scheduling was constructed around a diagrammatic clock system, using a pie chart and a flow chart which segmented each hour into programming portions, allocating set times to set musical categories, commercials, and news. The very term 'disc jockey' was born out of this continuity. The DJ was so called because he was expected to 'ride' the records, linking the separate segments of a programme into a unified whole. Unlike the British model this approach was concerned with continuity and cohesion and not the exclusivity of isolated cultural artefacts.

Gordon McLendon's KLIF Dallas was one of the first stations to introduce format, and the first to use station identification jingles in 1954.[29] These early jingles were mainly home-made items, generally put together by station employees, using just piano and voices. As technology grew more sophisticated so did the creative possibilities. KFWB Los Angeles developed the theory that the jingle should sound completely different from the music format it accompanied. Big band arrangements of film scores were favoured for this approach, and the jingles themselves began to grow in length from short burst promotions of 15 or 30 seconds to $1^1/2$ minute 'mini scores', complete pieces in their own right.[30] The jazz based sound was deliberately contrasted with the pop dominated sound of Top 40 radio. A similar juxtaposition was later applied, with minimal variation to the original formula, by many of the British offshore stations.

This programme style came to dominate the production values of almost every aspect of American commercial radio. News coverage, for example, was seen as one of the few ways in which radio could successfully compete with television. McLendon in particular recognized that it was cheaper both to produce and present on radio, and was more immediate and localized than anything the large television network newsreels could offer. McLendon's stations played on this low budget efficiency with some questionable promotional techniques; for example, even though KLIF only had two mobile news units they were numbered '5' and '6', to give the illusion of a large news gathering fleet.[31] Top 40 stations began to contrive an almost theatrical sense of immediacy in their news bulletins, with show-business style buildups and regular short updates usually preceded by fanfares.[32] Newscasts could be sponsored like any other item and became an integral part of the commercial ethos. Product advertising had to be similarly integrated in order to complement the station's output. The carefully crafted continuum could not afford its listeners to be driven away by what Chuck Blore, one of the first Top 40 DJs, called '60 seconds of dull'.[33] Format radio may have introduced programming innovations but it also reasserted commercial radio's familiar priorities.

Commercial radio in Europe took a rather different route in the postwar years. The IBC offices in London had been bombed in the blitz and the Normandie transmitter was destroyed in the D–Day landing. In 1945 the French Ministry of Posts and Telegraphs established the RTF state monopoly in television and radio. Radio Luxembourg, despite inheriting thousands of pounds' worth of state-of-the-art Telefunken equipment –

a legacy of the Nazi occupation which astounded its American liberators who promptly appropriated the technology for their own forces network – was beset with considerable economic and administrative difficulties in the aftermath of the Second World War. The postwar partitioning of the station into French, German, and English networks resulted in the French claiming the prestigious long wave daytime service, while English programming was initially restricted to one and a half hours per night. Listeners in Britain also had to contend with increased interference from foreign stations. In the prevailing atmosphere of economic uncertainty Radio Luxembourg's English service was slow to re-establish itself. Severe currency restrictions halted the flow of postwar capital and had a marked effect on advertising. Popular household products were not enough to sustain Radio Luxembourg during this period of recession and rationing, and sponsors were scarce in the late 1940s.

Luxembourg also suffered from the growing influence of television; many of its popular game shows, for instance, moved to more lucrative commercial pastures; in the space of two years Luxembourg lost *Opportunity Knocks*, *Take Your Pick*, *Double Your Money*, and *Candid Mike* (the UK forerunner to *Candid Camera*) to the newly formed Independent Television. More important, the station lost advertising sales which had previously brought in substantial American income. The situation was further exacerbated when the J. Walter Thompson agency advised its prestigious clients to switch from Radio Luxembourg to ITV.[34] The crisis of sponsorship initially meant that Radio Luxembourg were quite happy to pay the commercial piper. It didn't matter how the advertising slots were filled, as long as they were filled. The sponsorship vacuum was filled by religious programmes from fundamentalists such as Billy Graham and the Voice of Prophecy organization, sports quizzes, continental cabaret shows, even ballet. In the late 1950s, in an attempt to bolster falling audience figures, Luxembourg made an attempt to oust such shows and began recruiting 'personalities' from the entertainment industry to host programmes.[35] For a short time band leaders such as Joe Loss, Norrie Paramour, and Ronnie Aldritch found themselves simultaneously in the employ of the Mecca dance halls, the BBC, and Luxembourg, but by 1960 the quizzes and cabarets were back again.

Although in 1949 Radio Luxembourg had introduced the first Top 20 ever broadcast on commercial radio, there was little market potential in this innovation at the time. These early charts were simply a means of quantifying record sales, and were not perceived as something to build a popular format around. For although disc production was slowly replacing sheet music as the main indicator of sales, the music industry continued to pay more than lip service to tin pan alley practices. The music publishers' continued importance was reflected in the hit parades of the 1950s where it was not unusual to find four of five versions of the same song in the chart at any one time.

The record companies were no strangers to programme sponsorship, HMV having previously advertised extensively with Radio Normandie and Poste Parisien, Vocalion with Normandie and Toulouse,[36] but such sponsorship was slow to regain momentum in the postwar period. The big companies such as Pye and Decca only really began to solve Radio Luxembourg's revenue shortage in earnest once they had wound down their military obligations and resumed their interests in the leisure industry. The record companies soon brought cohesion and uniformity to Luxembourg's schedules. First they curbed a practice which had been common up until the mid-1950s, whereby presenters frequently played product other than the record companies' own on sponsored programmes. Those DJs who were found to be parading too much individual autonomy, including some of Luxembourg's best-known announcers, were brought into line or fired. The record companies' role rapidly spread beyond programme content and began to influence every facet of programme making. The selling of airtime, sponsored programme production, and the hiring of a presenter, had previously been separate concerns, all of them generating revenue and commission which was beyond the radio station's control. The record companies standardized the procedure by insisting on compulsory in-house production, echoing similar developments in the USA, where network control of sponsorship was increasingly usurping the influence of the advertising agencies. The record companies even began to influence the actual way in which advertising time could be bought. Regular block bookings rather than *ad hoc* individual slots favoured the disc manufacturers more than the makers of shampoo, cigarettes, or detergent, as they were the only clients with sufficient product turnover to justify buying consistent airtime week in week out. It was only a matter of time therefore before the record companies were totally determining the output of the radio station.

The UK entertainments industry

The commercial sector, despite some early tensions, has traditionally depended upon a reciprocal and assimilative relationship with the entertainments industry, whereas much of the BBC's early history reads like a catalogue of unsuccessful attempts to impose its rationale upon the workings of the commercial market. Its periodic and largely fruitless attempts to curtail the activities of song pluggers, for instance, go right back to the 1920s when there was a brief attempt to prohibit the announcing of song titles on air. By 1929, however, the Corporation was privately admitting that it was virtually impossible to prevent plugging. Throughout the 1930s the BBC attempted to counteract the trend, with bans on 'special arrangements' of songs (the particular copyrighted version favoured by a bandleader and his publisher) but this met with little success. In 1936 the newly formed Songwriters' Guild gave the fraught relationship between Corporation and commerce some semblance of gentlemanly respectability, but by 1939 the BBC was fighting a rearguard action, forlornly asking bandleaders for a written undertaking not to accept bribes from music publishers. In 1947 the BBC reached an agreement of sorts with the Music Publishers' Association; the MPA agreed to end song-plugging, in return the BBC agreed to a 60 per cent quota of 'contemporary material' in its dance music programme.[37]

The music publishers, along with the various copyright and royalties services, and the Musicians' Union, displayed considerable inflexibility in their negotiations with the BBC. As far back as 1926 the various bodies had expressed grave reservations about the nature of their relationship with the new medium. Radio in its infancy was viewed as the multi-faceted enemy, which would drastically curtail the shelf life of artistic merchandise and deny individual performances their uniqueness. Rapid technological advances took place during the 1920s and 1930s; the invention of the tape recorder, durable gramophone needles, cinema 'talkies', the microphone, and other developments in amplified sound, all threatened to transform the livelihoods of performers and writers. The various negotiating bodies believed that their members' contributions were being downgraded by the use of new technology, and lobbied extensively for services rendered to be adequately rewarded. By 'rewarded', of course, they meant 'compensated'. The decline of sheet music sales and the rise of disc production as a barometer of public taste in the early 1950s did little to ease the situation. The Musicians' Union reacted to rock and roll by adopting a rigidly protectionist stance. All aesthetic claims were subsumed in a chauvinistic championing of a 'British sound', and the airwaves began to reverberate with the rites and rituals of keeping jobbing musicians in business.

The Light Programme's cultural inheritance of cartelization, protectionism, and isolationism was made even more problematic by the sheer inconsistency of the dealings between the BBC and the various factions of the entertainments industry. The Composers' Guild, formed in 1947, distrusted the BBC, whereas the Performing Rights Society enjoyed a harmonious relationship with the Corporation.[38] The BBC in turn distrusted the trade press, particularly the Musicians' Union mouthpiece *Melody Maker*, yet depended upon MU members to provide the bulk of its light entertainment output. During this period, in complete contrast to the Light Programme's muddled policy, the BBC hierarchy gave clear and unambiguous directives to pursue prestige at the expense of popularity.[39] Sponsorship was bestowed upon the Royal Albert Hall Promenade concerts, and there was massive investment in the BBC's own symphony and regional orchestras which toured the major concert halls of Britain as ambassadors for the BBC's cultural policy. The BBC drew up rigid contracts for its concert musicians, outlawed the common practice of deputization (whereby a musician could withdraw from a performance at the eleventh hour if he found a better-paid engagement), and effectively creamed off the best concert players in the country. Apart from a half-hearted attempt to prohibit 'scratch bands' no comparable system existed for those working in the light entertainment field.

When BBC Radio was restructured into the respective lowbrow, medium-brow, and highbrow, facilities of the Light Programme, Home Service, and Third Programme in 1945, the cultural tripartitism implicit within these reforms was played down. But by 1952 the Third Programme, with less than 1 per cent of listeners nationwide, was accounting for 46 per cent of the BBC music budget. The Light Programme by comparison accounted for 15 per cent of the music budget, with 70 per cent of the audience.[40] Entertainment radio was indisputably increased in the postwar years but its development was carefully and paternalistically regimented; former high-ranking military personnel were given senior positions on the new Light service. In 1946, in line with the nationwide campaign to get women out of the factories and back into the home, the Light Programme introduced shows such as *Housewives' Choice, Workers' Playtime*, and *Music while you work*. These were to remain stalwarts of the network for the next 20 years. *Music while you work* and *Workers' Playtime* had both begun life on the Forces Programme during 1940–1 and continued to feature works and military bands quite heavily during the postwar period.[41] Other Forces Programme favourites like *ITMA* and *Variety Bandbox* were given peak time evening slots on the Home and Light services. The variety department, having won hard-fought concessions from BBC policy makers during the Second World War, continued to bank on wartime entertainers who had been good for morale, and the institutional appeal to nostalgia remained paramount long after hostilities had ceased.

In 1950 radio comedy provided the bulk of the peak hours output by the Light Programme, but by the mid-1950s, as in the USA, vast resources were being allocated to television. The advent of ITV in 1955 compounded radio's new-found role as the subservient medium. As on Luxembourg, most of the BBC's top variety shows moved to television, leaving light music, typified by the strict tempo of Geraldo, Victor Sylvester, and the sedentary Palm Court orchestras, as the new standard bearer for soporific diversion and passive amusement on the wireless. The Light Programme, although ostensibly a result of cultural streaming also had to fulfil a recognizably mundane monopolist function.

> The Third Programme then was little different to what Radio Three is now – always in danger of being called elitist and suchlike, and obviously not appealing to many young people, that wasn't its aim or its brief. The Home Service was very much the forerunner to Radio Four, and by and large its audience was very much the same then as now. The Light Programme was attempting to be all things to all men, in the sense that it had to have everything from Elvis Presley through to popular operatic arias, and *Your Hundred Best Tunes*. And the crucial thing of course was the amount of records you could play.
>
> (Teddy Warrick)[42]

Needle time: BBC pop rations in the 1950s

By the mid-1950s programmes of recorded music were fast becoming the norm for American listeners. This was not the case in Britain. New copyright rulings which came into force in 1956 favoured the record manufacturers. They were not only assured of income from consumer purchases but also received a fee every time a disc received radio airplay. This caused the BBC to introduce new processes of rationalization. The Light Programme's band show version of pop, shaped by years of rigorous auditions, selection committees, and policy units, was now being challenged not by format, but by an equally formidable factor.

> The needle-time arrangement is crucial to any study of popular music radio in this country. The history of the arrangement, if I can encapsulate it briefly, goes back to the days when the record companies themselves thought that if people listened to records on the radio they would never go out and buy them, so they instituted copyright restrictions on the

21

grounds that they thought record sales might suffer. They later came round to the view that far from record sales suffering radio stimulated record sales. It was a promotional device. But then they found themselves in a trap. Even if they had wished to increase the needle-time, because of the restrictions the BBC was having to employ a lot of live musicians in all fields of music. So you had the situation where live bands were re-creating the hits of the day themselves. But of course the MU weren't going to give up this source of employment lightly, and so although they weren't party to the needle-time agreement – that was totally between the BBC and the record industry through PPL (Phonographic Performances Ltd) – they were in a position to put pressure on the record companies not to allow the BBC too much needle-time. The record companies, perhaps fearing that the MU might not allow their members to make records, continued with the needle-time restrictions.

(Teddy Warrick)[43]

Teddy Warrick, an assistant in the BBC gramophone department during the 1950s, offers – as he says – an encapsulated view of a very complex argument. It is very much a pragmatic on-the-job account by someone then involved in the day-to-day running of the Corporation's light music service, but it demonstrates precisely the debilitating effect BBC administration, with its separate live music and gramophone departments, was now beginning to have on policy and output.

As a consequence of the BBC's continued reliance upon Musicians' Union session bands a peculiarly anachronistic 'house style' emerged, and its influence was audible throughout the entire network. Pop radio shows of the late 1950s and early 1960s like Drumbeat and Go Man Go ('your Friday tonic – the show with the most') featured resident session bands such as Bob Millar and his Millarmen, Arthur Greenslade and the G-Men, and Colin Day and the Hound Dogs. Compèred by David Ede ('your swinging man Friday'), Go Man Go was a typical example of the Light Programme's pop fare. Broadcast live from the BBC Playhouse in London the show's musical content consisted almost entirely of live cover versions, 50 per cent of which were contemporary pop, the other 50 per cent being standards. For a supposedly ephemeral subculture rock and roll fans proved to be surprisingly fickle when it came to interpretations of their music. In effect what the BBC was unknowingly offering them was a pastiche – which, in the light of the Corporation's policy on authenticity, was an irony of epic proportion, and contributed directly to the BBC's lack of communication with its young audience. On the surface it all sounded very chummy. The house bands would perform with apparent enthusiasm, linking their jaunty and robust material with 'in-house' indulgent humour (lots of scripted or terribly forced 'laughs off' etc – stale leftovers from the variety repertoire) but this could never completely conceal the fact that for the most part these bands, made up in equal parts of highly skilled jaded jazz musicians, and jobbing performers, held pop music in complete contempt. They were playing for their percentage, strictly from the copyrighted score – and it showed.

In the late 1950s the BBC still had only 28 hours per week of needle-time to share between its entire network. Because of the prestige value of high culture the Third Programme's share was disproportionate to its audience while the Light had to make do with something in the region of 14 hours a week. Only a smattering of programmes featured the newly emerging pop sound, fewer still featured it on disc, and because of its ties with the Musicians' Union the BBC reacted warily to the growth of the record industry. By the mid-1950s even the dance halls, still major employers of live musicians, were starting to adopt a more flexible policy. Mecca ballrooms, for instance, held regular once-a-week disc nights, the nearest equivalent British youth had at the time to a discothèque.[44] But long after the playing of pop records had become comparatively commonplace on Radio Luxembourg and in the ballrooms Light Programme presenters could still be heard announcing 'we have a couple of discs on today's programme' as if these were alien objects which would never find a proper context within the BBC. The terminology persisted right through to the early days of Radio One.

The chart programme *Pick of the Pops* (which was broadcast on Sundays at 4–5 p.m.), is often cited as the BBC's sole concession to popular taste in the pre-pirate era. This is not strictly true. Although the BBC undoubtedly gave pitifully low priority to the provision of any pop music at all, the Light Programme still had a virtual monopoly as a promotional outlet. Shows like *Saturday Club* (originally *Skiffle Club*) and its Sunday equivalent *Easybeat* effectively had the pick of top British and American acts, and many listeners heard the Beatles, the Rolling Stones, and many others make their first live radio broadcasts on such programmes (rubbing shoulders, it has to be said, with the BBC approved trad and Dixieland jazz of artists such as Acker Bilk, Terry Lightfoot, and Kenny Ball).

Both shows originally had a studio audience. *Easybeat* even had its own miniature 'juke-box jury' where a panel of young 'experts' would pass verdict on the current new releases. The overall effect was predictable and forced, rarely capturing the knowing exuberance of the typical pop audience. Studio participation was later dropped from both programmes. Along with weekly regulars such as *Workers' Playtime, Pop Inn*, and the daily *12 O'clock Spin*, both *Saturday Club* and *Easybeat* were later revamped with the minimum of modifications for Radio One. *Saturday Club* showed what could be done with pop rations and minimal resources – the programme was only allocated nine discs per two-hour show, three of which had to be non-needle-time new releases. It, and not *Pick of the Pops* (which in its original form was merely another shop window for the record industry) was the BBC's pop music showcase. *Pick of the Pops* was more notable for Australian Alan Freeman's idiosyncratic approach to presentation than it was for services to the record industry. He had taken over the programme from David Jacobs in 1961 and was frequently censured in the early days by the Corporation for his brash presentation, which sharply contrasted with Jacobs's sedate style.

Freeman aside, BBC announcers drew upon a variety of approaches to pop presentation in the early 1960s. Some distanced themselves from the new phenomenon, adopting a slightly disdainful tone towards the excesses of pop gimmickry and an equally patronizing attitude towards its teenage audience. Others offered a headmasterly variation on this, heaped scorn upon all aspects of pop modernism and sounded more as if they were interrogating their listeners than talking to them. Sometimes a genial uncle figure would host benevolent escapades into the youngsters' territory, addressing them overbearingly as 'chums' or 'mates', while leading them down the path of wise instruction and musical appreciation. The archetype for this was undoubtedly the *Children's Favourites* presenter 'Uncle Mac' (Derek McCormack). The approach, a mixture of Sunday School moral correctness and paternal *bonhomie* was also evident in the youth club ambience of BBC TV's first pop show *6.5 Special*, in *Crackerjack's* orderly participation and complete absence of pandemonium, and the Baden Powell ethos of the early *Blue Peter*.

On the whole light music enthusiasts were better served by the BBC, although some of the Light Programme's traditional musical terrain was slowly shifting, as BBC house orchestras began to include more contemporary pop tunes in their repertoire. Those who liked the Latin-American style, which was massively popular in the late 1950s, were well provided for, as long as they didn't mind their cha-cha and samba being played by BBC dance bands. Stage and film music also had a high programming profile; this was partly due to the continued influence of Hollywood and the music publishers, but it was mainly because show tunes and sound-tracks, like new releases, were exempt from needle-time restrictions. Shows like *Roundabout* catered for fans of the more sophisticated end of easy-listening music, and in the main the Light Programme fulfilled its obligation to its adult audience. Established programmes such as *Two Way Family Favourites* could command a Sunday lunchtime audience of 18 million listeners, *Housewive's Choice*, *Children's Favourites*, *Saturday Club*, and *Easybeat*, a further 8 to 10 million each. For pop fans, though, there had only ever been a smattering of what they desired spread meagrely across the week's output. By the early 1960s there were entire subcultures whose distinctive tastes were not being recognized. There was little acknowledgement of the new multi-racial audience brought about by postwar immigration or of the new forms of Afro-Caribbean music being enjoyed within the small and often illicit club scene of the big cities. This cultural exclusion had particular significance for fans of black American music because it was

25

largely out of this neglected dance culture that the Mersey sound and the subsequent British beat explosion were being forged. By the time the Beatles emerged during 1962–3, the BBC Light Programme was facing an insurmountable crisis of accommodation.

In 1963 radio still commanded an overall daytime listening audience of 7.5 million in the UK. Even in the evenings, competing with the BBC and ITV television networks, radio still retained 2 million listeners and 3 million people still possessed just a radio and no television. Equally significant was the increasing number of people listening on car radios and portable transistors. Historically the BBC and Radio Luxembourg had faced problems whenever they had attempted to transplant the audience's excitement and enthusiasm into their own studios. Such was the severity with which the Reithian aesthetic code was applied that the Corporation even faced internal criticism when it first invited studio audiences to attend plays and variety shows. Conflicts raged as producers and policy makers tried to decide whether the audience's physical presence added to the atmosphere or was merely an intrusion into the intimacy of the wireless–listener relationship. Retaining a good deal of this ethical distrust (and also because outside broadcasts were rather expensive!) the BBC rarely ventured into the dance halls, and tried instead to recreate the atmosphere of youth having fun in the supervised environment of its own Playhouse Theatre. Luxembourg fared slightly better in locating the young audience, but little better in trying to recreate its excitement. 'How to twist' lessons were perhaps not the best way of utilizing the medium's resources! The transistor radio transformed this relationship. To young people in particular radio no longer represented the permanent fixture in the living-room, it was an adaptable and dynamic accessory to their culture. It literally gave their culture mobility, and became an icon of intense significance. Its very existence anticipated new forms of cultural identity. By 1963 it was a symbol in search of substance. That substance was about to be provided by an unlikely new breed of maritime entrepreneurs.

European offshore pirates

British audiences had often looked elsewhere for their entertainment, as the commercial cartels of the 1930s, and the success of the American Forces Network in the postwar years showed, but it was not until the late 1950s that operations more directly clandestine in nature began to appear. And as with an earlier generation of commercial concerns the offshore radio phenomenon did not originate in Britain. The idea of circumventing legislation by situating a broadcasting vessel in international waters began in Scandinavia, and prior to the arrival of Radio Caroline in March 1964 there had been seven previous attempts to initiate offshore broadcasting in Europe. These were:

Radio Mercur (Denmark 1958–62)
DCR (Danish Commercial Radio) (Denmark 1961)
Radio Antwerpen (Belgium 1962)
Radio Nord (Sweden 1960–2)
Radio Syd (Sweden 1962–6)
CNBC (Commercial Neutral Broadcasting Company) (Holland 1961)
Radio Veronica (Holland 1960–74)

These stations enjoyed varying degrees of commercial success. Radio Mercur's alleged annual turnover was 6 million kroner. When Radio Syd purchased the outlawed Radio Mercur's ship and began broadcasting to Sweden it was quickly able to recuperate an initial investment of US $200,000. Radio Antwerpen, on the other hand, only survived three months before being grounded by the Belgian authorities and the North Sea elements. Similarly, when CNBC opened an advertising sales office in London, and attempted to broadcast a low-power English language service of jazz and easy-listening music to British listeners during 1961, the project only lasted a few weeks. CNBC was subsequently incorporated into the relatively solvent Radio Veronica, but the Dutch pirate only became a commercially viable proposition after 1965. Also in 1961, in more lucrative circumstances, Radio Mercur took over Danish Commercial Radio. DCR, started up by disaffected ex-Radio Mercur staff in the first place, had attempted to launch a highbrow talk show and classical music format in opposition to Mercur's light music programmes.

The European pirates broadcast a wide variety of services, oriented not necessarily to youth but predominantly to popular music. Some were simply halted by the elements, others were hampered by a lack of funding or insufficient advertising revenue. It became a truism of offshore radio that the desire to make a fast buck was backed up by an equal lack of desire to invest a slow one in the first place. Genuine investors often preferred to remain in the background, allowing others to test the legislative waters.

Inevitably the presence of pirate radio stations off the coast of Europe provoked considerable conflict. The offshore stations were challenged over their deliberately ambiguous interpretations of ownership and shareholder structure, and precisely how they generated their revenue. Tensions also arose over the blatant flouting of copyright and wavelength agreements, and the difficulty of establishing accountability of those who chose to work outside the law or inhabit its grey areas was acknowledged early on.

Eventually legislation was passed to outlaw the European offshore pirates (1962 in all of the above cases except for Holland, which didn't pass its own act until 1974). In all but one or two cases this was followed by the swift capitulation of the outlawed party. Radio Mercur recommenced transmissions shortly after Denmark had passed an anti-pirate bill, but its ship was immediately seized by the Danish authorities. Ignoring Swedish legislation Radio Syd made a more defiant stand, and continued broadcasting until 1966, when Sweden amended its laws in order to introduce Draconian new measures which made it possible to seize all of a station's assets if it continued transmitting. Most countries which passed anti-pirate legislation rapidly acknowledged the pirates' programming initiatives, many of which were incorporated into the existing broadcasting system. Belgium increased its own domestic output while Radio Antwerpen was still on the air, when the state-owned BRT extended its hours of transmission to midnight. When Denmark silenced its pirates the move was so unpopular that a third service was opened on the national network to cater for disfranchised lovers of light popular music. Sweden in turn introduced 'Melody Radio' when it outlawed Radio Syd.

Many of the procedures outlined above were to recur throughout the British offshore radio era of 1964–8, and there was a fair degree of continuity between these European prototypes and the British pirates. Gordon McLendon, one of the pioneers of American Top 40 radio, was instrumental in setting up Radio Nord, and was later involved in a consultancy capacity with both Radio Atlanta and Radio London. The Radio Nord broadcasting vessel was later used by Radio Atlanta and Radio Caroline South. Britt Wadner, owner of Radio Syd, was later to play a similar role in revitalizing the fortunes of Radio Caroline, by loaning the Swedish pirate's broadcasting vessel when the Caroline South ship ran aground in stormy weather in 1966. The same vessel would later have been used by the proposed Radio 390 North if legislation had not halted the venture. There were also direct parallels over the technicalities of maritime vessel registration. Radio Mercur was rendered stateless after Panama withdrew the right to a flag of convenience, thus anticipating what would happen to Radio Caroline two years later, and such occurrences were typical during the British offshore era. Arguably Radio Atlanta would have been the first British offshore pirate had not the forcible closure of Radio Mercur caused many of the station's original backers to withdraw their investment.

During the winter of 1961–2 various national dailies and music trade papers in Britain carried stories of a 'Radio GBLN', also later known as 'Radio GBOK'. The station, founded by two Canadian businessmen, John Thompson and Arnold Swanson, was said to be planning 'initial programmes lasting eighteen hours a day to be followed as soon as possible by a full twenty-four hour service'.[45] It was proposed that these programmes would be taped in a studio in Dublin and broadcast from a converted fishing boat anchored outside the three-mile territorial limit in the Thames estuary. Most of the European pirates were already taping their programmes on land and relaying them from a ship, and many British pirates were to do the same. Advertising revenue was said to be sufficient to keep the station going for one year. It was intended that the station would broadcast with a 5 kw Marconi transmitter to a radius of 100 miles. The backers were said to have put £100,000 towards the cost of the venture.

GBLN's intended programming policy also made it clear that non-stop pop music was not on the agenda. The station was primarily aiming to appeal to an adult audience, and its owners clearly had no more perception of the potential teenage market than the Light Programme had. Indeed its programme brief indicated that it was going to implement a much harsher degree of 'quality control' than anything exercised by the BBC: 'We will be playing discs by artists like Helen Shapiro and other modern beat singers with talent, but none by upstarts. And there will be plenty by people like Frank Sinatra and Ella Fitzgerald.'[46]

Despite Swanson having allegedly supervised the pre-recording of a number of programmes from converted stables at an Oxfordshire mansion the project ultimately foundered, on two predictable fronts. Firstly the expected funding failed to materialize in anything like the quantities required (then, as later, there was no guarantee that investors or advertisers were going to plunge into uncharted waters). But the main reason why GBLN never became the first operative British offshore pirate was that its owners had not fully thought through the full legislative implications of the venture. Thompson actually tried to negotiate with the British Phonographic Industry before going on air, perhaps naïvely expecting the GPO to hand out a broadcasting licence in the process.

At the moment we are having a bit of a problem with the major companies who are holding us up with permission to tape their records. This is the only delaying factor to us and means there is no possibility of getting some arrangement with them before the New Year, as mechanical rights permission is dependent on our arrangements with the British Phonographic Industry.[47]

The later generation of pop pirates undoubtedly learned from such tactics, and made sure they were safely established in international waters before they began negotiating for anything.

Meanwhile the Light Programme meandered along complacently, fortified by the findings of the 1962 Pilkington Report, which explicitly endorsed the BBC's public service provision and made the likelihood of the introduction of commercial radio recede even further. In the week leading up to Easter 1964 all the old familiar faces were there, reliably going about their business. Programmes like *Housewives' Choice* had been permanent fixtures in the schedules since 1946. The numerous BBC variety orchestras had been subliminally shaping the station's sound since the mid-1950s. On Good Friday 1964, the Light Programme was open for business as usual between 6.30 a.m. and midnight. Live guest on *Go Man Go* ('the show with the most') was Adam Faith, who came on and briefly promoted his new 'disc'. There was a place for everything predictable and everything was predictably in its place. And as evening approached, somewhere along the outer reaches of the Thames estuary a 702-ton converted passenger ferry, with a 165 ft mast, was getting ready to drop anchor . . .

CHAPTER 2

Action and reaction: Piracy and the pursuit of prestige

Purple heart radio

The hostile reaction to a succession of floating radio stations off the British coast during 1964 came, as might be expected, from the political parties, from established competitors in both radio and the press, and the vested interests of the music industry. Their objections were to do with the following main issues;

(a) The use of unauthorized wavelengths;
(b) The potential danger to shipping and interference with essential services;
(c) The non-payment of copyright to authorized bodies such as the Performing Rights Society (PRS) and Phonographic Performances Ltd (PPL);
(d) The adverse effect on the livelihoods of members of the Songwriters' Guild and the Musicians' Union;
(e) The adverse effect on record sales and newspaper advertising revenue;
(f) The qualititative questions of unethical and unprofessional broadcasting and the lowering of standards;

When the issue of offshore radio was first raised in Parliament in March 1964 the Conservative Postmaster-General Reginald Bevins promised 'action soon'. The first major objection to the pirates made in the House of Commons was that they interfered with essential maritime emergency services. Jamming their frequencies was considered as an early option but was quickly rejected. Robin Cooke, Conservative MP for Bristol West, and

Chairman of the Conservative Backbenchers' Committee on Broadcasting voiced much greater fears than mere interference with emergency services.

> The main objection to the pirate stations is that they are not obliged to keep to any recognisable standards on behaviour. There is nothing to prevent their pouring out Communist or Fascist propaganda, or perhaps more dangerous to the otherwise sensible British public, urging them to indulge in expensive self-medication with unnecessary potions and pills.[1]

Stephen Stewart, Director-General of the International Federation of the Phonographic Industry, expressed similar concern:

> So far there are only pirate ships broadcasting popular music, but if tomorrow a similar ship were to broadcast subversive political propaganda or obscene material the Government would – one hopes – wish to take action. Yet the legal position of such a ship would be exactly the same as that of Caroline.[2]

As these comments illustrate, the initial debate on the pirates was carried out in an atmosphere of indignation and moral panic. As institutional disquiet gathered momentum the audience for popular culture was deemed to be in more danger from 'unnecessary potions and pills' than it was from fascism and communism. A dominant strand within the parliamentary Labour Party, including the then Shadow Postmaster-General Roy Mason, also expressed concern over the possibility of unlimited pep pill and drug advertising on pirate radio. Amphetamine-based slimming pills (sometimes known as 'purple hearts') were still freely available over the chemist's counter, and thanks to the media attention on the Mods and Rockers, hedonistic drug use and abuse was making headlines. Initial reaction to the pirates was shaped within this context.

There was also concern as to what would actually replace the pirate stations if they were closed down. The Postmaster-General refused to accept that the establishment of pirate radio ships should precipitate policy decisions on local sound broadcasting in the UK. However, other Conservatives were not so reticent. Most prominent among the groups lobbying for the introduction of commercial radio was the National Broadcasting Development Committee, chaired by Sir Harmar Nicholls, Conservative MP for Peterborough. But as Nicholls also held directorships with Moss Empires and Radio Luxembourg the NBDC was careful to distance itself from the offshore stations and complained about the poor quality of pirate broadcasts. This somewhat dampened the notion that the Conservatives were going to be the natural ally of the pirates, and made a mockery of the subsequent bandwagon-jumping antics of some Conservative backbenchers. Certain strands within the Labour opposition also saw the Conservative populist stance as patently opportunist.

> Those MPs know exactly what the public wants. Their own interests include gardening, reading, fishing, ornithology, photography, music, theatre, and painting. They do not wish to share these interests with others. They want the public to hear about consumer goods with built-in obsolescence. They want us conditioned to hear nothing but pop records. They use their education and cultural background for the purpose of making money out of the less favoured.[3]

The Labour Party *Tribune* group condemned the NBDC's attempted appropriation of the popular sentiment, and staunchly favoured preserving the BBC monopoly. The feeling among the Tory hierarchy was that the party should not identify itself too closely with the 'candy floss' image of the offshore stations, but while distancing themselves very carefully from the illegality of the pirate operations the Conservatives, rather more shrewdly than Labour, were seen to favour in principle some form of legalized commercial radio. The Liberals had their own reasons for remaining wary of the pirates' clandestine 'image'.

A public relations man calling himself Major Cadow rang up several East Anglian Liberal candidates claiming that an anonymous client of his, a rich Norfolk Liberal, wanted to put up a lot of money for them to advertise on Radio Caroline. He said he had no telephone number, but would ring back on Monday. The Liberals were intrigued but are unlikely to take such an offer seriously; to advertise on an illegal station would hardly improve their reputation.[4]

Immediately prior to the October 1964 election the Welsh Nationalists, known to be annoyed by their lack of access to television, said that they too had been approached. However, unlike the major parties, they had turned down the opportunity to broadcast for more pragmatic reasons: Radio Caroline's reception was not sufficiently strong in the areas they wished to reach.

Direct political involvement would undoubtedly have brought a swift end to the pirates' adventures on the high seas. During May 1964 one incident made this look a distinct possibility. HMS *Venturous* visited the Caroline vessel and requested permission to board and inspect its bonded stores. This request was refused. On the assumption that their ship was properly registered, Caroline's crew had every right to refuse access under international law. Panama, however, had withdrawn its own registration as soon as the station went on the air, and it was later acknowledged by many of those involved in offshore radio in the early days that had the British government taken more forceful action there would have been little that the pirates could do. 'If they wanted to kill commercial radio they should have got at us in the first four days',[5] was a common sentiment. Certainly during these early weeks the offshore stations were at their most vulnerable, but while the authorities delayed, waiting for a Council of Europe agreement to be formulated in Strasbourg, the pirates were left to prosper.

The autumn election which brought the Labour Party to power with a narrow majority deprived interested observers of the opportunity to see how certain vociferous strands of Conservatism would have reconciled their free-market rhetoric with the legislation that would inevitably have to be drawn up to outlaw the stations. The new Labour Postmaster-General Tony Benn continued the work of his Conservative predecessor by initially placing great faith in the workings of the proposed Strasbourg agreement; but if anything this merely hindered

British legislation. The agreement was signed reluctantly by many member countries, some of whom reserved the right to opt out at a later date, and proved impossible to implement unilaterally. This prevarication occurred whenever the pirate issue was debated in the House of Commons during the early days of the Labour administration.

> Mr Blenkinsop: Does my Right Honourable Friend agree that a great deal of time has been taken and that other countries have carried out the agreement? Is not this delay causing trouble not only with agreements among the trade unions, the Musicians' Union, and others, but also causing a good deal of damage to broadcasting on the Continent? Is it not time he got on with the job?
>
> Mr Benn: . . . In fact four countries have carried through the legislation while another seven have not yet signed the agreement, so that our record in comparison with others is not as bad as my Honourable Friend suggests. This is a matter of legislation priorities.[6]

From the moment the offshore stations appeared it was inevitable that they would eventually have to disappear, Labour being as ideologically opposed to commercial radio as it had been to the introduction of commercial television in the 1950s. But it is apparent from the above exchange that the pirate issue was not exactly being treated as a 'legislative priority'. Unlike the more populist strand within the previous government the Labour administration at first regarded the pirates as a minor inconvenience. Debate within the new government was more concerned with a proposed non-profit-making 'university of the air', eventually to find form in the Open University. Apart from Benn's ill-fated idea for a National Broadcasting Corporation[7] Labour's only proposed concession to youth was a 'Radio Pop' to be run by the Post Office![8] It was as anachronistic as similar Labour initiatives to curry favour with youth, such as the Prime Minister Harold Wilson's miscalculated appearance at the Cavern Club with the Beatles to thank them for boosting Britain's export market. James Callaghan's refusal to endorse the Wootton Committee recommendation that marijuana should be decriminalized and his subsequent condemnation of drug-related deviance were perhaps more accurate indicators of the Labour Party's essentially problematic perception of youth.

The emphasis Labour gave to policing and controlling the airways was generally at odds with Benn's attempts to open them up in the name of democratic access. Apart from standard party line references to fly-by-night entrepreneurs, revenue dodgers, and wavelength cloggers Benn did at least acknowledge the part the pirates were playing in catering for the tastes of a sizeable proportion of the radio audience. He was adamant that the pirates could not be closed down without an alternative being put in their place. Benn also eventually acknowledged that legislation to outlaw the pirates could be a complex operation, and even floated the idea that the Light Programme should take advertising.[9]

Benn was already hampered by the inability of the Council of Europe to initiate anti-pirate legislation, and accused by the opposition parties of indecisiveness; but his disapproval of the restrictive practices of the Musicians' Union over needle-time agreements hardly endeared him to the entertainments industry either. He made similar criticisms of the record companies, and of the NUJ and the Newspaper Proprietors – whom he accused of 'looking at national problems from the point of view of their own strict personal financial interest' when they expressed traditional reservations about the introduction of local radio.[10] By March 1966 Benn was claiming that 'the BBC had exposed itself to pirate competition by policy refusal to meet what most people wanted'. Overall Benn was happy neither with what he called 'the quick buck people' nor with 'the colonial governors at the BBC'. He clearly regarded the pirates as 'a menace', producing little but 'audible wallpaper',[11] but did not share the repressive zeal of his successor Edward Short.

Apart from the political parties the pirates also had to contend with opposition from those organizations losing revenue through non-payment of copyright. Phonographic Performances Ltd announced in April 1964 that it intended to issue a writ against Radio Caroline to prevent it 'stealing' copyright material. All that transpired however was a flurry of activity as the pirates lined up to make offers of payment, thereby highlighting the extent to which they wished to be seen as legitimate business concerns. So eager were they to conform to accepted practices that in this respect, as the PPL General Manager Harold Walters wryly observed, the pirates' actions were far more placatory than many of PPL's long-standing clients.

> In our daily business we have to deal with a very large number of people whose liability to pay our fees is undoubted, but who do their best to evade us. It was therefore very refreshing indeed to find people, businessmen, whose legal liability was of the slimmest who came forward voluntarily and said they wished to pay our fees. In short from our point of view they are very gentlemanly pirates.[12]

However, despite such public utterances Phonographic Performances Ltd displayed a rather ambivalent attitude to the collection of revenue from the offshore stations. The organization, while eager to receive some sort of payment, still clearly disapproved of the pirate operations. In fact the whole PPL issue highlights the legal catch 22 that the pirates found themselves in. Those stations which offered to pay royalties on the records they played found that their payments could be refused on the grounds that, as pirates, they could not be recognized as 'legitimate' business. Yet those stations that flaunted non-cooperation were similarly condemned for breaking the very rules that the more respectable stations wished to conform to. The pirates' approach to PPL payment rarely went beyond the gestural anyway and there is much contradictory evidence, in statements issued both by the pirates and PPL, regarding figures agreed and amounts handed over. Many pirates also attempted to negotiate with the more formidable Performing Rights Society but reached no satisfactory agreement. In February 1966 a press statement from PRS condemned pirate radio broadcasts and opposed any form of token *ex gratia* payments.

The pirates were also condemned for their unauthorized use of medium wave frequencies. The abuse of such a supposedly scarce resource had a long history. Radio Luxembourg, for example, had seized a prime wavelength during the 1930s while negotiations concerning its allocation were still in progress.

The very concept of a wavelength agreement had historically proved itself to be a contradiction in terms. Early attempts to initiate a broadcasting 'League of Nations' to avoid the chaos of interference and wavelength overcrowding soon dissolved through a combination of self-interest and non-cooperation. Conferences held in Geneva in 1925, Brussels in 1926, Prague in 1928, and Madrid in 1932, were characterized by victories of political expediency over technical realism.[13] It was the Copenhagen convention of 1948 which was cited most frequently by those who objected to the pirates, but at this convention Austria, Iceland, Luxembourg, Portugal, Spain, Sweden, and Turkey, among others, refused to accept the frequencies they were allocated. As late as 1964 17 countries had not signed and ratified the Copenhagen agreement. It was estimated that by 1965 over 300 European medium and long wave frequencies were being used without authorization.

On the surface at least, the record companies were also 'cool' towards the offshore stations. Their official policy was one of non-cooperation, but of the groups who opposed the pirates they perhaps contrived the most ambivalent stance of all, unofficially falling over themselves to deliver exclusive pre-release copies of all new product to the stations.

It was total hypocrisy. They said 'we don't want any dealings with these dreadful people. They're totally illegal. They won't pay to play our records so we don't want to know. But by god, other people's product had better not be on there in preference to ours!'

(Tony Hall)[14]

In the early days, getting merchandise to the pirates was very much a cloak and dagger operation; the offshore stations often had to go and solicit the material themselves. As their potential as promotional facilities became more obvious tactics became far less shadowy. But even at the height of the phenomenon record company chiefs maintained an official line of non-cooperation, claiming that the existence of the offshore stations was leading to over-exposure of recorded material and harming sales. Any hope of a war of attrition, though, was completely undermined by the efforts of those employed at the 'bread and butter' end of the industry, the representatives and agents working on commission and initiative.

> It was lovely to hear senior executives and directors of gramophone companies haranguing about the pirates in the press and on the BBC while their own right-hand men were coming round saying 'would you like another dozen copies of this one or that one?'
>
> (Ted Allbeury)[15]

The first television programme to deal with the issue of pirate radio was Granada's *World in Action*. In May 1964 ITV's current affairs flagship was devoted to an examination of Radios Caroline and Atlanta. The *World in Action* team was granted exclusive access to Greenore Harbour in Dublin, recently vacated by Radio Caroline and still being used by the Radio Atlanta ship for fitting out, and was also taken to a secret location in London where Atlanta programmes were being taped. *World in Action* offered a concise and often wry account of the newly emerging situation, opening with adventure-film footage of sixteenth-century battleships juxtaposed with shots of the Radio Caroline vessel. By establishing a parallel between the pirates of old and their modern-day equivalents, Granada, like much of the popular press, promoted a buccaneer image for the stations. This literal interpretation of the term 'pirates', undoubtedly a convenient selling angle later on, was largely an invention of the media. The stations themselves were certainly not keen at first to exploit the image.

Although *World in Action* gave a fair hearing to the views of all the chief protagonists in the debate its musical sound-track reverberated with a deafening and inescapable irony all of its own. Accompanying location shots of the Radio Atlanta vessel as it made a precarious voyage round the English coast, and overdubbed on to the footage of real live Radio Caroline DJs going about their business in a real live Radio Caroline studio, were snatches of hit records of the day like '5–4–3–2–1', and 'Glad All Over'. They were not, however, the respective Manfred Mann and Dave Clark Five originals, which were Top 10 hits at the time, but Musicians' Union performed, PPL approved, PRS regulated, *cover versions*. It was both an unintended parody on Radio Atlanta's subsequent output and a perfect illustration of those aspects of BBC and music industry policy which the pirate stations appeared to be fighting against.

There is every indication that several of the offshore pirates would have relayed live group performances on a regular basis if the Musicians' Union had not had other ideas. Radio Caroline circumvented potential hostilities in May 1964, when American jazz organist Jimmy Smith performed live on the deck of the Caroline vessel, but the technical difficulties encountered rendered future live broadcasts unfeasible. Radio London met the limits of music industry tolerance when it ran the sponsored show *Call in at Currys*.[16] The show, hosted by Pete Murray, was to feature a daily outside broadcast from a Currys store. The electrical goods chain had been a long-standing advertiser on commercial radio and one of the first postwar sponsors on Radio Luxembourg, but when it attempted to run what was to be the first syndicated programme on offshore radio it experienced hostility on several fronts. Firstly the BBC objected to Pete Murray's involvement. (Murray was employed by both the BBC and Luxembourg at the time.) Then the Musicians' Union refused Radio London permission to broadcast performances from live groups on the show. (Similar planned tie-ups with the Marquee Club suffered the same fate.) Thirdly the technicians' unions clamped down on outside broadcasts in general. Both Radios Caroline and London made programmes at venues such as the Brands Hatch motor racing circuit and the Earls Court boat show in the early days of pirate radio, but were forbidden from relaying these live on air.

In May 1965 Rediffusion refused to accept a television commercial for a pop record because it mentioned Radio London. Similar restrictions prevented private disc jockeys from making prestigious personal appearances. Early on, Caroline DJs were guests on television pop shows such as *Thank Your Lucky Stars* and *Ready Steady Go!* but the entertainments unions soon clamped down on such activities. In January 1966 the BBC refused to allow Radio London's senior disc jockey Tony Windsor to appear on *Juke Box Jury*. In May of that year, with anti-pirate legislation slowly being formulated, the BBC refused to allow its own Head of Engineering Information to appear on the same conference platform as the Radio London chief Philip Birch.

The positions of the main participants in the offshore radio debate can be summarized as follows: the Songwriters' Guild and the Performing Rights Society upheld the sanctity of intellectual copyright; the Musicians' Union reasserted its right, established by generations of cartelization and protectionism, to determine how many records could be played in any one day, how many interpretations of them could be performed – and by whom; the Conservative government complained about the illegal poaching of frequencies, and the apparent threat to shipping posed by a tiny flotilla of expensively maintained 'floating juke-boxes'; the commercial radio lobby championed free enterprise and made its bid for the populist vote while carefully distancing itself from the full *laissez-faire* implications of the pirates' cause. The Labour Party, starting with the same initial premise, that these stations must be closed down, differed only in its definition of what would replace them. Labour's policy options ranged from leaving it all to the BBC, to leaving it all to the parish pump, or the municipal reformists, or the polytechnics. None of these options had been fully debated when Labour won the October 1964 election. The parliamentary battle against the pirates continued to be waged in the familiar areas of frequency interference and copyright infringement, and regardless of who was in power, floating juke-boxes remained firmly on the agenda.

Locating the addicts

One felt that maybe this was an idea that would never get off the ground, because it did sound a little bit ludicrous to have a radio station broadcasting from a ship off the coast. But once it became apparent that they were there, and they were going to persevere, and try to make a success of their operation we started to listen.

(Teddy Warrick)[17]

Within weeks of Radio Caroline coming on air the BBC began negotiating for more needle-time, asking for an extra 94 hours a week for all its services. It got roughly half of that, with an increase from 28 to 75 hours a week, which was then distributed across the Light, Home, and Third Programmes. Light Programme staff made the best of it, knowing that the BBC network allocation for an entire week could be slotted into Caroline's daily 6 a.m. to 6 p.m. schedule. The fact that there would inevitably be an expansion in pirate transmissions meant that BBC staff knew that they would not compete on anything like equal terms even if they had wanted to.

We envied the pirates. The BBC paid for its needle-time. They were able to broadcast as many records as they liked without making any payments to the record companies via PPL or to the composers and publishers via PRS, or indeed any of the usual copyright payments. One envied them the fact that they could act outside the law rather than break any law. We still had our hands tied behind our back. Whenever we were trying to negotiate new needle-time agreements, even in these days increases were only being given very reluctantly, and not enough to make any real difference.

(Teddy Warrick)[18]

Given the BBC's preoccupation with the three Rs (resources, revenue, and rationalization) it was fitting that its staff should emphasize the needle-time arrangement as the main stumbling block to network reorganization, but this inconvenience deflected attention from more telling areas of the Corporation's cultural policy. It helped to obscure both the low priority given by the BBC to expanding its pop provision in the first place and the kind of material it deemed suitable for public consumption. The emphasis on needle-time negotiation, although a major contributory factor to the BBC's problems, indicated that the conflict was purely administrative and therefore did little to confront the anachronism that BBC popular music policy had become by the early 1960s. There was certainly no overwhelming desire within the BBC to emulate the offshore stations, and policy priorities at the time indicated little expansion in pop provision. Reacting as much to the resurgence of pressure from the National Broadcasting Development Committee as to the existence of the pirates, the BBC outlined proposals for a local radio system consisting of:

(a) Community service, representing all the local interests of each area: social, industrial, business, and every form of public activity;
(b) Education, in co-operation with local schools, as well as working with universities, colleges, and similar bodies, correspondence courses of study for adult education;
(c) Light entertainment, local as well as national.[19]

Local radio, an institutional priority for the next four years, was intended to revitalize the public service flagship, and scant attention was paid to what kind of programmes, if any, would ever replace the pirates. Naturally the official line on Caroline *et al.* was to condemn them for disregarding the law, but it was also noticeable that their professional initiatives were not dismissed so readily. On the contrary, BBC staff recognized the unique training opportunity that unlimited broadcasting hours could allow, and were not slow to acknowledge the effect this would have on the offshore stations' raw recruits. Simon Dee, for instance, estimated that he put in over 1,500 hours of programming during his twelve months with Radio Caroline.

Their DJs, who were totally unknown to us, could be on the air for 50 hours a week, three hours a day (or longer) with doubling up shifts. And so an ease came about in their presentation. If we wished to give anybody a programme in those days he was lucky if we could say 'here's thirteen half-hour programmes for the next three months'. Nobody could ever be in the position of gaining the sort of experience the pirates were getting. So that style of presentation came about through the massive exposure and experience that they were able to get over a very short space of time.

(Teddy Warrick)[20]

Radio Caroline had commissioned a Gallup poll within weeks of coming on air which showed that out of a potential audience of 20 million an estimated 7 million had tuned into the station at some time. In the late summer of 1964 Caroline, by then running two stations, commissioned Attwood Statistics to carry out a further study. This survey revealed that out of a potential audience of 13.5 million people over the age of 12, Caroline South was reaching an average of 999,000 (7.4 per cent), peaking during the weekday lunchtime period with 1,350,000 (10 per cent), and on Sunday mornings with 2,025,000 (15 per cent). Out of a potential audience of just under 16 million Caroline North was reaching an average of 976,000 (6.1 per cent), similarly peaking during the weekday lunchtime period with 1,360,000 (8.5 per cent), and on Sunday mornings with 1,440,000 (9 per cent).

The Attwood figures are significantly lower than anything the pirates publicly claimed at the time. As the offshore stations' polls were largely aimed at the business community figures were often massaged to produce favourable results. Many of the surveys generated under the auspices of policy research naturally served the advertising industry more than the listeners. In the general clamour to claim what were often outlandish audience figures the finer points of demography and methodology were obscured. Most polls commissioned by the pirates took unreliably small samples, and while there were endless promises of more elaborate research to come such schemes were always being indefinitely shelved. Individual stations' listening figures were often added together and passed off as the accumulative total listening to all the pirates. For example, at their peak during 1966–7 both Radio Caroline and Radio London were claiming an audience around the 12 million mark. It did not take long for these figures to be interpreted as a combined audience of 24 million.

Many also inflated their potential audience 'reach', exaggerating both density and breadth of regional coverage. Radio 390, for instance, commissioned its own survey in 1966 and claimed that its signal was not only stronger than all of the other offshore stations, but in several areas, including much of Kent, Sussex, and East Anglia, was stronger than that of the Light Programme itself. In its promotional literature 390 claimed 'an effective output' of 35 kw. In October 1965 even the BBC publicly assumed that the station must be running 60 kw, and credited it as the most powerful offshore station. It was in fact acknowledged among the station's principal commercial competitors that 390 never actually put out more than 5 kw.

Another common tactic was to round up figures to the nearest million. In March 1965, for instance, an NOP survey estimated Radio London's audience to be 2,170,000, compared to Caroline South's 1,090,000. In subsequent publicity literature Radio London's audience was said to be 'nearly 3 million'. One reference book,[21] by substituting potential audience reach for actual audience figures, took this massaging of demographic realities to its illogical conclusion: it stated that in 1964 Caroline North and South had audiences of 17 million and 15 million. Out of regional populations of 16 million and 13.5 million respectively this was truly a remarkable achievement!

The Caroline organization even claimed that at times its listenership exceeded that of the Light Programme. Radio London was careful not to do the same, even issuing a memo in July 1965 forbidding DJs from making such boasts on air. The BBC not surprisingly refuted both Radio Caroline's claim and the NOP audience figures. A study carried out for the BBC by Continuous Survey estimated that overall the Caroline audience was probably about one third of that of the Light Programme.

As a mark of how seriously the Corporation took the pirates it commissioned a further survey during the autumn of 1964; it was carried out by Mass Observation, into what was termed 'the Caroline phenomenon'. The audience research department of the BBC took a sample of 1,000 people over 11 years of age during November 1964 and set out to establish:

(a) Who listens to Caroline?
(b) How much is Caroline listened to?
(c) The nature of Caroline listening;
(d) Attitudes towards Caroline.[22]

This survey gave both Caroline and the BBC higher listening figures, while broadly agreeing with the Continuous Survey estimate of audience ratio, that is about 1:3 in the BBC's favour. But the Mass Observation findings also admitted that perhaps Continuous Survey had not used the most appropriate method to measure Caroline's audience: 'This was done merely as an experiment, it being recognised that Continuous Survey interviewers were inexperienced in "logging" a service of this kind where identification by programme title is impossible'.[23] Continuous Survey did not know how to 'read' the new style of programming, or its audience. Coming to terms with new formats was not the only methodological shortcoming to be exposed by a study of this kind. It also raised serious doubts about the ability of quantitive analysis to offer anything meaningful about the offshore radio audience beyond the most obvious crude head count. The BBC admitted as much in its survey, pointing out that the definition of an 'audience' spanned those who gave a programme their full attention to those who just happened to be within earshot of it. What the BBC survey failed to acknowledge was its own inherent cultural bias.

The BBC approach to surveying the precise constituents of the pop audience in the 1960s was similar to its response to the emergence of a distinctive youth culture in the 1950s. Using socio-anthropological terminology to locate and isolate 'the tribe' (or what the BBC termed 'Caroline addicts') the survey defined this group, which constituted about one fifth of the sample, as:

(a) largely working class in origin;
(b) mostly under 30 years of age (split fairly equally between male and female);
(c) better supplied with portable transistors than the rest of the population;
(d) ITV oriented in their choice of television programmes;
(e) 'less choosey' than the average listener about what they listened to;
(f) tending to use radio as background listening.[24]

The above reads like a caricature of the average pop music audience, and reveals far more about the poll's hidden assumptions than it does about the nature and circumstances of this audience's listening. The survey simply attempted to 'read off' the extent to which the pirate audience conformed to the stereotype and the extent to which it passively fulfilled the assumed exploitive needs of the offshore operators. The survey was actually carried out during a period when much of its potential sample was in school and unavailable for questioning but despite this flaw throws new light on previous assumptions. Perhaps its major finding, although not one which should have surprised the Corporation, was that 'Caroline audiences by no means consist entirely of truants from the BBC'. As there had only been a marginal effect upon the Light Programme audience the inescapable conclusion was that the pirates were catering for what had been, up until 1964, a largely disfranchised audience.

The BBC tempered such findings by focusing on a supposed lack of audience allegiance to the pirate stations. It reached this conclusion after it was found that a significant proportion of the sample appeared to be indifferent to the pirates' fate. Audience allegiance is notoriously difficult to measure: the danger is either of falling back on the same commonsense notions of consumer needs and wants which fuel the broader assumptions of much market research, or more ironically, of reasserting the Reithian maxim of people supposedly not knowing what they want. The BBC's attempt to come to terms with this problem was at best superficial. During the survey the interviewees were presented with a set of adjectives from which they had to choose the ones best describing the 'image' of Radio Caroline and the Light Programme, as if they were rival soap powders. Predictably the 'addicts' found Radio Caroline to be 'lively', 'friendly', and 'cheerful', while they thought of the BBC as 'square', 'stuffy', and 'dull'.

Offshore pirate radio was an atypical broadcasting phenomenon and it is therefore very difficult to draw meaningful conclusions from polls carried out either by the stations themselves or 'official sources' because their criteria for measuring both quality and quantity was suspect. Technological variables also played a major part in distorting findings. Radio 390 was fortunate in one respect in having chosen a relatively clear frequency to broadcast on. Radio London, although indisputably the most popular offshore pirate, shared its wavelength with a powerful East German station. Interference was rarely audible during hours of daylight but by the evening Radio London's broadcasts were accompanied by a piercing heterodyne whistle which worsened as night fell. This interference was evident even during the relatively trouble-free summer months, and was not just confined to the outer reaches of the station's transmission area, being clearly audible on the Kent and Essex coast, and logged in some cases less than four miles from the ship. Radio London tacitly acknowledged the detrimental effect this had on night-time listening figures – a fraction of what the station could command during the day – by never introducing a full 24-hour service during its two and a half years of broadcasting.

Another factor to be taken into account was the equipment that people were listening on. Many wirelesses in operation in 1964 were table mains sets or radiograms, bought, in many cases, in the pre-television era. These were mostly connected to outside or loft wire aerials and would give good reception, even to relatively weak medium wave stations on clear channels – hence Radio 390's survey findings. By the time the offshore radio era was in full swing many people had replaced their obsolete sets with portable transistor radios, without external aerials, which naturally had less sensitivity to weak medium wave signals. The service area of Radio 390 would therefore have been much less than its survey estimated. Radio 390's technical criteria for such findings remain unclear; its 1966 report concludes, with a vagueness that was characteristic of the pirate operations, that the signal had been 'accurately recorded on reliable measuring equipment'.[25]

One thing the 390 survey did clearly indicate was the relatively weak signal that many of the pirate stations were getting into London. Because of a combination of geographical factors, most notably the lie of the Thames basin and the density of commercial and industrial property characteristic of any business capital, London was not the strategic success for many stations that it should have been. Many of the pirates found, for instance, that they could often be heard as well, if not better, in the Midlands than they could in London. One of the lowest readings in the 390 survey was for Leicester Square, and for some stations reception in West London was virtually non-existent. Radio City in particular suffered from this, and was often inaudible at its Denmark Street headquarters. There was also the so-called 'Radio Luxembourg effect' to contend with. Atmospheric vagaries played havoc with radio waves during hours of darkness and a station could often be received as clearly in remote areas of Northern Scotland as in its own immediate vicinity. Assisted by a superior signal across water, and the flatness of East Anglia, listeners on the East coasts of England and Scotland were in the anomalous situation of receiving as good a quality signal from the pirates as did the main target area, the South East.

Nobody loves the pirates – except the listeners

The offshore stations adopted a variety of strategies to combat official disapproval. They pursued prestige not merely through profit maximization (indeed the stations that interpreted the profit motive most crudely were often the least successful financially, so pirate radio's *raison d'être* and subsequent ability to survive cannot simply be deduced by a perusal of company accounts) but also by the manner in which they negotiated the status quo. Given the range of creative opportunities available to them within an ill-defined legal framework most of the pirates behaved remarkably unpiratically for most of the time. Although not all complied completely with the law (the situation attracting more than its share of mavericks, opportunists, and individualists), and although levels of compromise and restraint varied considerably, once the pirates' existence had been defined as problematic the majority quickly revealed incorporatist tendencies. They made placatory gestures in order to appease authority rather than act out the rebellion they paid lip service to. For example, on the day of Sir Winston Churchill's funeral, 24 January 1965, Radios Caroline and London both suspended normal programmes in order to play classical music and broadcast unofficial tributes. Radio London even closed down while the funeral took place. Only a month before this Radio Caroline had made a request to the BBC for a copy of the Queen's Christmas Day message, but was refused on the grounds that it was an unauthorized station. Several pirates were later to make equally futile requests to the GPO for broadcasting licences.

The degree to which the pirates conformed to existing business norms could be most accurately measured by the way in which most stations, even those who swallowed the buccaneering rhetoric wholesale, presented themselves as respectable concerns, eager to pay their taxes and copyright royalties. In their eagerness to conform to recognized broadcasting standards some pirates constructed for themselves codes of behaviour every bit as restrictive as those observed by the legal broadcasters. Self-regulation took varying forms but remained a prominent feature during the pirates' three-and-a-half-year life span. Up until the final stages of the offshore era most stations carefully avoided broadcasting anything which could be construed as politically sensitive. The indiscreet airing of dirty City linen and some unsavoury business practices may have surfaced once in a while; on the whole, though, the more respectable pirates steered clear of controversy.

A total of 21 offshore stations operated between 1964 and 1968 under little more than half a dozen management syndicates. The ownership patterns of the pirate stations was therefore analogous to the wider commercial market they operated within. There were frequent mergers and take-overs, and boardroom friction regularly occurred. Without legislation, expansion would undoubtedly have continued unabated. It was not uncommon for shareholders from one station to make legitimate business approaches to others. For instance, several investors in the Radio Atlanta project offered their services to Radio London while it was still at the planning stage during late 1964. There was also an undue concentration of stations aiming at southern England, a justifiable objective and theoretically lucrative in most industries, but fraught with technical and administrative difficulties in the case of marine broadcasting. Not one offshore station ever achieved national coverage, a situation which encouraged further boardroom mergers.

The first year of British offshore radio was characterized by cautious and steady growth. In an address to the Publicity Club on 2 October 1964, the Project Atlanta director Allan Crawford, mindful of the dangers of adopting too high a business profile, stressed that the Caroline organization had no further plans for expansion or increased transmission hours. In deference to television's vast audience limited daytime broadcasting remained the norm throughout 1964. Crawford also indicated that the newly-named Caroline South, like the majority of pirates, was not getting a very good signal into London. Despite this he claimed that Caroline had an audience of 4 million during peak listening hours.[26]

By the end of 1964 only a handful of pirate stations had become fully operational. With the exception of Carolines North and South and Radio London there was little evidence that any of the stations which periodically appeared on the medium waveband were going to threaten anything other than the Copenhagen Wavelengths Agreement. The smaller stations in particular depended upon the popular press's desire for a novelty, and devised a succession of publicity stunts in order to maintain a media profile. Radio City's managing director, for example, claimed at one point that he was going to start a station from a submarine. The scheme was, needless to say, as unfeasible as it was ludicrous, but it got Radio City a smattering of national newspaper covering. There was little to worry the government unduly in such pranks, and similar wild proposals elsewhere were also proving that getting a pirate station beyond the boardroom planning stage was no easy task. Financed by a consortium of Liverpool club owners, Radio Red Rose allegedly broadcast for just one afternoon in July 1964, and was typical of many similar fly-by-night ventures which made the obligatory single test transmission from an undisclosed location (Southend beach was said to be a much favoured spot) and then disappeared. As anonymous hobbyists indulged in a little harmless fun at the expense of the Wireless Telegraphy Act, numerous stations arose with names such as Radio Albatross, Radio Caesar, Radio Alf, and Radio Sheila, but Radio Marie Celeste would have been more appropriate in most cases.

In the 1920s and 1930s the Newspaper Proprietors' Association had sought to prevent the competing medium from receiving news coverage. Since the late 1950s, though, the NPA had begun to relax its embargo and the *Daily Mirror* and *Titbits* began carrying Radio Luxembourg's programme schedules. Similarly, with the advent of the pirates several of the popular papers proved willing to advertise. Commercials for the *News of the World*, *People*, and *Daily Sketch* were prominent in early pirate broadcasts. Few of the press barons saw legalized commercial radio as an opportunity to expand their media holdings, but their newspapers did begin to give the pirates a cautiously favourable response. The smaller regional and local papers were more scared of losing advertising revenue and couldn't afford to duplicate the nationals' populism. The NUJ was firmly opposed to the introduction of commercial radio, while William Kidd, Director of the Newspaper Society, insisted that newspaper proprietors should take precedence in the event of franchise allocations. The commercial television companies were also uninterested. ATV and Rediffusion expressed indifference to any possible expansion, although Granada did state a guarded interest. Significantly the J. Walter Thompson agency said that it would give serious consideration to tendering for licences if the chance arose. Other groups who expressed an interest at the time, albeit in muted form and only at a localized level included the Rank–Bush–Murphy group, and Lords Thomson and Bessborough. The one group obviously not about to be trusted with the future of the commercial sector was the pirates themselves.

While the popular papers appeared keen to advertise with all but the smallest pirate operations the quality press, in direct contrast, remained distinctly aloof. *The Times* carried the formidable voice of establishment condemnation: 'the motives of these operations is profit, cloaked with the assertion that such vessels provide a radio service which the public wants. There is not a shred of evidence for this.'[27] The *Guardian* likewise was contemptuous of the pirates' efforts and left its readers in no doubt as to who should be the only source of sound broadcasting.

> Does any community feel culturally deprived in being denied its own disc jockey? And is the commercial radio lobby really animated by a sense of cultural mission? . . . Facilities for local radio should therefore go to the organization most likely to make best use of them . . . There might be more demand, on an audience count, for commercial candy floss. But on likely quality the BBC has it.[28]

This was what the voice of liberal left journalism sounded like in the days before papers began actively to court a youth readership. The *New Statesman* made a more savage attack, revealing pure contempt for the pop audience.

What a bottomless chasm of vacuity they reveal! . . . bloated with cheap confectionery and smeared with chain-store makeup, the open sagging mouths and glazed eyes, the hands mindlessly drumming in time to the music, the broken stiletto heels, the shoddy, stereotyped 'with-it' clothes.[29]

Such editorial sneering provided the pirates with ready-made ammunition in the battle for the hearts, minds, and pockets of the pop audience. The legislative procedure was grinding imperceptibly but inevitably into action, and all interested parties were apparently united in their desire to condemn the offshore stations. The ailing *Daily Sketch* summarized the situation on 14 May 1965 with a simple headline: 'Nobody loves the Pop Pirates – except the listeners.' The sentiment could be reversed with equally telling effect because until the pirates came along the listeners had 'no body' to represent them. Even though the station owners were largely interested in their purchasing power they also recognized the prestige to be gained from such sentiments. As consumers the audience's existence had meaning. Listeners were participants in a new emerging youth culture but 'no body' had so far given them much of a voice. They were simply presented with a litany of prohibition, a discourse on all that was forbidden: not to conspire in the stealing of copyright, not to listen to unlimited amounts of recorded music, not to deprive musicians and artists (especially BBC session men) of the right to earn a living, not to encourage the attention of informal disc jockeys who addressed them as 'pussycats'.

What the literary establishment objected to most about the commercial ethos was formularization, the idea that radio output could be streamlined to suit demographic common denominators and to deliver such audiences to the advertisers. These same critics who seemed entirely content with the formula of the well-made play, the rites of the salon, the stylistic nuances of commissioned court composers, or the affectations of modern folk music, clearly did not believe that their perceptions had been damaged in the way that audiences of popular culture had been. It was permissible to embrace the sanitized routines of vaudeville in order to signify empathy with working-class culture, or 'appreciate' the recognizably classical motifs of jazz orchestration (such an insidious critical device made jazz respectable, watered down its radical tradition, and conveniently removed the music from its political context) in order to signify empathy with black culture. But generally there was extreme disapproval of contemporary forms of popular music and their various machine-age outlets. A distrust of all things Afro-American, and the elevation of functional cultural accessories like the juke-box into mechanical manifestations of the devil's own technology were pervasive both among broadcasting policy makers and cultural commentators.

The BBC's unwillingness to endorse specific areas of popular culture mirrored the academic misgivings of a generation of postwar reformers. There are parallels to be drawn between the BBC's institutional complacency (including an increasingly outmoded reliance on previous technology and administrative imperatives) and the cultural establishment's inherent faith in Welfare State social democracy and all its Keynesian Arts Council initiatives. The radio historian Paddy Scannell sees the postwar years as a turning point for public service broadcasting and talks of 'the [BBC's] shift towards popular and entertaining programming [becoming] unstoppable' in this period. He links postwar reforms in politics and broadcasting, depicting them in similarly epochal terms.

In 1945 the landslide victory of the Labour Party at the polls showed the strength of the collective will that there should be no going back to the economic and social conditions that had prevailed before the war. No more could radio hope to return to its prewar ways.[30]

Critics who in other areas of their field-work had enriched the study of popular culture were often dismissive of pop music, making it evident that the democratization of culture, like political democratization in general, had its limits:

There is the lowbrow-gang-spirit of some gramophone record features in which young men, accompanying their items with a stream of pally patter, offer programmes whose whole composition assumes that whatever the greatest number like most is best and the rest are aberrations of eggheads.[31]

Reactions to the postwar rise of the affluent teenager were uniformly negative among cultural commentators. The mere existence of the juvenile delinquent was problematic, threatening the idealized portraits of working-class life which had emerged from such writings as Richard Hoggart's. The dismissive tone of the above quote reflected a formidable orthodoxy, its style permeating every facet of the media. On BBC television the interrogative edge of the populist current affairs style, championed by presenters of *Panorama* and *Tonight*, encapsulated the approach. The archetype, evident now only on grainy archive footage, depicts a six-foot-tall old Etonian presenter in a grey raincoat, standing on a school rugby field on a foggy day, bending down from the clouds brusquely to ask little Johnny what he would do when he left school. On the radio, the corporation's opinion of pop was more likely to be accurately conveyed by the dismissive tones of the panelists on the brains trust type of programme than via the contrived exuberance of *Easybeat*. In the teen exploitation movies of the early 1960s a patronizing approach to popular culture was personified by the adult figure who played 'straight man' to the teasing but essentially harmless japes of the young pranksters.[32] Once it had been established that the youth phenomenon had potentially menacing implications, its energies were diluted in these movies with the wholesome integrity of an enthusiastic clergyman or welfare officer, who would be drafted in from a genteel leafy suburb, pitched into a postwar inner city slum area, sent out into the youth clubs to find out why the kids vandalized property and didn't go to church any more, only to find that the kids weren't a bad lot after all as long as they were treated with respect.

Within popular music radio there was an attempt to rekindle the values of the family, church, and education, by transplanting the middle-class ethos of the youth club into light entertainment programming. Such initiatives were supposed to compensate for a sentimentally depicted communal loss and to supplement the supposedly undernourished cultural diet of the masses; without this instructive element, it was suggested, popular entertainment provision would only induce mass conformity. The dour British critical orthodoxy of the 1950s evokes an image of a thousand technical college liberal studies classes resentfully being force-fed aesthetics when they would rather have been out jiving, groping, eating candy floss, and enthusiastically embracing all the other iconographic flotsam of the age.

In other areas, such as sociology (where the social work case-study became the social scientist's substitute for the working-class novel) writers similarly talked of cultural deprivation and compensatory education for the poor. Suddenly the whole of the educational ethos was seen as unquestionably good compared with the dangerous new forms of indoctrination which were allegedly being manufactured by unscrupulous advertisers. Denys Thompson talked of a 'distinctive national culture' and delivered the prescribed constituents of cultural heritage in Leavisite and Reithian terms. All the listener had to do was choose correctly from the options available. Advertising expenditure was compared with the education[33] and health budgets[34] but never, for example, with military expenditure (or indeed the private sector of education and health provision). Such explicit parallels would perhaps have highlighted the inconsistencies in Labour policy that allowed the Welfare State to be quasi-egalitarian but not socialist.

Some critics made claims for advertising's influence which were more outlandish than the very advertisers' techniques they were attacking. Even traditional enemies of the municipal working class like rent and debt collectors or urban planners were not portrayed so scathingly. They merely had to be endured with the kind of weary resignation and stoical resilience that gave the working class its 'character'. Advertisers, on the other hand, were depicted as psychic intruders into working-class communities; these commercial hucksters had to be repelled at all costs, because, as was made abundantly clear, working-class people and working-class teenagers in particular were vulnerable and could rarely be trusted to make rational decisions. Advertisers apparently possessed a deadly psychological armoury capable of all kinds of emotional manipulation.

To postwar critics the particular model of public service

broadcasting developed by the BBC became synonymous with public service broadcasting *per se*. The commercial model, although equally adept at creating its own ideals, came to be defined as everything the public service model was not. Oppositional relationships were postulated between 'public information' and 'the market', between public funding and sponsorship initiated by the business community, between active participatory 'listeners' and passive populism-fed 'consumers'. Adorno saw 'the language of promotion' replacing 'the language of evaluation'. In the creative domain the qualities of 'professionalism' were pitted against a particular pejorative notion of 'amateurism'. Radio's supposed organizational schism was informed by a literary aesthetic which contrasted the acquiring of 'taste' with the consuming of 'merchandise'; appreciation was desirable, base enjoyment was to be distrusted. Culture confronted barbarism, and the continued colonization of the public service by the postwar literary establishment echoed the Corporation's essentially Arnoldian notions of culture as 'the pursuit of perfection' and 'the best that is thought and known in the world'.

Whatever else the concept of commercial radio may entail it has never simply meant a licence to print money. Economists rarely agree on such matters as the volume of advertising that the market can absorb at one time, and even the most sophisticated market research can rarely predict the audience's capacity or willingness to consume the services on offer.[35] There is also considerable disagreement about the degree of correlation between advertising outlay and subsequent company profit, the volume of advertising and the size of a company, and the volume of advertising and a product's overall market share. Nor is there any consistent evidence to suggest that massive expenditure on advertising exercises a greater influence than minimal expenditure. What little evidence there is merely suggests that high advertising costs are eventually passed on to the customer, despite advertising initially being offered to the consumer at no cost. The organizational goals of commercial radio have been built on this legacy of imprecision. The postwar critical establishment talked of all these factors as if they were constants. Patterns of consumerism are not so predictable, and consumers do not always conveniently slot into the neat demographic categories that either media planners, social policy makers, or indeed the commercial purveyors of dreams and desires would seem to require.

Broadcasting history in Britain, particularly radio history, needs to be seen in a less simplified way than the arguments about ownership and cultural policy have traditionally allowed. Confining the debate within such narrow conceptual parameters relegates crucial tensions to an inventory of charter ideals and market distribution. 'State' and 'privately owned' regimes are accorded a polarity of intent, measured by recourse to some emblematic notion of the value systems they supposedly represent. Academia continued in the postwar years to be informed by this false dichotomy between the competing forces in radio's mixed economy. The mass communications debate was reduced to a tactical argument about the quality of provision. The analysis of entertainment was not seen to be a purposeful activity even though it was here, in light entertainment's supposedly non-controversial, non-problematic, non-epochal, day-to-day cultural production and distribution, that constraints and potential could be most accurately located. The recipient mass audience who selectively received this output exercised its prerogative to enter into contract with its sins and pleasures at will. From jazz age to jitterbug, from bobbysoxers to Bob Dylan the public has generally shown itself to be willing to indulge first and suffer the cultural condemnation later. For some schools of critical inquiry the spectacle of sub-cultural sacrificial lambs lying down with the lions of commercial exploitation continues to throw up some unpalatable truths.

CHAPTER 3

Method actors versus multinationals

Anyone who can remember anything at all about pirate radio in the 1960s can usually remember two names: Radio Caroline and Radio London are synonymous with the offshore era. Between them they accounted for the majority of the audience who listened to the pirates, and the majority of sponsors who advertised on them. But although they basically shared the same market rationale Caroline and London approached their respective tasks completely differently. London sought respect, prestige, and accommodation. Its every move was geared towards being legitimately incorporated into the existing system of broadcasting, and its main purpose seemed to be to lay the groundwork for a legal commercial radio system in Great Britain, built on the American model. Radio Caroline had a very different rule book and a very different guiding ethos. By a series of acts which culminated in a defiant stand against what it saw as repressive legislation Caroline made explicit underlying tensions which anticipated the wider ideological tensions of the 1960s counter-culture. For Radio London respect would eventually be won and the station's influence and programming legacy would endure in the shape of both its immediate replacement – BBC Radio One – and the independent local radio system which followed in the 1970s. For Radio Caroline there would be nothing like the same degree of influence. This contrast of approaches and outcomes between the two major pirate stations is at the epicentre of the story of offshore radio.

Radio Caroline

Without the capitalist pigs of the City of London there would have been no Caroline. There's no way on this planet that I could have got the money from a central committee or a Wedgwood Benn to start Caroline.

(Ronan O'Rahilly)[1]

Prior to Radio Caroline going on air in March 1964 its founder Ronan O'Rahilly had dabbled in several ventures. The first of these was an acting school in Knightsbridge called Studio 57; it was set up to teach 'the Method', a component of Stanislavski's 'system' as preached through the works of the post-Russian Revolution Moscow Arts Theatre, that had been imported and adapted to American film and theatre by Lee Strasberg at his legendary Actors' Studio in New York. In the late 1950s there was money to be made out of the Method. Schools opened up all over London in order to satisfy once-sceptical thespians who had reluctantly come round to thinking that there must be theatrical life beyond farce, comedy of manners, and the well-made play. The Method approach offered introspective and intense self-absorption, which involved tearing up the rule book of correct intonation and stage direction and instinctively becoming the part. O'Rahilly and some of his Studio 57 colleagues were later to show that the Method was as applicable to radio as it was to theatre. This radical and fervently resisted break with the formal tradition and techniques of theatre became a crucial metaphor, which Radio Caroline alone among the pirates was to make explicit in its spontaneous approach to pop radio.

In the early 1960s O'Rahilly ran the Scene Club, a former jazz venue in London's Soho. As Club Eleven in the late 1940s and early 1950s it had been one of the few venues catering for a multiracial audience and had attracted notoriety when it received London clubland's first drugs raid.[2] The resident DJ at the Scene Club was Guy Stevens, who, with Chris Blackwell, also ran Sue Records, Britain's first independent record label; it catered for *aficionados* of rare soul, blues, and Jamaican bluebeat. Those individualists who turned into modernists long before the media discovered 'Mods' were the Scene Club's clientele. They were also the subcultural link between the burgeoning micro-economy of London's upper-class bohemians and the newly affluent working-class youth.

Ronan O'Rahilly had previously managed Alexis Korner's Blues Incorporated, which included Mick Jagger and Charlie

61

Watts of the Rolling Stones and provided the nucleus of the early 1960s British blues boom. The kind of groups O'Rahilly booked for the Scene Club (the Rolling Stones, Them, Georgie Fame and the Blue Flames) had their roots in rhythm and blues and jazz; their influences were artists such as Muddy Waters, Sonny Boy Williamson, Lightnin' Hopkins, Ray Charles, Jimmy Reed, Mose Allison, and Jimmy Smith. Although Ronan O'Rahilly's club was in Soho his social clique centred on Chelsea, and a consideration of the role that the Chelsea set played in the emergence of both Radio Caroline and 'swinging London' is crucial to any analysis of the 1960s.

> Chelsea was the centre of everything, all those facets of Ronan's social life, the acting set, the King's Road set, everyone seemed to live within one hundred yards of the King's Road. You met people and set up plans. It was the generation maturing, the early days of all that, and there wasn't any of the paranoia that exists today. It was open and colourful, and it was the start of Mary Quant and all those people, putting seeds in that later grew. And there was Ronan's energy. He knew that he had sufficient links to raise finance, get a boat, and get it fitted.
>
> (Simon Dee)[3]

Radio Caroline's original board of directors included C. E. Ross, owner of the Ross group of companies, and John Sheffield, Chairman of Norcros. Ross and Sheffield controlled 83 per cent of Radio Caroline shares. The most influential of Caroline's original backers, although not a major shareholder, was Sheffield's son-in-law Jocelyn Stevens, then Editor-in-Chief of *Queen* magazine. Radio Caroline temporarily used *Queen*'s Fetter Lane offices as a base during the launch period. Interviewed in these offices for the Granada TV's *World in Action* early in 1964 Stevens dominated the documentary footage, his formidable presence completely outshining that of his associates. The fresh-faced O'Rahilly now comes across as tongue-tied in comparison with Stevens, with his bullish business acumen.

Before Stevens's involvement, which began in 1957, *Queen* was operating very much in the shadow of another society magazine, the *Tatler*. Stevens transformed the magazine, as Chelsea itself was being transformed, and the innovative stylistic devices and carefree juxtapositions which *Queen* utilized at that time captured both the depth and superficiality of the 1960s. In print, pithy ephemera coexisted with genuine investigative journalism. In pictures, *Queen*'s astonishing succession of commissioned photo imagery set the visual tone for the decade to come. Cecil Beaton glamourized dowdy debs. Norman Parkinson flew models over the Eiffel Tower for Cardin or Ricci, Armstrong-Jones snapped Eton College, Cartier Bresson revealed communist China. The magazine, which carried features on the jet-set excursions of the elite, on what were then fashionable, even bohemian, resorts such as St Tropez, Ibiza, and Majorca, still found time to develop what was probably the first designer social conscience. When *Queen* ran an 'austerity issue' to counteract its earlier 'boom time issue' it was printed on ration book paper![4]

Pseudo-anthropological surveys mocked the follies and foibles of the upper classes' tribal archaisms; its nepotism, philistinism, and narcissism were favoured targets. *Queen* was constantly redefining the social mores of the Establishment and the dividing line between *nouveau* and not so *nouveau riche*; particular attention was paid to the obsessive question of what constituted 'with-it-ness'. Such concerns also made up a major component of the burgeoning Oxbridge satire boom, and *Queen* was happy occasionally to accommodate the collective irreverence of *Private Eye* and TW3 contributors Richard Ingrams, Christopher Booker, Bernard Levin, William Rushton, and Paul Foot.

An unmistakable hybrid of New Right and New Left libertarianism also ran though the magazine, thematically anticipating the counter-culture in all its contradictory splendour and ideological failings. *Queen* was, for instance, the first magazine to do an in-depth feature on casual drug use. Written by John 'Hoppy' Hopkins, later an important figure in the English underground, and best known for running the UFO club, the piece broke new ground by emphasizing leisure-time hedonism over social problems. *Queen* was also one of the first magazines to deal with feminist issues (or as *Queen* referred to them, using the appropriate apolitical vernacular of the time 'feminine issues'), such as abortion and birth control. As Chelsea was being 'discovered' so too were Chelsea set authors.

The Chelsea novel, with Virginia Ironside and Nell Dunn as its ambassadors, mostly offered introspective accounts of the Chelsea set. Occasionally, as in Dunn's *Up the Junction*, it took off on inquisitive escapades into neighbouring Battersea for glimpses of working-class life. Side by side with *Queen*'s gossip grapevine and its 'Debs' Diaries', subcultural snapshots of a weightier kind could periodically be summoned from Colin MacInnes, Antonia Fraser, Mark Boxer, Penelope Gilliat, James Cameron, or Angus Wilson.

Queen also gave valuable publicity to David Bailey, Terence Donovan, Jean Shrimpton, and Mary Quant, names synonymous with 'swinging London'. The patronage offered by Chelsea's rich bohemians to the new generation of actors, musicians, designers, models, photographers, and writers that was beginning creatively to uncoil in the early 1960s, enabled an entire artistic community to live on the periphery, maintained by the autonomous wealth of philanthropic heiresses, lords, and earls. Invisible income sustained some very visible spending; if things went wrong the Chelsea norm was to expand operations rather than cut back. Economically reckless schemes could be indulged on a whim, without a care for their viability or their future; security came from the knowledge that everything from subterranean values to finishing school could be subsidized by private incomes and inheritances. The older Chelsea order offered privilege permanently in season, a world in which remnants of aristocratic lines walked out with their débutante daughters pursued by enigmatic socialites (enigmatic because they appeared to do little other than socialize). It is precisely within such affluence that the hedonistic origins of Radio Caroline can be located. By 1964 that whole microcosmic Chelsea world was starting to become public knowledge.

This then was Ronan O'Rahilly's cultural milieu. A 22-year-old citizen of the Irish Republic, whose grandfather had been killed in the Easter uprising, and subsequently eulogized in verse by W. B. Yeats, he had entered into Chelsea's exclusive bohemian clique in the late 1950s. O'Rahilly also brought with him an

Irish-American cultural identification with the Kennedy clan, which was in the first instance responsible for the actual naming of Radio Caroline. In a typical photo-opportunity, John Kennedy's daughter had been depicted in *Time-Life* magazine apparently holding up important White House business with her mere presence and a smile. O'Rahilly's empathy with Caroline Kennedy's quasi-innocence and the idealism embodied in her father's political vision was transformed in the conspiratorial aftermath of the President's assassination. He maintained his rebel's instinct and an undaunted naïve optimism but these were now fuelled by a shrewdly opportunist desire for a little entrepreneurial action. O'Rahilly also allegedly held a grudge against Radio Luxembourg because it would not accommodate his Georgie Fame recordings into their fully booked schedules – although many believe O'Rahilly's plans for a radio station were formulated long before this much-documented, but possibly apocryphal incident. This was Radio Caroline's cultural lineage, an ancestry of gestures, symbols, impressions, and attitudes. O'Rahilly regarded freedom of expression as a political birthright, and his radio station as the symbolic embodiment of this birthright.

The overall sound of Radio Caroline in those first few months of broadcasting couldn't help but reflect the likes and life-styles of its staff and its backers. O'Rahilly never lost contact with the philosophy of, or indeed the participants in, the Method venture. Simon Dee had previously been a student at Studio 57, and many of Caroline's early DJs, like Carl Conway, John Junkin (who had been with Joan Littlewood's experimental East End theatre company), and Doug Kerr, came not from the music industry but, as had so many commercial radio recruits before them, from the acting profession. Few of the station's early DJs liked pop music exclusively. O'Rahilly's Scene Club heritage and the tastes of the Chelsea set were also audible in station output.

From March 1962 *Queen* magazine began to carry a Top 20 – the most requested numbers at Annabel's, the recently opened nightclub in London's Berkeley Square. This Top 20, with its heavy emphasis on jazz and quality singers (Barney Kessel to Ella Fitzgerald), bore a marked resemblance to the music listeners heard on those very first broadcasts from Radio

Caroline. The Caroline station theme was the jazz organist Jimmy McGriff's arrangement of Thelonious Monk's 'Round Midnight'. Simon Dee's theme tune was 'On the street where you live' by Tommy Dorsey and his band. Bryan Vaughan and Jon Sydney both used Henry Mancini pieces. Gary Kemp used Ray Charles's 'Let's Go'. Along with a preponderance of jazz, rhythm and blues, and ballads, pop had to take its place with a smattering of blue-beat, trad, folk, and Latin-American music.

The Merseybeat boom was at its peak during the early months of 1964, and the Top 20 for the week that Caroline began broadcasting, (21–8 March), contained records by Cilla Black, the Merseybeats, the Searchers, Billy J. Kramer and the Dakotas, the Hollies, Freddie and the Dreamers, the Beatles, and Peter and Gordon. For the first six months of 1964 Merseybeat records, or discs by artists generally associated with the beat boom, accounted for the number one spot for all but two out of the 26 weeks, but neither Radio Caroline, nor any of its early rivals, was predominantly concerned with pop music. It is a major misconception about the pirates, actively encouraged both by hostile authorities and aggrieved representatives of the music industry (and, of course, the offshore stations' own myth-making) that they were merely 'floating juke-boxes', playing a non-stop diet of pop. Although the rise of offshore radio could undoubtedly be attributed in part to the low priority the BBC gave to pop music there was in fact always a great deal of diversity in the pirates' programming. Caroline was content to call itself 'your all day music station', rather than 'your all day pop music station', and during its first three or four months of broadcasting (up to the merger with Radio Atlanta in July 1964) leaned very strongly towards what would now be called hip easy listening or quality middle-of-the-road music. Ronan O'Rahilly's radio station, initially at least, bore all the hallmarks of an attempt to corner the sophisticated end of the adult market.

Many of the station's early programmes were taped on land and therefore did not immediately have the exuberance and freshness of style that people generally associate with the pirates. The majority were stockpiled by DJs Simon Dee and Chris Moore weeks before Caroline actually went on air, and when the station did make its first broadcasts most of the records featured were at least three or four months old. The few programmes that were done live on the ship entailed the disc jockey announcing the music, while an engineer was responsible for all manual operations. This was standard practice at that time. In later years, DJ 'self-op' became the norm and was the essential difference between a disc jockey and an announcer. As these were, give or take the odd force nine gale, the same conditions that the BBC staff operated under, it is not surprising that the presentation styles were not significantly different. Listeners certainly heard a greater quantity of non-stop music on Caroline during its first few weeks of broadcasting than they had previously, on the Light Programme, together with a hint of the mid-Atlantic patter that was to become a hallmark of the pirates' presentation. But apart from a few asides about the weather conditions and the uniqueness of location the pacing of programmes was rather stilted. Disc jockeys on the ship would occasionally interject time checks into the taped shows, but topical comments were not risked.

Some typical programming from Caroline during those early months is illustrated in Table 3.1. Without getting too embroiled in purist definitions of musical forms one can see that there are, by any stretch of the imagination, only a few records among them which can be strictly classified as pop. Although some Caroline programmes were more pop oriented than others none of those illustrated here are untypical. They are not significantly different from one or two of the more adventurous shows on the Light Programme at the time.

Table 3.1 Radio Caroline programming, early 1964

Discs played	Type
Simon Dee and Carl Conway, 10.45 a.m. to 11.15 a.m., April	
'Blueberry Hill', Ray Conniff	(light orchestral)
'Nutty Squirrel', Billy's Bag	(jazz)
'I call your name', Billy J. Kramer and the Dakotas	(pop)
'Side by side', Ray Charles and Betty Carter	(jazz)
'I love you because', Jim Reeves	(country ballad)

'Pushover', Etta James   (rhythm and blues)
End of Simon Dee programme (theme: 'On the street where you live',
   Tommy Dorsey)
Start of Carl Conway programme (theme by Ray Conniff)
'Needles and pins', Searchers   (pop)
'With a little bit of luck', Stanley   (musical sound-track,
   Holloway   *My Fair Lady*)
'Young and Foolish', Paul Anka   (ballad)

Chris Moore, 12.00 noon to 12.30 p.m., April

Opening theme: 'I've got a woman',
   Jimmy McGriff   (jazz organ instrumental)
'I'm so in love', Frank Sinatra   (ballad)
'Wheel of fortune', Ray Conniff   (light orchestral)
'Peanuts', Gene Pitney   (pop)
'Take the A train', Mantovani   (light orchestral, arrangement)
'Ain't misbehavin', Nat King Cole   (ballad arrangement)
'As usual', Brenda Lee   (pop ballad)
'I'm the lonely one', Cliff Richard   (pop)
'Pushover', Etta James   (rhythm and blues)
'Hey look me over', Cy Coleman   (jazz)
'Stars fell on Stockton', Shadows   (pop instrumental)

John Junkin show, 4.30 p.m. to 5.00 p.m., April

'The Preacher', Billy May   (big band jazz)
'You and I,' Billy Davies   (pop)
'Limehouse Blues', Tony Bennett   (ballad)
'The Reverend Mr Black', New Christy
   Minstrels   (commercial folk)
'Living it up', Murray Ross   (jazz vocal)
'Hello little girl', The Fourmost   (pop)
'Lover', Johnny Dolittle   (ballad, jazz arrangement)
'Falling in love', Big Jolly Trio   (jazz)
'If I were you', Peter and Gordon   (pop)
'Confessin', Louie Prima and Keely
   Smith   (jazz style ballad)
'I could write a book', Ella Fitzgerald   (jazz vocal)

Carl Conway show, 12.10 p.m. to 12.40 p.m., May

'Anytime is the right time', Ray Charles (gospel-tinged rhythm
    and blues)
'Something special', Dusty Springfield   (pop)
'Baby don't cry', The Puppets   (pop)
'Summer Place', Andy Williams   (ballad)
'America', Trini Lopez   (musical sound-track, *West Side Story*)

'I just wanna stay here and love you', Mike Sammes Singers	(light orchestral)
'Yesterday and you', Ellenka Balluska	(continental ballad)
'Sunday', The Stringalongs	(Hawaiian-style instrumental)
'My favourite things', Mark Murphy	(musical sound-track, *The Sound of Music*)
'Little Egypt', The Marauders	(pop)

Radio Atlanta

Radio Atlanta, which began broadcasting in May 1964 but was merged with Radio Caroline within two months, illustrated during its short existence one of the ways in which pirate radio was tempered by traditional music industry thinking. Its owner, the Australian Allan Crawford, had been working both in Britain and Australia as managing director of the American-owned music publishing company Southern Music between 1955 and 1959. By the early 1960s he had formed his own independent company, Merit Music, and recognizing the lack of promotional outlets in Britain was looking there for fresh exposure for his product.

> The reason he [Crawford] started Radio Atlanta, at some considerable expense to himself, and much greater expense to many of his associates, was that he had a feeling – a deep rooted instinct which was quite wrong – that the only way to sell a record was for it to be heard by people incessantly. And he felt that any record, provided it had his copyright on it, played a sufficient number of times a week to an enormous audience, would sell in vast quantities, and would reach the Top 10. Now this theory was completely wrong . . . And that was one of the things, apart from all the general skulduggery, that seems to be part of any unofficial attempt at organizing entertainment, that killed Atlanta. Most of the records that he played from his own company and group of publishing houses were just not popular.
>
> (John Ridley)[5]

The three record labels featured most prominently, Rocket, Sabre, and Canon, were all owned by Crawford, and featured cover versions of the hits of the day by unknown artists. Therefore, as on the Light Programme, listeners to Radio Atlanta were far more likely to hear a cover version of the Beatles' or Rolling Stones' latest record than they were the Beatles or Stones original. In fact Allan Crawford's approach was still very much the norm in the early 1960s. Sheet music was still widely available and cover versions of songs were a much favoured way of generating income. Radio Atlanta's programming philosophy reflected the interests and backgrounds both of its owner and several of its backers from the entertainment world. This also explains the predominance of film and show tunes in early Atlanta broadcasts. The continued importance of Hollywood and Broadway as promotional vehicles for new tunes guaranteed a flow of published material which remained lucrative even at the peak of the pop boom.

Project Atlanta Ltd issued approximately 150,000 shares at £1 each. There were initially 38 individual investors, holding from as few as 50 shares to as many as 10,000. The latter belonged to the largest private shareholder, the financial director Frank Victor Broadribb. The next largest interest, 4,000 shares, was held by Major Cecil Lomax, a publisher and Lloyds underwriter. Other notable investors were: Sir Robert Barlow, Chairman and later President of the Metal Box Company, who with Lady Barlow held 1,000 shares, Atlanta's accountant William Wells (of Amsdon, Cossart and Wells) with 1,250, and Lord Hazlerigg with 1,000. In many cases, though, genuine investors preferred to shield their identities, delegating their capital to trust funds and investment companies. A syndicate of well-known boxing and wrestling promoters was one such group which invested in this discreet manner. Kelling Investments, of Hatton House, London EC1, held 20,338 shares. Various stock exchange syndicates held a further 20,000. Hidden among these nominees was the Port of London Authority Pension Fund. There was also a strong rumour of involvement from the Rothschild family. Another prominent shareholder was Major Oliver Smedley, in 1955 a founder member of the Institute of Economic Affairs, an avowed free-trader, and former Vice Chairman of the Liberal Party. As a private individual he held only 1,250 shares, but companies of which he was a director (Investment and General Management Services Ltd, and Mise-en-Scene Ltd) held a further 30,000 shares. Like Smedley, the theatrical impresario Kitty Black held a stock of 1,250 shares, but her company CBC (Plays) Ltd was the largest overall investor, with 36,000 shares. Both Smedley and Black were to figure prominently in subsequent pirate dramas.

At the planning stage of Project Atlanta Allan Crawford and Ronan O'Rahilly had briefly been part of the same team. But when Crawford's venture suffered a series of setbacks and many of its original backers nervously pulled out, the King's Road crowd went their own way. While being fitted out at Greenore in the Republic of Ireland, a port owned by Ronan O'Rahilly's father, the Atlanta organization did undoubtedly suffer from periodic petty sabotage, but the 'general skulduggery' referred to above, and the rivalry said to have existed between the two stations, have been vastly overplayed. Being fitted out in the same port in mutual secrecy is not generally symptomatic of bitter enemies. Caroline even used to feature several of Crawford's cover versions in its programmes long before anyone was talking openly about merger.

On Atlanta, as on Caroline, there was initially little evidence of any demand for 24-hour pop programming, but unlike Caroline which presented jazz, pop, rhythm and blues, and easy listening, pot-pourri style within the same programmes, Atlanta tended to separate the styles into distinct segments within the schedules. There would be a programme of pop music, followed by a programme of Latin-American music, followed by a programme of country music. The overall effect was similar to the output of Radio Luxembourg, that is, separate slots, contrasting in style depending on the sponsor, and ranging in length from 15 to 90 minutes.

Table 3.2 illustrates the extent to which Allan Crawford's record labels were plugged during Radio Atlanta's general programming, the variety of music promoted on the station's new releases show, and the scope of Atlanta's specialist programming. Brief analysis of each example indicates a lack of hard sell at variance with Crawford's more obvious entrepreneurial tendencies. Due emphasis was certainly given to product licensed by Radio Atlanta's owner, yet there was little blatant promotion, beyond a customary name check for the label concerned, even in programmes where Merit Music

71

material was featured prominently. The first example in Table 3.2 was one of the few programmes where it was possible to log full content information, as disc jockeys on other shows constantly neglected to mention the artist's name and often played anonymous cover versions of popular songs which, as far as can be ascertained, were not on the Sabre, Rocket, and Canon labels. The lack of priority accorded to Allan Crawford's material indicates that tin pan alley thinking was the predominant influence on Radio Atlanta's programming ethos. Publishing revenue was primarily generated by songs, not artists or record labels. In the second example, a new releases show, the DJ gave copious biographical details of many of the artists and groups featured, but omitted the name of the record label. Instead the listener was given the general advice, 'available from your record store now'.

Table 3.2 Radio Atlanta programming

Discs played	Type
Bob Scott, Johnnie Jackson, 6.55 p.m. to 7.30 p.m., 25 May	
(Merit Music material in parenthesis)	
'Gloria', Kenny Bardell	(Sabre)
'The poor people of Paris', Chet Atkins	
End of Bob Scott show/beginning of Johnnie Jackson show	
'What am I gonna do without you?', Lynn Collins	(Sabre)
'Save the last dance for me', Drifters	
'Let the four winds blow', Fats Domino	
'Hippy Hippy Shake', Frank Bacon	(Rocket)
'Yellow Rose of Texas', Stan Freburg	
'Perfidia', Ventures	
'Don't throw your love away', Tony Stevens	(Canon)
'Tonight I fell in love', Tokens	
'My Boy Lollipop', Laura Lee	(Canon)
'Crazy', Patsy Cline	
'Love my life away', Gene Pitney	
'You can depend on me', Brenda Lee	
'Mocking Bird Hill', Frank Bacon	(Canon)
Tony Windsor, new releases show, 3.30 p.m. to 4.00 p.m., 30 May	
'Stop, look and listen', Wayne Fontana	(pop)
'I don't want to know', Shirley and John	(pop ballad)

'Rock around the Clock', Bill Haley and the Comets	(rock and roll re-release)
'Dimples,' John Lee Hooker	(rhythm and blues)
'Rosalyn', Pretty Things	(rhythm and blues)
'Hickory Dick and Dock', Bobby Vee	(pop)
'I wish you would', Yardbirds	(rhythm and blues)
'Please little girl,' Heinz	(pop)
'Be anything but be mine', Connie Francis	(ballad)
'Why not tonight?', Mojos	(pop)

4.00 p.m. Clive Burrell, Latin-Americana	
4.30 p.m. Richard Harris, Best of the Ballads	
5.00 p.m. Johnny Jackson, Country and Western	
6.00 p.m. Mike Raven, All Systems Go	(beat music and specialist rhythm and blues)
7.00 p.m. Neil Spence, Music of the moment	(pop)

Radio Atlanta also gave early indication that the British public was going to be presented with a considerable variety of presentation styles, ranging from an unadulterated American, through broad Australian (a constant yet consistently overlooked influence on British radio from the 1930s right through to the early 1970s) to immaculate actor's RADA-speak and Received Pronounciation. During its first few weeks the only disc jockeys on board the ship doing live programmes were the Texan father and son team Johnnie Jackson and Bob Scott. The fact that Jackson had worked as a DJ and engineer in Dallas radio was revealed in his snappy delivery and throwaway catch-phrases like 'the most on the coast', 'the ship that rocks the ocean', and 'the music queen of the seven seas'. Jackson's son had a tendency to refer to himself as 'Mrs Scott's little fat boy Bob'. Unfortunately what was standard Texan *bonhomie* back home sounded faintly ridiculous to British ears. What was being projected as homely merely sounded corny to listeners who were more used to the rather staid and formal 'I'm now calling Mrs Elsie Lockett – are you listening Elsie?' BBC style, which Atlanta approximated during its request programmes. As the more perceptive press reports accurately noted, if a broadcasting revolution was coming it was obviously taking its time. A *Daily Telegraph* columnist noted,

> in West and South West London Atlanta is giving the strongest signal, but it is shyer of announcing its identity than

Caroline ... Atlanta it seems is putting out a plausible imitation of the BBC's *Housewives' Choice* with postcards, loving messages and the lot.[6]

Radio London

The few times I'd turned the radio on and listened to British radio I'd been bored up the wall. The more I thought about it, and I thought of the free enterprise radio system in the United States and what it brought to the people over here, that it would also bring pleasure to people in England. And this offered a vehicle, if it were possible to do, to bring both a pleasure to England, plus make a capitalist profit ... I knew nothing about commercial radio, nothing about shipping.

(Don Peirson)[7]

The Texan oil buccaneers and gas barons of the postwar years were aggressively populist in outlook and *laissez-faire* in their dealings. They also constituted a powerful Conservative political lobby. Texan oil dollars dictated the rural economy of the Lone Star state, and the oil and gas industry was linked with several formidable subsidiaries, all dependent on oil revenue. Oil funded the transport industry, particularly automobiles, construction (dams, power plants, and pipelines), and more significantly, because it helped fund rural electrification and irrigation, it also helped create media markets. Radio London was funded by such money.

The station's initial investors were: Don Peirson, conservative mayor of Eastland, Texas, who owned various automobile agencies (selling Dodge and Oldsmobile) and the Abilene National Bank; Tom Danaher, also an automobile dealer (Volkswagen) and airport owner in Wichita Falls; Mal McIlwain, owner of the McIlwain Cadillac Company and a Ford agency; and Jack McGlothlin, a Texan oil mogul. Peirson was project overseer, McIlwain put together the sales organization, McGlothlin dealt with legal and financial operations, Danaher supervised the outfitting of the station's broadcasting vessel.

These four raised the initial $500,000 for the venture and held controlling voting interests. Each sold splinter shares to other partners, and there were in all 17 shareholders with financial interests chiefly in construction, automobiles, and banking. Gordon McLendon had been partly responsible for inventing Top 40 radio, for setting up one of the first promotional jingles companies (PAMS) in the 1940s, and for launching one of the first offshore stations in Europe (Radio Nord) in the 1950s. He was involved in the background in a consultancy capacity, particularly over programming, where he advised London's first station manager Ben Toney, himself a former programme director of the leading Fort Worth stations KCUL and KJIM, and a budding political careerist at Junior Chamber of Commerce and county government level. In 1964 Toney campaigned for the conservative Barry Goldwater in the presidential primaries.

'Ladybird' Johnson, the US President's wife (owner of KTBC–TV Austin, and a chain of CBS-affiliated radio and television stations in Texas) was also rumoured to have a financial interest via her trust funds. This was not so ironic given the cross-political loyalties of Texan money. Oil dollars transcended party allegiance and early in his political career Lyndon Johnson had acted as a conduit for conservative wealth, appeasing Republicans and manœuvring oil revenue necessary for his political advancement into Democrat campaign coffers. Radio London management did little actively to discourage rumours of Mrs Johnson's involvement. In fact the story has no foundation but does illustrate how adept Radio London was at generating its own mythology. Ladybird Johnson's media holdings, although purchased in her name, were wholly owned by her husband.[8] Philip Birch, hired by Mal McIlwain as Radio London's Managing Director, had spent time on the Johnsons' Texan ranch though, and his venture had received the President's approval and encouragement, if not his hard cash.

The fact that presidential involvement could be cited in such a way while Ronan O'Rahilly could only compete on an emblematic level by naming his station after the daughter of the recently assassinated John Kennedy, is one of the most potent symbols of the entire offshore era and reveals much about the two stations' contrasting intentions and expectations. Radio London could draw upon powerful multinational allies for its support, postwar capital from newly rich oil entrepreneurs. London's credentials for such an expansionist venture were therefore impeccable. Caroline was funded by old money, and bohemian benefactors, who operated within the autonomous public sphere of hip capitalism. While Caroline emphasized offshore radio's symbolic value and took on board the kind of nebulous philosophy and hedonistic politics consistent with its embryonic swinging London origins, Radio London was pursuing pragmatic incorporation.

> When Radio Caroline went on the air I was interested enough to check into the legal aspect, and I found out from a firm of international lawyers and my own solicitors that what they were doing was perfectly legal. I felt Caroline wasn't doing it very well and I thought it could be done a lot better . . . Caroline was running a pop station, but I felt the people running Caroline really didn't understand how pop music works on radio.
>
> (Philip Birch)[9]

Philip Birch, London's Managing Director, had a proven track record in advertising, having worked for 14 years as Media Director and accounts executive for the J. Walter Thompson organization, most prominently on the Ford Motors account in the early 1950s (hence the link with McIlwain). Once a managing director had been acquired from the largest advertising agency in the world, prestigious recruitment and efficient organization were to become hallmarks of the Radio London project. Alan Keen left Fleetway Publications to become head of the station's sales division. Dennis Maitland, another advertising man with a proven track record, later joined from Odhams, having previously worked for the *Daily Mail* group. The Radio London project was staffed by people who were steeped in advertising and marketing experience. Keen had reached middle management level with the IPC group as Assistant Advertising Manager with *Woman's Mirror*. Maitland was Advertising Manager for *Woman's Weekly* and *Housewife Magazine*. Both were recruited for their expertise in targeting the women's market.

It was in the area of sales that Radio London was most able to maximize efficiency. Radios Caroline and Atlanta had tentatively opened the advertisers' eyes to offshore radio's possibilities but it was the London project that was able to capitalize on this potential growth area most effectively. It was decided that Radio London would generate advertising ahead of launch and would go on air with a full account book. The first clients were familiar names in the world of commercial media, many of whom, like Reckitts, Palmolive, and Gibbs, had previously advertised on Radio Luxembourg and Radio Normandie in the 1930s. Gibbs SR toothpaste had been the first product advertised on ITV in 1955. Negotiating through its British agencies for predominantly American clients Radio London offered a facility where multinational capital could continue to flourish. The other benefit of such a strategy was that Radio London could go on air sounding like an established radio station.

Financially the London project was made economically watertight right from the start. This had entailed setting up a trust fund in the Bahamas for the station's investors, which accounted for the actual purchasing of a ship and broadcasting equipment. Once purchased, ownership and operation were kept separate. The ship itself was actually owned by Panavess Incorporated, operating from Panama. This side of the venture maintained a corporate structure and issued shares to the four principal financial overseers of the station. Radio equipment on the ship was owned by the Marine Investment Company Incorporated, based in the Bahamas. Sales were managed by a British company (Radlon), which also remained legally independent from the rest of the operation. Such a structure allowed a great deal of financial autonomy within the project. Panavess Incorporated was not liable to pay income tax in the USA. The Bahamas trust fund was similarly free of US tax obligations and American employees were not liable to pay income tax in Britain. Because of an arrangement whereby all British advertising fees were channelled through a Swiss account, sterling being converted to US dollars in the process, advertising income was subject to minimal British taxation, while the trustees remained free of exchange controls in the Bahamas.

This was a rather crazy venture because the real problem was that while it was perfectly legal the government, sooner or later, would make it illegal, and this would mean closing down. And of course buying the ship and fitting it out with an enormous transmitter, generator, and ship's crew, as well as broadcasting staff, [was] a very expensive proposition, and if in fact the legislation had come very quickly we would have lost all our money.

(Philip Birch)[10]

In all an estimated £1.5 million was invested, an awesome amount of money for a venture which was taking shape against murmurings of government legislation to outlaw the stations. Nevertheless Radio London was clearly a potentially lucrative venture, and with the kind of company the station's management was keeping it turned out to be a remarkably low risk project. Various reciprocal deals were struck which kept overheads to a minimum, and indicated the organization's priorities. The broadcasting vessel had been purchased for £28,000, RCA transmitting equipment was installed for £90,000; rented premises in London's Mayfair were also obtained cheaply. Expensive promotional jingles were purchased from PAMS of Dallas, but management decided early on that they could do without the expense of renting an apartment for the marine crew and DJ staff when on shore leave.

Continuing the legacy of American Top 40 radio similar cost-cutting occurred in the areas of news provision. It had originally been the intention of the London organization to provide a comprehensive news service (Radio Caroline at the time was not running news bulletins), but the London project encountered major difficulties when attempting to negotiate such a service. Reuters was dependent upon existing GPO landlines and was not willing to jeopardize this arrangement by getting involved with pirate radio. UPI, on the other hand, made a provisional offer, subject to the legal position being clarified, but Radio London decided that both the proposed cost of this, and the subsequent copyright problems which would be encountered, would be prohibitive. A further representation to Associated Press also came to nothing. One final deal was attempted with the *Sun* newspaper.

It is an independent paper which leans to the left, and is published by IPC as a sop to the Labour Party. It started publishing on September 15th [1964] . . . since we want the Labour Party on our side I don't think we need to worry about the leftish nature of the *Sun*, particularly since half the population and possibly two-thirds of our potential audience votes Labour . . .

(Philip Birch)[11]

Such a shrewd reading of the political temperature showed the degree of forethought that was going into the London venture. However, when the *Sun* pulled out of the proposed deal – aware, like many others, of its legal and political sensitivity – Radio London decided that in this instance at least it could do without prestige and resorted instead to what became standard practice among most of the offshore stations: stealing the news from the BBC.

Station identification and music policy was problematic too. Indeed the project was not even known as Radio London until Philip Birch pointed out to his American employers that a definite name was needed for the station's advertising rate card. Initially some shareholders had wanted the station to have an all-American image. Don Peirson favoured 'Radio KLIF London' ('The Big K') after Gordon McLendon's KLIF Dallas. Among numerous other criticisms of this idea Birch pointed out the unfortunate connotations of 'Dallas' after the Kennedy assassination the previous year! They settled for the 'The Big L', Radio London.

The boardroom wranglings over the precise definition of an American format were significant for the subsequent course taken by offshore radio. Peirson is believed to have wanted to interpret the 'Americanization' brief quite literally by relaying recordings of KLIF to British listeners. The inevitable watering down of this approach would eventually lead to Peirson, and others involved in the original London project, setting up a new station, Radio England. The repercussions of this uncharacteristic indecisiveness regarding music policy would also audibly spill over into Radio London's early broadcasts. The main conflict at this stage of the project was over the degree to which an American style of presentation would be utilized, a situation which was resolved with the withdrawal, in time-honoured boardroom fashion, of Peirson from all decision making. He retained a major financial interest in the actual Radio London ship, however.

Immediately prior to commencing transmissions Philip Birch hired the services of the public relations firm Patrick Baker Ltd to organize Radio London's advance publicity. An elaborate public relations campaign was devised, consisting of plans for initial press liaison and an associated follow-up campaign of station-related promotions; they involved the tried and tested populist formula of talent competitions, radio bingo, and promotional tie-ups with magazines, record companies, and related media. Among other proposals was a suggestion that prominent members of the 'Big L' management team, and Philip Birch in particular, should be groomed for more sophisticated areas of public relations. This would entail lecturing and after-dinner speaking to responsible bodies and organizations, and generally building up rapport with those who might be sympathetic to the cause of commercial radio. Particular emphasis was placed on Birch's exemplary military record. His biography in the first Radio London press release mentioned that 'he was reputed to be the youngest commissioned officer in the Second World War'.

Like everything else on the publicity side the campaign was well organized and guaranteed to put the station in a favourable light. A crucial underlying theme of the campaign was the emphasis on selling Radio London as a respectable business proposition. The station's management were keen to distance themselves from the buccaneering image which had largely been foisted upon the pop pirates by the media. Considerable emphasis was placed upon courting the Establishment, and not doing anything which might jeopardize the station's position.

This then was Radio London's organizational milieu. In the main it honoured established practices. It was unquestionably efficient, it had recruited from a position of strength, it had shown great foresight and a shrewd understanding of the political temperature in most of its decision making, and it had marketed itself in a favourable light. The overriding institutional goals were to maximize profit and bring legal commercial radio to Great Britain. While sales revenue for Radio London could be generated by picking up a telephone and talking to any one of a number of well-established multinational contacts, security in the Radio Caroline camp was largely restricted to Ronan O'Rahilly getting his ship fitted out in the relative secrecy of his father's Dublin harbour. The Caroline team had wealthy titled contacts and assurances of patronage from the Chelsea set, but Radio London was always going to achieve more as an organization. In theory Radio London was a pirate radio station. In all other respects it was a major business concern which just happened as a matter of legislative convenience (or inconvenience) to be operating from a ship.

1964–5   Programming and promotion

After a month of test transmissions Radio London began broadcasting regular programmes, on 23 December 1964, and it soon became apparent that the station's approach to pop radio was as new to some of its disc jockeys as it was to its listeners. The sales force may have been well versed in the methods of media marketing, the station's image may have been fastidiously cultivated, but there did initially prove to be one or two serious inconsistencies in the thinking behind the Big L format. The first problem was gauging the level of Americanization appropriate for a British audience. The uneasy mishmash of on-air styles which listeners heard while this was resolved varied from stilted interpretations by British staff of how an American announcer would sound, to the slick, sharp, wisecracking, effortlessly authentic patter of those DJs who were obviously versed in the real thing. Somewhere in between lay the style that Radio London was eventually to settle with, a predictable mid-Atlantic watering down of the verbal pyrotechnic excesses of American pop radio into something palatable to the untrained English ear.

It was the very notion of format itself which initially gave the disc jockeys most problems. Some seemed ill at ease when attempting to approximate the seamless continuity of the American approach. There was an abundance of contrived links, characteristic of those unavoidably steeped, and in many cases actually trained, in the formal BBC style. All the pirates were afflicted with this in the early days and it was a long time before any really broke free of its conventions and nuances and began to create an identity of their own.

> Of course we didn't want to sound like the BBC. What we were doing was taking an American Top 40 format – *and there were at least half a dozen others we could have chosen* – and we were adapting it to the British ear. I think at times we sounded very transatlantic.
>
> (Philip Birch, emphasis mine)[12]

After considerable interpersonal wrangling at management level Radio London had decided on one particular interpretation of the American Top 40 format; not surprisingly it was the one then being relayed by KLIF Dallas. London's chosen 'Fabulous 40' package consisted of three categories of records: an 'A' list, consisting of the Top Ten records of the week, a 'B' list consisting of the remainder of the Top 40, and a 'C' list consisting of new releases. In addition to this there were slots for LP tracks, and hits from the past – the first time 'oldies' were played as a distinct category on British pop radio. DJs were forbidden from choosing their own records, and had a 'Top 40 climber' selected for them each week by station management. In time-honoured fashion the presenter simply had to endorse the product.

When Radio London began broadcasting it was rumoured that the station possessed a totally inadequate supply of discs. The story was quickly seized upon by the popular music press and was shrewdly encouraged by London's management to illustrate how well the disc jockeys coped in those first few months. The implication was that the format structure itself and the professionalism of the station's disc jockeys compensated for the scarcity of records. The estimates that have entered offshore folklore, of just how many (or how few) records Radio London did initially have, vary from 27 to 40. Needless to say the stories are not true. Analysis of recordings of those early broadcasts reveals that a more accurate estimate would be nearer 90. Admittedly the station appeared to have no more than ten discs from the current hit parade, and consequently many of the records that were plugged incessantly would not have received such extensive exposure in normal circumstances.

The preponderance of material associated with the already dying hot rod and surfing crazes, most of which had not even been issued in the UK, came from the personal collections of those London DJs who had previously worked in North America. But 90 records was actually a great deal more than a typical Top 40 play-list required, and right from the start Radio London programming displayed considerable variation. Among the original batch of records there was a sufficient number of Beatles and Beach Boys discs to ensure familiarity; more important, there was also a fair proportion of records by black American artists who, until the arrival of the pirates, had received little exposure on British radio. Fans of the newly emerging soul sound could now hear Mitty Collier, Mary Wells, Little Anthony and the Imperials, or Candy and the Kisses, at an hour of the day normally reserved for *Housewives' Choice* and *Morning Story*.

At times during those first few weeks Radio London presenters conveyed a lack of hard sell at variance with the station's stated intentions. The whole venture may have been meticulously planned at boardroom level but for the disc jockeys responsible for conveying a new programme style to British listeners there were major flaws. Simply through unfamiliarity some of the London team approached the idea of format as if it were a minefield, each fresh category containing a potential pitfall: 'We have several categories of 45s here. We have flying 45s, favourite 45s, and revived 45s. Well this one comes into both the Fabulous 40 section and my personal favourite section' (Paul Kaye).[13]

Format radio is by nature a highly systematized construction, involving a planned schematic approach to radio airtime. American Top 40 radio at its most refined presented the listener with a seamless cultural montage of advertisements, music, news, and patter. Radio London disc jockeys, unfamiliar with the formula, were literally reading the menu. For a station that was supposed to be modelled on the slick hard sell of American commercial radio its presenters too often stumbled over their superlatives. Radio London was supposed to be 'Wonderful'. The Top 40 was supposed to be 'Fabulous'. It took a while for some DJs to get this simple requirement the right way round. Even when they got the categories right there was often a curious hesitancy in the salesmanship: 'Here is a climber that we think, *rightly or wrongly*, will do very well' (Paul Kaye, my emphasis).[14]

Another feature of those early tentative broadcasts was the extent to which Radio London newsreaders were prepared to add editorial comment to news stories. Having failed to secure a major sponsor for news broadcasts the station had taken to pirating the news from BBC broadcasts, and what had initially been intended to be one of the most impressive features of London's programming never really transcended the unethical nature of its gathering. As the station's popularity increased editorial freedom was curtailed but before the disc jockeys' self-censorship and sense of duty got the better of them many made unethical but daring forays into editorial judgement. On one occasion the newsreader Paul Kaye commented on Adam Faith's expulsion from South Africa for refusing to play to segregated audiences. The situation only arose through announcers being unclear as to how familiar they were expected to be with their material and their audience. It was only during those first relatively unprepared weeks of broadcasting, when ground rules were still being defined largely through trial and error, that Radio London employees felt able to take risks. The station's objective was to get permanent land-based commercial radio on the statute books of Great Britain, not to allow its presenters a political platform. But in those early and somewhat hesitant broadcasts, in the midst of all that British reserve and trepidation, the foundation for British pop music radio of the future was being laid.

Radio London did, as planned, go on air with a full quota of advertisements. The most prominent sponsor during early transmissions was Reckitts, whose Germolene, Beechams, and Settlers brands ensured the continued high profile on commercial radio of a staple diet of cuts, grazes, headaches, and flatulence. Regular exhortations from the disc jockey to 'see Vic at Modern Home Makers in Gravesend' sat incongruously next to the syndicated agency efforts of the large companies, but such a mix was what gave offshore advertising its particular character over the following four years, for in addition to attracting multinational clients the pirates also gave small advertisers the opportunity to promote their products inexpensively in a new growth area.

The initial range of sponsors on Radio Caroline also included a mixture of familiar and unknown names, indicating the *ad hoc* nature of offshore radio advertising in the early days. The station's first Sales Director was Michael Parkin, then married to Molly Parkin, who was at that time Fashion Editor of the innovative *Nova* magazine. When approached by Jocelyn Stevens and offered the post with Radio Caroline, Parkin was Managing Director of Attwood Statistics, part of the TAM group (Television Audience Measurements). Previously he had worked in commercial television with Channel and Rediffusion. Also on the Radio Caroline sales staff at this time was Jose Scudder, who had worked with Grampian Television and Unilever. Caroline's other sales executives during this formative period were drawn from the Chelsea clique and included Robin Courage of the Courage brewery family, the heir to the Earl of Denbigh (Viscount Fielding), Major Murray Robb, and Ian Ross, son of Caroline backer C. E. Ross. Radio London was able to provide simultaneously local, regional, and national markets for its advertising clients. It had a network of agents covering the whole of the UK, despite not being able to guarantee nationwide transmission coverage. Radio Caroline had a plethora of sales executives but they had less specialized knowledge of the markets they were covering. Lack of direct sales expertise was to have severe repercussions for the Caroline organization later on.

Among the first promotions on Radio Caroline were advertisements for Harp Lager, the *News of the World* (a prominent advertiser on all of the early pirates), William Hill's Turf Accountants (who had been one of the first advertisers on Radio Luxembourg in the 1930s), Ecko Radios, Bulgarian Holidays, Peter Evans Eating Houses, and Kraft Dairylea Cheese. The latter was placed by the J. Walter Thompson agency as part of its campaign to introduce soft cheese to the British market. Until the launch of Radio London involvement of the large agencies in offshore advertising was sporadic.

How much revenue came from these sponsors is unclear. Radio Caroline claimed its initial contracts to be worth £30,000, but was actually selling advertising at half its specified rate;

some were simply dummy advertisements. Reciprocal 'meal-ticket' deals were also commonplace. The original pioneers of format radio in the USA had found that a free meal could always be traded for a free plug and this practice was continued by the pirates. Prestigious groups like the finance houses, banks, and building societies steered well clear of the off-shore stations, nor were any advertising campaigns for major products ever launched on the pirates. Many agencies were never fully convinced of the importance of radio as a selling vehicle; consequently the pirates were never considered a primary medium for promotion. The agencies preferred to give radio a supporting role, saving their main campaigns for commercial television and the most popular newspapers and magazines. When agencies did use radio they allocated the bulk of their advertising budget to Radio Luxembourg. Beechams for example, one of Radio London's most consistent advertisers, always launched its seasonal campaigns on Luxembourg.

Even products which were direct subcultural spin-offs from the rise of pop usually took the legitimate route in the initial stages of promotion. In May 1965 Philips Electrics launched its new transistor radio, the 'Popmaster' by placing advertisements in the *Daily Express, Mirror, Mail, Sun,* and *Sunday People.* For the youth and music industry audience they chose *Rave Magazine* and *Showtime,* and ignored Radio London and Radio Caroline.[15] A reciprocal deal was made during the same period by Pye, who advertised its 'Swingalong' transistor portable on Radio London, alongside a competition to win an evening out with a top recording star or tickets to a live concert. Variants on this kind of deal usually involved the chance to win records from the Big L chart or night out at a club with a Radio London DJ.

Radio London succeeded in finding the appropriate level of Americanization for British listeners, but a mere toning down of excesses was not enough to turn London into a successful operation. The station's management was also well versed in the dominant demographic trends of commercial radio, and the majority of advertising on Radio London was pitched not at teenagers (the station only had a notional interest in 'youth' as an ideological and economic construct) but at the adult market, particularly at the housewife. Pirate programme schedules in general faithfully reflected this with endless variations on 'elevenses', 'coffee breaks', and 'tea-time tunes'. During Radio London's first year of broadcasting the majority of the station's advertisers were conspicuously aiming at the older audience. A representative sample of new advertising clients for the period April to September 1965 includes Kempton Park Racecourse, Shell Petrol, Player's 'Richmond' Cigarettes, Reckitts' Windolene (and other household products), Carreras 'Guards' Cigarettes, Omo washing powder (and various other Unilever household brands). CEMA Bingo was responsible for the first sponsored request programme on the station. Other sponsored programmes at this time were paid for by Currys, Peter Stuyvesant Cigarettes, Vernons Football Pools, Brooke Bond Tea, and S & H Pink Trading Stamps. Oxo, through an account managed by J. Walter Thompson ran its 'Oxo family' campaign for the first time on offshore radio. Various IPC magazines, including *Reveille* and *Bride* also advertised on the station, the latter sponsoring a weekly half-hour programme preceding the Top 40 show every Sunday. In November 1965 Radio London increased its advertising rates, and by the end of its first year 250 products had been aired on the station.

Radio London's *Fab 40* bore little resemblance to any other recognized listing. The BBC at the time was using an amalgam of the hit parades of the three leading music papers: *New Musical Express, Melody Maker,* and *Record Mirror.* This method of selection was supposed to eliminate the effect of chart rigging. Record pluggers could, and often did, hype their product into the lower regions of the chart, thus guaranteeing national airplay and setting into motion sufficient promotional momentum to secure a hit. Naturally the BBC was more wary of ethical dilemmas than any of its offshore competitors, most of whom were not unduly averse to promoting those discs that arrived metaphorically wrapped in £5 notes, but was no more successful at keeping the fixers at bay than it had been with the sheet music pluggers thirty years earlier. All that the *Pick of the Pops'* 'Top 30' did was keep new entries and mobility within the chart to a minimum. Its laborious and cumbersome mechanism constantly failed to register pre-release advance sales of records. Radio London's *Fab 40*, in contrast, was positively buoyant with weekly chart placings and new entries registering dramatic rises and falls. It also had an explicit market function, and unlike the BBC chart, which was there simply to reflect sales, Radio London's had more directly promotional objectives.

> A format that has been enormously successful in the States is the Top 40 format. And this means simply playing the top 40 records of the week – and incidentally this is nothing to do with the charts, nothing to do with which records happen to be selling, because in fact those aren't the top 40 records of the week. They are the top 40 records of about three or four weeks ago. By top 40 we really mean the best of the new records that are coming along now.
>
> (Philip Birch)[16]

The Radio London chart, promoted as a more up-to-date barometer of public taste than its BBC counterpart, was essentially a prediction 'Top 40', signifying efficiency and 'know how' to the music industry it served. At its peak the Radio London chart was said to be six weeks in advance of the established national hit parades being used by the BBC and the popular press. During its final week in August 1967 the *Fab 40* contained more than a dozen records which were not even due for release until the following month, so eager were record companies to air their product through such a prestigious formula.

The contrast, however, between Radio London's public pronouncements and actual station practice was considerable. Business within the music industry was then, as now, often undertaken in the informal social whirl of parties, press conferences, promotional campaigns, and live shows. It was largely within the casual terrain of launches and lunches that plans were formulated and contracts were cemented. The Radio London organization was extremely scrupulous in this area of negotiation. The official line on record promotion was that disc jockeys could be wined and dined by potential pluggers, agents, and managers, but they were not to allow their integrity to be undermined by bribes or similar inducements, no matter how great the temptation, or how blurred the boundaries between acceptable and unacceptable conduct. However, a shrewd understanding of the flexible ethics of salesmanship permeated every stratum of the Radio London operation, and the image of corporate responsibility personified by the presenters was all part of the station's meticulously crafted game plan. The degree to which it was adhered to can be measured by referring to the Radio London *Fab 40*, which consistently contained records which never registered on any other hit parade. The Radio London chart was, theoretically at least, compiled by Radio London staff. Records would arrive on the ship with various directives from head office, and the final selection would be made on a Saturday afternoon by the station's senior presenter. DJs would be allocated their 'climbers' – new releases which would be featured on the station's play-list the forthcoming week – and at peak listening time on a Sunday afternoon a jingle would announce, 'After extensive research and tabulation Radio London is proud to present the new Fabulous Forty'.

Radio London's claim that it helped launch the career of many subsequently successful artists cannot be easily reconciled with the counter-claim that it never accepted payola for airplay. Correspondence obtained from Radio London's files between grateful clients and the station's management is couched in the terminology of showbiz gratitude. It unsurprisingly makes no mention of fiscal favours received or services rendered. Artists or agents wrote company-prescribed 'thank you' notes, thanking the disc jockey for 'choosing' the artist's record as a climber, ('we realise it must be hard choosing which records you are going to plug on your programme, as you must receive hundreds'), thanking the Radio London programme director for attending the recent record company launch, ('and hope to see you at *X* and *Y*'s party on December 23'), thanking Big L for making the record number five in its *Fab 40* ('although sadly it failed to register on the national charts'). The station defended its entire selection process as if it was a series of negotiations governed by free will and based wholly on an aesthetic consideration of whether the merchandise in question was of a sufficiently high quality to justify airtime. The cut and thrust of promotion was reduced to an over-simplified eulogizing of quality. The curiously untypical and implausible constitution of Radio London's charts was apparently all down to charity and benevolence.

The extent to which advertisers could influence station output was clearly indicated when Pepsi Cola took over sponsorship of part of the *Fab 40* show. A memo from the Radio London management to station disc jockeys instructed them to hastily override changes made to the programme schedule because, in the case of the *Fab 40* show, the rescheduling clashed with Pepsi's current campaign strategy.

> As you know the Fabulous 40 programme from this Sunday 5th of December is being brought forward to 2.00 p.m. It is now imperative that the programme continues until 6.00 p.m., as Pepsi Cola, who sponsor the last half hour of this show, have had 12,000 leaflets printed and distributed saying 'Listen to our programme on Big L each Sunday between 5.30 and 6.00 p.m.' The only answer is to include more climbers etc. for the first 3½ hours. On no account must the Top 10 be transmitted before 5.30 p.m.[17]

The fact that the Radio London management was prepared to delay programme schedule changes and allow the running time of its most popular show to be dictated by a sponsor to suit its own promotional campaign clearly indicates the station's marketing priorities. The ethos applied whatever the merchandise, as the Radio London 'Top 40' constantly revealed; it was as applicable to records as it was to any other consumer purchase.

Disc jockey recruitment

Several of Radio Caroline's original DJ team were recruited from the wider sweep of the entertainments industry, predominantly from acting, but the curricula vitae of other early recruits also reveal a number of scriptwriters, songwriters, stage hands, theatre managers, and commercial artists. While recruiting announcers for Radio London Philip Birch even used the appropriate vernacular, speaking of hiring disc jockeys who were merely 'resting' between creative engagements. For many in this position the pirate stations, like their commercial precursors of the 1930s, provided the broadcaster's equivalent of repertory, a facility where jobbing announcers might find good short-term prospects with free board and lodgings and on-the-job training.

Caroline and London also employed a high quota of staff with experience of overseas commercial radio, chiefly in North America or Australasia. Of the original Radio London team, Dave Cash had worked at CJAV in British Columbia, and with station manager Ben Toney in Texas. Pete Brady, like Cash, had spent his formative years in Canada before working for Jamaica Radio. Another Canadian recruit, Duncan Johnson, had previously worked on Radio Bermuda. The senior disc jockey on Radio London, Tony Windsor, had been a leading presenter on 2SM in Sydney. Windsor had also worked on the BBC Light Programme during the early part of 1963, presenting the lunchtime pop show *Go Man Go* from the Playhouse Theatre, and for Allan Crawford's Radio Atlanta, but left when it merged with Radio Caroline in July 1964.

There was another much overlooked category of broadcasters, which had a crucial bearing on Radio London's particular style of presentation, and its subsequent niche in British sound broadcasting. This included those who had already gained experience of 'establishment' media, usually in British television, or the forces and colonial broadcasting network overseas. Paul Kaye (another former actor) had experience of both, having worked on the African Broadcasting Service in Kenya, and for BFN in Cyprus, before moving to the newly established BBC 2's arts programme, *Late Night Line Up*. Earl Richmond had worked for ITV as a transmission controller, and for forces broadcasting in Trieste. Radios Caroline and Atlanta also had their share of ex-BFN recruits.

At this time [1959–60] there was no other recognised way into radio, unless you had a university degree and joined the BBC as a studio manager. Quite a number of well-known names came the BFN route; Cliff Michelmore, Raymond Baxter, Keith Fordyce, Don Moss, David Jacobs, Bill Crozier, David Hamilton, Brian Mathews . . .

(Keith Skues)[18]

Skues, who worked with both Caroline and London, learned his craft with BFN in Cologne, starting as a presentation assistant (emphatically 'not cleared for broadcasting') before becoming a successful announcer. BFN was one of the first stations to have 'self-op' broadcasting: the presenter operated programmes without assistance, whereas normally an engineer would put on a record following a visual cue from the DJ. This kind of 'hands on' experience undoubtedly allowed those who 'came the BFN route' to become conversant with the pirates' approach, helping to develop familiarity and a relaxed style.

Forces broadcasting in the late 1950s revealed a paradox more widely apparent within National Service as a whole. On the one hand programming was heavily scripted and strictly controlled. Broadcasts were scrupulously monitored for everything from a potential security risk to a dropped aitch. On the other hand forces broadcasting couldn't help but be suffused with National Service ennui. There were many recruits at this time who saw broadcasting as an escape route from the drudgery with which conscription had become associated by the late 1950s. In a previous generation the Goons had been spawned by ENSA. Now a whole new generation of mavericks was again rising through the ranks, blending surrealism and populism while displaying a certain disregard for red tape and petty authority.

During the entire 32 months of its existence Radio London only employed 30 disc jockeys, half of whom worked for the station for over a year. This indicates both a very settled working unit, and, for the turbulent and transitory world of media professionals in general an extremely low staff turnover. During its 48-month life span Caroline South employed at least 67 DJs, only thirteen of whom stayed with the station for over a year. During the 44 months of its existence Caroline North employed at least 38 DJs, 22 of whom also worked at some time on Caroline South, making a known total of 83 for the entire Caroline network. It has to be stressed that the figure given for Radio Caroline can only be an estimate. With such a high turnover it is clear that some temporary staff would not have been registered on any existing documentation. The task of historical reconstruction is made doubly difficult by the fact that, unlike Radio London, who on the whole preferred 'tried and tested' announcers with a proven track record in broadcasting, Caroline was often prepared to send DJs out to sea on a week's trial; some of these lasted considerably less than the full seven days. In this respect Caroline's hiring and firing policy more closely resembled that of the smaller pirates, such as City and Invicta, than it did that of a major radio station.

Job mobility between the pirate stations was always fairly fluid, but it was noticeable that the more successful and ambitious announcers gravitated towards Radio London, and from there to Luxembourg or the BBC. In pirate circles working for Radio London was seen as the supreme accolade, and it paid better too, normally double what a DJ could expect on Caroline. Simon Dee recalls leaving a £45 a week (plus commission) job with an estate agent to go and work for Caroline for £15 a week in 1964. At its peak in 1966 London was paying an average of roughly £50 a week to Caroline's £25.

Despite being supposedly eclipsed by the pirate stations, Luxembourg found that its audience, which had dropped to 3 million by 1960, actually increased between September 1964 and September 1965, from 5,760,000 to 6,410,000. Its airtime sales showed similar increases, rising from £616,085 in the first nine months of 1965 to £650,000 in the corresponding period during 1966.[19] More important, Luxembourg still offered a direct link with the established music industry and a 'way in' to legitimate broadcasting for many announcers. As with Radio London a number of Caroline staff also worked for Luxembourg; similarities in career structure and professional outlook between the two pirates tended to transcend their differences in programming style.

The most discernible difference between London and Caroline initially was that London planned its formula first and then required its disc jockeys to adapt, while Caroline tended to work more intuitively with whatever talent was available. What this amounted to in programming terms was a disparate quota of creative individuals in Caroline, bonded by a collective desire to be involved in a potentially exciting form of broadcasting, but with no natural programming empathy between them. There were also a number of organizational factors specific to the setting up of Radio Caroline which had a crucial bearing on the way the station developed during its first two years. One of these was the merger which took place between the controlling bodies of Radios Caroline and Atlanta in July 1964.

During 1963 there had been genuine, albeit brief, collusion between Ronan O'Rahilly's venture and Allan Crawford's Project Atlanta. As Crawford laconically revealed in the Granada TV *World in Action* programme transmitted in May 1964, 'We both gave each other a great deal of advice. It could be that I took less of his than he of mine.' Despite the inter-organizational rivalries that ensued the two projects shared much common ground, and as previously noted, the sharing of the same harbour in Ireland to convert their ships into vessels suitable for broadcasting hardly constituted the actions of bitter enemies. It plainly made little sense from a business point of view to have two expensively fitted ships anchored less than a mile from each other beaming a similar style of programme to exactly the same audience, and the British press openly speculated about the possibility of a merger from the moment the two ships set sail. Radio Caroline had even made provision for a northern sales office and staff in its original budgeting.

Under the terms of the merger Radio Caroline took over Radio Atlanta's debts, and claimed one third of any profits made after the deal. The original Radio Caroline sailed north to a location off Ramsey Bay, Isle of Man, and continued as Radio Caroline North. The Radio Atlanta vessel remained at roughly the same anchorage off the Essex coast and continued as Radio Caroline South. In theory the newly amalgamated organization would offer a vastly expanded and fully networked service to potential advertisers and comprehensive coverage of the British Isles to listeners. In fact the merger brought with it new and unforeseen problems. Some, like staffing allocation, and the fact that the Radio Atlanta ship had been primarily geared towards taped programmes and only offered limited facilities for live output, were merely technical hindrances and were soon overcome. Others, like Caroline's necessarily placatory relationship with the authorities on the Isle of Man and in Ireland (which involved running a constant series of unpaid advertisements for the Isle of Man and Irish Tourist Boards) were matters of expediency. But the differences in philosophy between the two operations were not so easily overcome. Several Radio Atlanta disc jockeys refused to join the new network and the Project Atlanta General Manager Leslie Parrish resigned shortly after the merger, stating 'My own views are completely incompatible with certain policies being pursued.'[20] Parrish had previously worked for Channel, Granada, and Rediffusion television and had been pencilled in for the job of Northern Sales Manager.

From the late summer of 1964 there was little coordination between the North and South ships, and so different approaches to programming began to evolve. The North ship, ostensibly being controlled from an office 200 miles away undoubtedly became the chief beneficiary of this organizational confusion. It maintained a fairly settled staff line-up, more programming autonomy, and little pirate competition. Caroline North sounded more authentic than its southern counterpart, more in tune with the prevailing pop mood of the period, and faithfully reflected north-west England's beat-group heritage. Daytime scheduling was brash and upbeat, while late night shows such as Jim Murphy's *Midnite Surf Party*, Tom Lodge's *Rave Party*, and Don Allen's *Country and Western Jamboree* catered specifically for the region's specialist audiences. After midnight programming was particularly innovative. Most pirates, when they expanded into nocturnal broadcasting, offered easy listening tunes and soporific sentiments. Caroline North treated its post-midnight provision as an extension of the discothèque, featuring a high quota of black American music.

The South ship in my opinion was not being programmed well. It was boring. Too much of the old style of music that the BBC was playing on the Light Programme. Not even Luxembourg, more Light Programme stuff, and I assume some of the Crawford records from the old Radio Atlanta. Meanwhile we up north were having a phenomenal time.

(Tom Lodge)[21]

Although the motives behind the merger had been expansionist the Caroline organization proved to be equally protectionist in other ways. Just weeks before Radio London came on air Ronan O'Rahilly approached Philip Birch with a view to a merger, not of the actual organizations or station programming, but of Radlon and Caroline Sales, the rival advertising departments. Birch effectively called O'Rahilly's bluff in his reply by shrewdly making a whole series of prohibitive demands. These included making the Caroline organization responsible for all marine vessel maintenance expenses, all legal fees incurred in setting up the merger, and a request for a £40,000 deposit on top of the actual ship's rental costs. The Radio London organization never seriously entertained the idea of a merger. It is revealing, though, that Caroline management chose to make such an attempt in the first place and that the initial strategy was to combine forces on the sales rather than the programming front. Similar attempts by the Caroline organization to instigate a joint Caroline–London–Luxembourg sales cartel and a commercial radio equivalent of the Independent Television Contractors' Association were also spurned.

By April 1965 Caroline South was having to come to terms with the formidable presence of Radio London. It introduced a regular news service and also attempted to emulate London's style of programme presentation. Caroline's ex-BFN and Equity-card-carrying disc jockeys were also suddenly transformed by a blundering initiative of uncertain origin into New-York-style 'good guys'. In major US cities the clan image of hit stations like WMCA and WABC – with the legendary DJs Big Dan Ingram, B. Mitchell Read, and Jack Spector – was a winning formula in the intense ratings battle. During the spring of 1965 Caroline began syndicating daily programmes sponsored by Roulette Records and hosted by Jack Spector on both of its stations. The radical change of Caroline's image was an attempt to bring the station into line with Spector's own cheerleader approach, with its true-to-your-school style 'pledge of allegiance', so beloved of many Top 40 stations in the USA. But whereas the original 'good guys' were convincing as image ambassadors for their respective stations the English version sounded rather less plausible.

This ill-judged institutional directive transformed comparatively mild-mannered individuals into gibbering, frenetic, and singularly unconvincing provincial 'good guys', whose programmes sat ill at ease with existing ones; it was to have wide-reaching repercussions by the end of the year, culminating in a series of drastic staff purges. While some DJs attempted a passable imitation of what was required the whole procedure merely induced hostility and lingering resentment in others. Caroline's answer to Radio London's chart was *Sound Sixty-Five*, an attempt to emulate the success of the *Fab 40*. In order to cram 65 records plus new releases into one three-hour chart show it was often necessary to play just a short section of each record, which was hardly progressive programming, but more of an ironic reminder of what Radio Luxembourg had been doing since the mid-1950s.

The 'good guys' image was further undermined by the kind of sponsored programmes the station was carrying at the time. These 15-minute features, very much in the Luxembourg style, were produced by the J. Walter Thompson and S. H. Benson agencies, broadcast daily, and were sponsored by, among others, Player's 'Anchor' Cigarettes, Andrews Liver Salts, Fynnon Liver Salts, Princes Foods, Chappell Pianos (which was owned by EMI, prominent opponents of offshore radio) and Miners Make Up. As on Luxembourg a decade earlier there was little editorial say by Caroline in the music policy of these shows, as individual responsibilities were delegated to the respective advertising agencies. The *Chappell Show* for instance, featured only 'music from the shows' and the emphasis in several of the others was on the kind of light music which would supposedly not scare away potential consumers. Another feature of such shows was that they were often hosted by well-known personalities from the world of show business. Kenneth Horne introduced *Talking Shop*, an advertising magazine programme of the type outlawed on British commercial television since 1961. There was a motoring show hosted by Stirling Moss. *Down Memory Lane*, the programme sponsored by Fynnons, was compèred by Anne Shelton. *The Ognib Show*, a radio bingo game, was hosted by Charlie Drake. Perhaps most incongruous of all, *The Miners Make Up Show*, the programme most likely to appeal to a teenage audience, was hosted by Vera Lynn!

Ted Allbeury, former head of Radio 390, maintains that Radio

London was a success because Philip Birch was a good businessman rather than a good radio man. Caroline promoted an altogether different ethos. Ronan O'Rahilly's idiosyncratic approach and the station's guiding *laissez-faire* philosophy were perceived by some to be too *ad hoc* and caused a great deal of dissent among those who wanted a more disciplined, businesslike structure. Such unease contributed directly to the staff upheavals which occurred at the end of 1965. Roles were further obscured by the fact that after the merger some employees were paid by O'Rahilly's Planet Productions while others continued to be paid by Crawford's Project Atlanta. The organization now had two managing directors and considerable boardroom friction.

> Once again it would be nice to know when decisions are made. Simon Dee now terms himself Assistant Programme Director. The last I heard was that he had been fired, which brings one to the point of programme policy which seems to be non-existent ... I think one must accept that we are in for a rude shock when eventually audience research figures for the two stations [Caroline and London] are revealed.
>
> (Michael Parkin)[22]

Dee, who broadcast from the South ship for the last time in March 1965 but continued to work in Caroline House for a couple of months gives his account of the prevailing atmosphere at that time.

> By then it was becoming more professional and I saw things going on that worried me a little bit. People making a little bit too much money ashore, while we were making too little on the boat. I mean the most I earned on that boat was £20 a week and sometimes we didn't get paid for weeks and weeks on end. And I could see the impetus was building in the wrong direction. It was going into ... I won't say corruption, that's a hard word, but it wasn't being ploughed back. A little rip-off alley was taking place and young guys were dealing with situations a little bit higher and faster than they could handle.
>
> (Simon Dee)[23]

Many people involved in the early days of offshore radio possessed no other qualification for the job beyond the fact that they had access to revenue or credit. Caroline's Chelsea set clique merely displayed indifference towards the finer points of business know-how, relying on bravado, initiative, and general King's Road *Zeitgeist* to sustain creative momentum. Nepotism on the payroll and giving inexperienced employees their head would lead to both programming innovation and organizational chaos.

With its executive suites, intercoms, and enough memos to rival Broadcasting House for bureaucracy, Caroline headquarters became a sprawling and unwieldy centre of operations, employing 60 people compared with London's equally efficient 18. In addition to housing the entire Caroline network staff the seven-floor building in London's Mayfair also leased office space to the actor Terence Stamp, the Moody Blues, and the Rik Gunnell agency. On the lower floors were the engineers, the administrators, and the over-staffed advertising department. On the upper floors 'the young guys' were holding court, and getting out of their depth in a manner which anticipated more serious ideological flaws to come. The contrast between Caroline and London was not matched by a contrast of intent within Caroline, creativity versus accountancy, idealism versus pragmatism.

The believable part of it all was that there was music coming out of a transmitter, which to me made it valid, and there was no bureaucracy on the boat. But there were a lot of times when we weren't paid. One day we almost turned off the transmitter because we hadn't been paid for something like seven weeks, and it was getting a bit moody. I was putting out 30-second commercials for cigarettes and *Woman's Own*, and I knew the money was coming in, so where the hell was it going? I said pay your bureaucrats in London but pay us first because we are going through the force 10 gales, and snow storms and transmitter failures. When I went ashore and found all the bureaucracy I thought 'My God, this is amazing'. This seven-floor building in Mayfair, people dashing backwards and forwards with files, commercials being made, dolly birds being photographed outside holding

99

Caroline Club stickers, and I'm thinking 'Oh really? Meanwhile back on the North Sea right now . . .'

(Simon Dee)[24]

This was the first manifestation of what was to occur frequently over the next three years. The confrontations came in different guises, but in essence only the names of the adversaries changed, the chaotic procedures and eccentrically managed responses would remain constant. The enduring irony was that Caroline's own shortcomings echoed the same organizational conflict the BBC had first had during the prewar years, a conflict between dedicated programme makers and detached policy makers. Simon Dee's sentiments could have been expressed with equal validity 30 years earlier.

We were terribly much a part of the centre, yet we were treated more or less as the fringe. They were so busy in the middle being bureaucratic and making money that they actually forgot who was responsible for the image of the boat. I noticed that when I went ashore. They had lost touch.

(Simon Dee)[25]

In matters of finance Caroline's seemingly permanently ramshackle affairs could be put down to simple inefficiency. Ronan O'Rahilly's freewheeling approach certainly cut across the regulated ebb and flow of formal economics, but Caroline's whole existence went against the grain of standard boardroom practice. It therefore becomes necessary at this point to consider the much deeper reverberations of what was by the end of 1965 emerging as an embryonic form of anarchic capitalism with no clear hierarchy of control. Radio Caroline was less than 18 months old when Ronan O'Rahilly started citing the Declaration of Human Rights in defence of his station. Clear differences were therefore beginning to be articulated between the two major offshore stations, which transcended programme policies. They were differences of spirit and they could be traced right back to the stations' contrasting origins. Radio London was planned and financed at multinational level. The Big L ethos came out of the boardroom. Caroline in contrast emerged from the dilettante whims of the King's Road and the unfolding possibilities of the swinging sixties. The geographical divide mirrored a much greater philosophical divide. London reflected the industry back at itself. Caroline reflected attitude. 'The industry was in Soho. The industry never was in the King's Road. London had its act together and was much better organized, whereas Caroline kind of reflected Ronan's attitude to life' (Tony Hall).[26]

Radio Caroline's net advertising income from both ships for the period March 1964–March 1965 was £294,320 with running costs for the same period estimated at £100,000–150,000. These figures obscure the fact that a disproportionate amount of the revenue had been made in the nine months before Radio London began broadcasting. By the end of 1965 Radio Caroline's running costs had virtually doubled, while advertising had completely stagnated. Radio London on the other hand was said to be grossing £60,000–75,000 a month with significantly lower overheads. By November 1965 the station was even being promoted in a full-length feature film called *Dateline Diamonds*. While London prospered, Radio Caroline, in financial jeopardy, lurched from one minor organizational crisis to another. The *Sunday Telegraph* of 14 November 1965 reported that the entrepreneur John Bloom, whose Rolls Razor company spectacularly went into liquidation with debts of 'over £4 million', had tried to buy out C. E. Ross's controlling interest in Planet Productions. Ross, and his partner John Sheffield, were said to be dismayed at Caroline's falling advertising revenue and rising overheads. Bloom knew Ronan O'Rahilly through the London nightclub circuit, but with his former financial exploits still the subject of a Board of Trade inquiry the deal fell through. Tom Lodge, programme director of the relatively unscathed Caroline North, sums up those first 18 months.

I would ascertain that people were listening to Caroline South at that time because at least it was better than the BBC and it was romantic, but in my personal opinion the music was terrible. So they switched right over to Radio London. I think in the autumn of 1965 there was a survey done by Gallup and it estimated that London had seven listeners to Caroline's one. All advertising just went from Caroline South to London. Naturally! Why advertise on Caroline South? You could advertise on Caroline North and London. This is when Ronan approached me and said, 'Tom, I want you to go down south and be programme director and put that station back on the map.' I said what I've got to do is have a brand new staff. There's two reasons for that. One is a very basic obvious reason; there was a certain amount of influence from the existing staff about the music that was being played. The other is that whenever you have an organization that changes direction as completely and drastically as I was going to do the old staff are going to drag their heels and subvert it, and undermine it in any way to justify that the past was right. So I had to change virtually the whole staff.

(Tom Lodge)[27]

The listenership survey by Gallup which Tom Lodge referred to formed part of a wider internal inquiry into the workings of the troubled Caroline organization. Its findings, which were not made public, were a savage indictment of the entire Caroline set-up. It criticized management malpractice, the sales operation, and music policy. The inquiry confirmed Planet Productions directors' worst fears. Radio London had, in a matter of months, decimated both Caroline's audience and its advertising. In the Anglia ITV region, for instance, where signal strengths were said to be equal, the BBC Light Programme accounted for 30.4 per cent of the audience between 7.00 a.m. and 9.00 a.m., Radio London took a 14.3 per cent share, and Caroline South held a meagre 0.9 per cent – an estimated listenership of 40,000 in its prime reception area. Radio London's audience peaked at 780,000 between 11.00 a.m. and 1.00 p.m. Caroline's peaked at 160,000 between 5.00 p.m. and 7.00 p.m., a figure largely attributable to the imported Jack Spector show.

Advertising figures were equally disastrous. The bulk of advertising money came through networked advertising mainly provided by the agencies but even these campaigns were rarely sustained. Direct sales income was negligible. Caroline North reflected a similar pattern but generally took twice as much advertising as Caroline South. Even during the period when it had no significant pirate competition Caroline South was only taking eight to ten minutes of advertising a day. Once Radio

London came on air Caroline South's advertising slumped. Within three months of London's first broadcast Caroline South was averaging less than £1,000 a week in advertising revenue. The station had originally estimated yearly profits of £1 million, and it had been envisaged that these would rise by £1 million a year.

Caroline's decline was attributed to various factors. Apart from the poor performance by sales and programming staff, poor quality advertisements and payola records, and the arrival of Radio London with its better broadcasting signal, it was also pointed out that the station had not sustained the novelty value and emotional appeal it had gained from being the first pirate. Low morale was also attributed to the high staff turnover, the inability of management to communicate decisions, and some of the less than savoury business practices being carried out by certain station employees. The continued influence of Project Atlanta shareholders on music policy, with incongruous advertisements appearing for Wigmore Hall concerts and Mermaid Theatre productions was also criticized. One recommended solution entailed streamlining the sales organization and closing down the direct sales operation completely. Direct sales only brought in £1,000 a week at their peak, and by the summer of 1965 net takings were less than £100 per week after commission was deducted. Commissioned agents on the North ship, for instance, brought in little sponsorship other than occasional advertisements for hoteliers, car hire firms, and turf accountants. It was also strongly suggested that the 'little rip-off alley' which Simon Dee alluded to was indeed taking place. The survey's summary castigated Caroline's 'pirate image' and made particular criticisms of the station's 'highly questionable business ethics', and the less than loyal 'get-rich-quick' philosophy of certain employees, whose activities in the sales department were likened to those of 'second-hand car salesmen'.

As a symptom of the disenchantment which was beginning to spread through the whole Caroline DJ staff Tom Lodge actually left the Caroline organization for a brief period at the end of 1965. He planned to go into films and had gained the services of a manager Kenneth Pitt, who also had on his books at the time an unknown singer and mime artist called

David Bowie. When this career move came to nothing Lodge freelanced for Radio Luxembourg for a short time, presenting a programme called *Ready Steady Radio* during January 1966, before rejoining Caroline. The resistance which Lodge envisaged facing from discontented station staff was in fact already well under way before he became programme director of the South ship. The lack of morale seemed to have begun with the 'good guys' policy, and its programming implications. This had entailed the introduction of strictly formatted three-hour 'slot' scheduling to replace the old 30- or 60-minute segments. Disc jockeys on the station were also aggrieved when new duty rostas were introduced in August 1965 which cut shore leave entitlement by 50 per cent.

In successive weeks during August and September of 1965 long-serving disc jockeys Doug Kerr, Gary Kemp, Jon Sydney, Mike Allen, and Roger Gale, were sacked or resigned from Radio Caroline. Nine weeks after this first 'mutiny' they were joined by Keith Skues, Bryan Vaughan, and Paul Noble. In the space of just four months Radio Caroline South lost the services of an entire generation of announcers. Doug Kerr, Gary Kemp, and Mike Allen, who had all been fired, were particularly outspoken about their employers. Kemp and Allen had sent up advertisers on the air, Allen simulating a coughing fit during a cigarette commercial. Cigarette advertising, banned from television, was at the time accounting for 12 per cent of all offshore radio sales revenue. Allen also firmly believed that the 'good guys' image and its accompanying pop music policy was a mistake. He was quoted at the time as 'fed up of being a screaming moron'.[28] Many of the disc jockeys were audibly unsuited to the kind of slick presentation normally associated with American commercial radio. Unwilling, or unable, to comply with the strictures of format, several had been criticized by the station's damning internal inquiry for sounding unenthusiastic and inarticulate, perpetuating a 'square' station image and playing too much inappropriate music 'obscure musical comedy numbers, Noel Coward, and Russ Conway'. Where they were supposed to be brief they sounded indulgent, and where they were supposed to project 'personality' several sounded as phoney as the 'BBC scripted automatons' that they had previously decried.

Few of this first generation of pirate disc jockeys were mould-breakers. Two years after leaving Radio Caroline Graham Webb, for instance, was back in Australia presenting the Sydney portion of *Family Favourites* for the BBC. Most were in fact highly regarded traditional broadcasters of the old school. Allen, previously a hit songwriter, had been largely responsible for the bulk of Caroline's jazz and blues input and he sold the concept of musical appreciation like a true Reithian. But his tendency to deride pop music over the air clearly did not endear him to his employers. Keith Skues was immediately offered a spot on a Southern Television pop show, and a record company show for CBS on Radio Luxembourg, where he recalls earning more for a 15-minute slot than for an entire week on Caroline. CBS paid him a guinea a minute, whereas Caroline at the time was paying £12 a week. Kenny Everett, having been fired from Radio London for sending up sponsored programmes was also hired by Luxembourg, which was actively recruiting from the pirates at a time when the BBC was still objecting on ethical grounds to employing disc jockeys who had such close links with the record industry (as many undoubtedly did). Of the others who left Caroline Bryan Vaughan went to work for Philips in Australia and Paul Noble joined the Luxembourg-owned Radio Antilles in the Caribbean.[29]

These major upheavals marked the end of the first phase of Caroline South's broadcasting history. Between late 1965 and the spring of 1966 the station entered a period of transition, a period which was prolonged in ways which could not have possibly been foreseen, when on the night of 20 January 1966, the South ship, the *Mi Amigo*, ran aground on Frinton beach after breaking its anchor and drifting during heavy North Sea storms. Such hazards were always a possibility, given the precarious nature of offshore broadcasting. Early in 1965 the Radio Caroline North ship had drifted in similar circumstances, and only days before the *Mi Amigo* ran aground Radio London had drifted into territorial waters on successive nights during blizzards when its anchor system failed.

The vessel used by Britt Wadner's Radio Syd was 'loaned' to the Caroline organization while the Caroline South ship underwent essential repairs in dry dock in Holland. But there was little charity involved in the transaction. The Syd organization was paid a fixed sum of £750 per week in cash for the loan, even though the boat was hardly suited to the rigours of a North Sea winter and was frequently off the air itself during this emergency period. But with a skeleton staff Caroline was at least able to run a stop-gap service. When it did return, fully operational, in May 1966, it was with some of the most genuinely spontaneous pop radio ever heard in Britain.

1966

> The establishment in England was always trying to get rid of us and there were a number of ways we prevented that or made it harder. Every operation within Radio Caroline was run by a separate company. Programming was run by Planet Productions for instance. Every little segment was a different company separately incorporated. There was no entity called Radio Caroline! It didn't exist legally. It was just words on the air.
>
> (Tom Lodge)[30]

What occurred on Radio Caroline during 1966 illustrated the difficulty of pursuing radical objectives while remaining dependent upon traditional methods of funding, and during this period Caroline unwittingly constructed a prototype for the subsequent failings of most oppositional impulses of the 1960s. After all if there was no entity called Radio Caroline then the station was materially and conceptually up for grabs. Such libertarianism was a two-edged sword which ultimately allowed economic realities to succeed over station philosophy, permitting those who were less than scrupulous ideologically to plunder the underlying naïvety of the 'swinging sixties' and appropriate its cultural territory to serve their own ends. This then is the story of the failings of the 1960s counter-culture in microcosm.

> In February 1966 I'd really had my lot. I was not only the longest serving person in pirate radio at that point, but I was also the only one left of the originals, and the whole thing

was going in a way I didn't like. It was getting into the acid scene and it's not the music I'm thinking of but some of the people involved. There was a certain type of person and a certain type of philosophy which wasn't quite me.

(Colin Nicol)[31]

The two factors which helped most to regenerate the station at this time were a fresh approach to recruitment and the adoption of a programming style which more accurately reflected the freewheeling mood of Ronan O'Rahilly's King's Road cultural milieu. It gave voice to the latent intent and nebulous ideals which had previously lost much of their potency in the translation from Chelsea set whim to the business realities of the music industry. What happened to Radio Caroline during 1966 clearly reflected wider social upheavals. Something fundamental was now occurring out on the North Sea. Caroline was putting into effect particular programming objectives which could perhaps only be realized outside the reaches of formal broadcasting policy, administrative rationalization, and political legislation. The floating radio pirate as a working environment suddenly became the sole focus of attention and this microcosm began to be resonant with possibilities; the station whose founder had begun London life dabbling in the fashionable self-absorption of method acting now began to translate Stanislavsky's 'system' into something tangible and audible. The means of mediation was the disc jockey:

Something I always felt very strongly about was that a DJ should always listen to his own programme. You'd be surprised how many disc jockeys do not listen to their own programmes. They turn the monitor on when the record comes in and say a few words and then turn it off again so they aren't tuned in to their own programme. We used to stand up when we did a show! We used to be so into the music that when the music ended we would have the same feeling that the audience had. You would be part of the whole show and the audience picks up on that. It was essential that you had the monitors on. We used to have our headphones on full blast and be dancing around to the show. And of course when you are doing that you are playing a piece of music and saying 'what do I want to hear next?' And you know exactly. You have that pile of records sorted into categories around you and you find that next cut and bang bang bang you're always ready. That was an infectious feeling that I don't think any other radio station had.

(Tom Lodge)[32]

The formal assumptions that had previously constituted the DJ's orthodoxy began to be eroded. Lodge continued to pay lip service to the requirements of the profession, a good radio voice, enthusiasm, personality, etc, but they were no longer regarded as prerequisites. Instead Lodge articulated a new set of priorities, talking of the right spirit, attitude, commitment, and involvement. One of the prominent features of the team Lodge assembled to instigate this free-form agenda was the number of recruits without any previous radio experience, but who then became successful DJs. All had sold themselves to their prospective employer on dedication alone. Lodge was dismissive of the conventions which most of the other offshore stations were holding to:

I don't think experience has anything to do with being a good disc jockey. I think it's all to do with attitude and state of mind. It's a certain type of personality and attitude which is essential. You also have to have enthusiasm but that alone is not enough. It's also a feel for the music: an empathy.

(Tom Lodge)[33]

Lodge introduced to the South station something of the infectious enthusiasm he had long been used to on the North ship, which had enjoyed a relatively continuous run of success, free from pirate competition and suffering none of the lurches in policy or staff purges which had hindered Caroline South. The predominant accents on Caroline North were either undiluted Mancunian or Canadian, and the rejuvenated Caroline South team was built around a similar nucleus of North American experience and provincial enthusiasm. With just one or two exceptions the whole unit revolved around this North American–Lancashire hybrid. Lodge attempted to instil in his new team an approach built upon intuition and spontaneity. He based a programming policy almost entirely on these notions, promoting the maxim that if spontaneity and empathy were compatible then the ideal preparation was not to prepare, but just to be:

> My whole approach to programming was totally different to anything else. The DJs have to be totally involved with the generation they are playing to. This meant that you have to be the kind of person who goes to the concerts, who wants to meet the new people who are coming on the scene, and be involved in the music in every way. And then you give the on-air personnel total control of their show.
>
> (Tom Lodge)[34]

For the first time Radio Caroline was accurately capturing the essence of its circumstances. The mechanics of the approach celebrated the ever-passing present and therefore embraced the cultural paradox that pop music is built upon. It successfully provided a context for ephemera which elevated rather than denigrated pop's necessary obsolescence. In its most lucid moments it acknowledged that there was more to an audience than a passive entity, a demographic convenience, collectively drying the dishes while musing upon the range of consumer durables available for purchase. All the tired assumptions about playing it safe, built largely on the premise that what the audience wants is familiarity, were radically reassessed. The format, that totem of conformity, propagated by the music industry, and faithfully valorized by Radio London, was transformed by its new irrelevancy:

> I used to tell them pick out and put in piles around you the kind of music they wanted to play, but to categorize it into Top 40, albums, new releases, plus the way out stuff they liked, etc, etc. *Choose the record when the record before is playing. No other preparation. You listen to your show and that way you will be playing what's relevant at that moment. And you will be in tune with your audience if you are the right kind of person.*
>
> (Tom Lodge, emphasis mine)[35]

Radio Caroline's idea of format had always been somewhat elusive, and aspirations towards streamlined uniformity had never sat easily on the station's agenda. The 'good guys' initiative of early 1965 was hampered by an unwilling and unsympathetic staff and the experiment had lapsed into resentment and inconsistency. Now, given completely free reign, Caroline DJs had to rely on intuition in order to regain their notions of professionalism. The nearest anyone came to defining a working model of what was practised during Tom Lodge's reign as programme director was 'one in, one out', that is, one chart record followed by one non-chart record. The brief was as simple as that, but even that meagre guideline was less than rigidly applied and few concessions were made to the trappings of format radio. Daytime programming maintained recognized slots for children's requests, coffee break, factory call, etc., but these were token gestures. Unlike the other stations who followed convention by playing the obligatory selections of nursery rhymes in their children's slots, or family favourites like Jim Reeves or Ken Dodd in their housewive's sections, Radio Caroline was just as likely to present psychedelic rock in both!

In July 1966 Radio London announced that it had reached its self-imposed advertising threshold of six minutes per hour. In fact the volume of commercials aired per hour was far higher than this. As can be seen from Table 3.3 the figure could be nearly double the station's stated maximum even during off-peak weekend broadcasting. Radio London grossed an estimated £1 million in advertising revenue during 1966, but even at the height of its most successful period of programming it was noticeable that Caroline South hardly saturated the airwaves with commercials. In-house advertising for T-shirts, Caroline Club membership, etc., and promotions for the station's own functions significantly outnumbered product commercials. Table 3.4 indicates that Radio London carried a high number of in-house promotions but even here London's sales expertise and superiority were evident. While Caroline hired Wimbledon Palais for its nights out, Radlon Sales was arranging extensive promotional tie-ups with Top Rank, then one of the largest leisure organizations in the country.

On Caroline there were occasional advertisements for *Disc and Music Echo*, for which several Caroline announcers wrote guest columns, and for the magazine *Paris Match*, to reciprocate

Table 3.3 Advertising on Radio London

Time	Disc	Advertisement, duration

Chris Denning Show, 9.00 a.m. – 10.00 a.m., Saturday, 21 May 1966

Time	Disc / Advertisement, duration
9.00	Weather forecast, DJ theme tune and introductory patter
9.02	'Sloop John B', Beach Boys (10) (2)
9.05	Players' Weights' Tipped Cigarettes, 30 secs
	Mother's Pride bread, 30 secs
9.06	'Wonderboy', Bruno (39) (–)
9.09	Top Deck soft drink, 30 secs
	Evette deodorant, 30 secs
9.11	'Little man in a little box', Barry Fantoni (climber)
9.14	'Is this the dream?', Zombies (revived 45)
9.16	Generation Boutique, 70 secs
	Big L Marquee Beat and
	Disc Show promo., 90 secs
9.20	'I love her', Paul and Barry Ryan (9) (–)
	Mother's Pride bread, 30 secs
9.23	'Message to Michael', Dionne Warwick (30) (–)
9.26	Harry Fenton Stores, 30 secs
9.27	'River deep mountain high', Ike and Tina Turner (climber)
9.30	News
9.31	'Hey Girl', Small Faces (5) (15)
9.34	Bri-Nylon 'Impact' shirts,
	Burton's Mail Order, 30 secs *
9.35	'Promises', Ken Dodd (21) (14)
9.39	Top Deck 'Rumba' drink, 30 secs
	Outspan fruit, 15 secs
9.40	'To make a big man cry', P J Proby (climber) (34)
9.43	Mother's Pride bread, 30 secs
	Morgan: A Suitable Case For Treatment,
	film trailer, 30 secs *
9.44	'Revenge', Ray McVay Sound (revived 45)
9.45	South-east Jazz and Blues Festival, 70 secs
	Bride Show promo., 15 secs
9.47	'Sorrow', Merseys (3) (9)
9.49	Generation Boutique, 70 secs
	Top Deck 'Rumba' drink, 30 secs
9.51	'Got to find another baby', Force West (33) (–)
9.54	Mother's Pride bread, 30 secs
9.55	Promo., Radio London Club, Disc of the Week
	'Don't bring me down', Animals

Total advertising time in 60-minute period: 11 minutes, 30 seconds

Lorne King Show, Radio London, 6.00 p.m.–7.00 p.m., Sunday, 21 May 1967

6.00	Weather
6.01	'Silence is golden', Tremeloes (8) (1)
6.04	Vidor batteries, 15 secs
	Speedwood stock car racing, 45 secs *
6.05	'Two Streets', Val Doonican (11) (–)
6.08	West Sands Caravan Park, 30 secs
6.09	'Lola', Los Brincos (climber) (–)
6.11	Silexine paint, 30 secs
	The Double Man, film promo., 25 secs
6.12	'My old car', Lee Dorsey (climber) (–)
6.15	Vidor batteries, 15 secs
6.16	'There goes my everything', Engelbert Humperdinck (climber) (–)
6.19	Uppercut Club 'Discoveries of Tomorrow'
	competition, Philip Birch
	Agency, 40 secs
6.20	'Patterns', Small Faces (climber) (–)
6.22	Costa Brava Holidays with DJs, 90 secs
6.24	'A day in the life', Beatles (LP track)
6.28	'Knock on wood', Eddie Floyd (Radio London soul set) (–)
6.30	News
6.32	'Get me to the world on time', Electric Prunes (4) (–)
6.35	Rothman's 'Crown' Filter Cigarettes, 30 secs
6.36	'Don't sleep in the subway', Petula Clark, 25 secs
6.39	*The Double Man*, film promo., 25 secs
	Big L catamaran offer, 30 secs *
6.40	'No good to cry', Jimmy James and the Vagabonds (climber)
6.42	Vidor batteries, 15 secs
6.42	'Everyday I have to cry', Dusty Springfield (revived 45)
6.45	Wimpy Bars, 15 secs
6.45	'Whiter shade of pale', Procol Harum (5) (–)
6.49	*The Double Man*, film promo., 25 secs
6.50	'Then I kissed her', The Beach Boys (20) (12)
6.52	Rothman's 'Crown' Filter Cigarettes, 30 secs
	Radio London T-shirt offer, 65 secs
6.54	'To be loved', Casinos (climber) (–)
6.56	London School of Broadcasting, 60 secs
6.57	'Here comes my baby', Tremeloes (LP track)
7.00	'The World Tomorrow', Garner Ted Armstrong (30 minutes of sponsored religion)

Total advertising time in 60-minute period: 9 minutes, 45 seconds

First number in parentheses refers to position in Radio London *Fab 40*
Second number in parentheses refers to position in BBC chart
 * indicates advertisement read live on air by disc jockey

the deal which DJ Emperor Rosko had with both Caroline and the French service of Radio Luxembourg (M. Jean Provost, the owner of *Paris Match*, was also a shareholder in Radio Luxembourg). Slot advertising, such as it was, was confined to make up, tights, and television rentals – teenage disposables and the growing 'never-never' economy of hire purchase. In August 1966 Ronan O'Rahilly brought in the Canadians Terry Bate and Alan Slaight to reorganize the Caroline sales department. Bate, a former vice-president both of Stephens & Townrow and CBS Radio Canada, had the kind of North American commercial pedigree previously absent from the Caroline operation, and the effects of his new policies were soon felt. Bate and Slaight (nicknamed Batman and Robin by Caroline's more cynical DJs) were ostensibly drafted in to sell radio time, create commercials, promote merchandise, and advise on station administration. The sprawling sales department was immediately scaled down in the name of efficiency, and by November 1966 a whole new set of promotions started to shape the station's daytime output.

Of all these shows the highest profile was given to 'Caroline Cash Casino'. Bate brought in a comprehensive package deal, drawing upon sponsors from different advertising agencies, and then selling separate spin-off shows under the 'Cash Casino' umbrella. The main 'Cash Casino' competition offered the largest cash prizes ever given away on pirate radio at that time, over £4,000 in some cases, and was sponsored by popular household name brands such as Weetabix, Findus Frozen Foods, Galaxy Chocolate, VP Wines, Nabisco Shredded Wheat, Alberto VO Shampoo, and Libby's Canned Fruit. Other examples of competitions included in the package were 'Partners in Profit', sponsored alternatively by Weetabix and Ajax, and 'Lucky Birthday Bonanza', sponsored by Golden Wonder Peanuts. Some of these shows ran simultaneously with the 'Cash Casino' campaign, others, like 'Enva Merry Christmas', sponsored by Enva Cyprus Sherry, were seasonal one offs. During the winter of 1966–7 these segments effectively reintroduced 5- to 15-minute programming slots to Caroline South.

'Cash Casino' was undoubtedly the most successfully marketed deal that Caroline had ever embarked upon. It was also universally unpopular with disc jockeys, who complained that it was too long and spoiled the flow of their programmes. Broadcast five times daily on weekdays between the peak listening hours of 9.00 a.m. and 1.00 p.m., each instalment of 'Cash Casino' lasted anything up to 15 minutes, taking 45 minutes out of a three-hour programme. There was never any market research evidence to suggest that it increased either Caroline's audience or the sales of its products, but to the marketing men it symbolized prestige. There had been indications after a year or two of programming lucky dip that the initiative was back with the King's Road mavericks. By July 1966 the renaissance appeared to be in full swing, but by November the free-for-all was over. Station management cut back on all costs including, for a while, the hiring of new disc jockeys. For Caroline's programme director the ultimatum came when he was asked to take a 50 per cent pay cut:

> Ronan was a visionary, a romantic, a pioneer, but he wasn't an astute accountant. I don't know if there was a problem with money but Phil Solomon just cut everything down, all costs. He obviously felt this was a short term thing and he would make as much money as possible and cut everything to the bone. The thinking was the momentum of the past would give you the profits and you don't put anything back at all, and by the time the effect of those cuts is realized you've taken out your profit. I think that was the basic philosophy. It meant that all the things we had been doing in the past were suddenly curtailed and at that time I decided it was time to leave. The whole show was changing dramatically.
>
> (Tom Lodge)[36]

Phil Solomon joined Planet Productions as a full-time working director in February 1966. Previously he had worked in record distribution with Decca and as an agent and concert promoter, managing Irish groups such as Them and the Bachelors, putting on regular summer shows with the latter at the ABC in Blackpool. These shows were widely advertised on all the pirates and the Bachelors themselves were no strangers to offshore radio, having been previously linked to a takeover bid of the ailing Radio Invicta in December 1964. Solomon claimed when he joined the Caroline organization:

> I am selling most of my other interests to join Radio Caroline so that I can devote my time to the exciting prospect of contributing to the growth of this company. We are about to put into effect a new development which we feel will give Caroline a new boost.[37]

One of the first schemes that Solomon put into operation was one for Radio Caroline to start its own record label. He negotiated with Ember Records to distribute the new label's product. Ember's own records were at the time being distributed by Selecta, a subsidiary of Decca, Solomon's former employer. It had been planned to start the new label in September 1966 but Selecta was sensitive to the wider implications of establishing an explicit distributive link between offshore radio and the record industry: prolonged negotiations delayed the launch until late November 1966. Selecta had already refused to distribute a single called 'We love the pirates' which had been recorded by members of the Ivy League under the alias 'The Roaring Sixties' because of its pro-pirate sentiments. The record naturally became an anthem on all the offshore stations but not a Top 20 hit.

Solomon's label was finally launched on 25 November 1966. Called 'Major Minor', its product was to be manufactured by CBS and distributed by the suitably placated Selecta. The plan was to lease cheaply, from American labels, product which was not otherwise available in Britain, in addition to home-produced items by new groups. The first two releases on the Major Minor label, by unknown Irish groups the O'Brien Brothers and Odin's People, were both extensively plugged on Radio Caroline but neither made the national charts. Records by promising British and Irish artists such as the Wheels and the Gibsons also met with little success, and it became immediately noticeable that apart from its high profile on Radio Caroline Major Minor product received no airplay on any of the pirates.

Major Minor later embarked upon several adventurous leasing

deals with American record companies, bringing names such as the Isley Brothers, Kim Weston, and Johnny Nash to UK prominence for the first time, but a high proportion of the material initially released on the label featured Irish showbands and ballads. The majority of them would not have sounded too incongruous on Caroline North, whose catchment area took in audiences who had traditionally always enjoyed Irish and country music (indeed Caroline North had a substantial Irish listenership), but Caroline South featured Major Minor material just as prominently.

The boardroom changes of 1966 and the subsequent reorganization of Caroline's sales department were the most visible manifestation so far of the underlying contradictory forces which had always threatened the precarious infrastructure of the Caroline organization. The conflict between, on the one hand, a spontaneous creativity rooted within Caroline's embryonic anarcho-capitalism, and on the other, an imposed accountancy (and accountability), designed only to balance the books, had now been more clearly defined and situated. Caroline had been born out of nebulous motives and its two ships had given substance to an unlikely whim, but such ill-defined and hazy origins were always likely to be susceptible to a dose of economic reality. Although financed by traditional city resources Caroline's very existence symbolized a striving for alternatives. Its claim to cultural territory had been as valid as that of the Beatles, its place in the iconography of youth as secure as Carnaby Street or purple hearts. But by late 1966 the pirate radio issue was becoming a convenient means by which the vested interests of the entertainments industry could talk to each other. The pirates themselves had become a focal point, providing concrete linkage between all of the music industry's newly mobilized capital. There was obviously going to be some sort of role for Radio London's brand of organizational efficiency, and given the range of subcultural initiatives already on display there was no reason why Caroline's particular hip capitalism should not have been assimilated. But by late 1966 there were signs that Caroline's defence was dwindling into little more than moral indignation, a naïve demand for the right to broadcast and be left alone. Swinging sixties rhetoric was plainly going to be insufficient if Caroline's campaign for survival was to be anything other than bluff and bravado. There were also clear indications that with the ascendancy of Philip Solomon as director and Terry Bate's salesmanship the King's Road crowd was becoming an idealistic luxury.

In September 1966 Ronan O'Rahilly's promotion company joined forces with former business associates in the Rik Gunnell agency (the Gunnells had previously run the legendary Rikki Tik clubs during O'Rahilly's Scene Club days) to look after the interests of Georgie Fame, the Alan Price Set, Chris Farlowe, and Zoot Money. There were signs that Caroline's chief was becoming a mere figurehead in his own organization, and that Caroline House was now no more than an administrative convenience where the Chelsea set could continue to indulge its whim. Reports that O'Rahilly was looking at the feasibility of using an ancient charter to establish land rights in Cambridgeshire did little to alleviate this suspicion. In August 1966 the Caroline boss made contact with Leonard Warren, who, in addition to being a caretaker employed by Cambridge University also claimed to be Overlord of the Ancient Kingdom of Reach, and cited a Rogation Day Charter signed by King John in 1201 to justify his title. The charter, like hundreds of other pieces of obsolete legislation relating to compulsory archery practice on Sundays and suchlike had never been erased from the statute books. Warren seemed convinced that a pop pirate station could legally and technically operate from the new kingdom. Little more was heard of the venture, although it wasn't to be the last time that Ronan O'Rahilly would explore the possibilities of establishing an independent state.

1967

Nothing should be done to overload the memory with sense-less and compulsory work ... Man himself, the whole of him is the book of creative art. And the longer you give him the wrong kind of tuition at school, the less conscious does he become of the creative powers within him, and the more will he rely on textbooks and external circumstances to make a career for himself, forgetting what it was that first drew him to the studio and how great his love was of the career he had chosen for himself when he entered the studio.

(Stanislavski)[38]

I would say there is a relationship between the Stanislavski school Ronan was running and Caroline. His whole life when I knew him was very influenced by that type of philosophy. He ran Radio Caroline along those lines, bringing in the people who had the energy. And of course you make lots of mistakes that way, so you get rid of the people who don't lock in and you've got fluidity that way as well. A corporation like General Motors cannot afford to do that so they have to go with a much more rigid format. In my mind Caroline's is a far more natural way. It's also going to lead to more interesting and innovative things. At the same time you are going to fall on your ass more often.

(Tom Lodge)[39]

Disc jockey Emperor Rosko later claimed that he was always being sacked for refusing to play Major Minor material only to be reprieved by Ronan O'Rahilly whenever he went to collect his final pay-cheque.[40] Rosko eventually put personal integrity before company profits and left Caroline in January 1967. Those of a like mind who chose to stay with the station remained secretly antagonistic towards what was perceived to be editorial intrusion but only began to offer audible resistance when the new strategy became public. Shortly after Rosko's departure it emerged that Caroline was charging £100 a week to plug new releases. Under the conditions of this blatant payola system a record would be plugged for two weeks. If it had not entered the Radio Caroline Top 50 by then it would be dropped from the play-list. It was the refusal of Caroline to continue to promote a new Cliff Bennett single, and the subsequent outrage which ensued, which brought the matter to light. This episode did little to allay music industry suspicions that highly unethical practices were being indulged in by most of the pirates, not only Caroline.

There was a fair degree of eccentricity and personality problems on London. There were all sorts of things going on on Big L. There were several levels of dynamic. They ranged from certain senior disc jockeys chasing certain junior disc jockeys round the bunks right through to the political level of whether or not they were going to continue to support a record label that was perhaps less than helpful in terms of supplying particular records.

(Tim Blackmore)[41]

Throughout 1966 Radio London had continued to issue strenuous denials that it was operating a payola system, even though some curious movements were taking place in the Radio London chart. An array of new and unknown artists made regular appearances in the 'Big L *Fab 40*', their records often reaching the top five without registering success elsewhere. As a prediction chart and barometer for future music industry trends the Big L hit parade had clearly developed a logic of its own. In March 1966, during the week that Nancy Sinatra's 'These boots were made for walking' reached number one in the music press and BBC charts the record dropped out of the Radio London *Fab 40*. Throughout the summer of 1966 those music papers sympathetic to the pirates' cause such as *Disc and Music Echo*, and *Record Mirror* pointedly observed the frequent anomalies. During July and August half of the BBC Top Ten had already disappeared from the London chart, while anything up to half of the records in the *Fab 40* were absent from the *Record Mirror* Top 50.

The whole pay-to-play issue has to be seen in the context of a concerted campaign to discredit the offshore stations. By 1967, with legislation looming this campaign was really beginning to gain momentum. The Marine (etc.) Broadcasting Bill had received its first reading and prominent members of the record industry such as Sir Joseph Lockwood (head of EMI) were lining up to support the pirates' suppression. The Cliff Bennett disc which had provided the catalyst for condemnation was an EMI recording. Caroline even retaliated by placing a temporary ban on the Beatles' 'Penny Lane – Strawberry Fields Forever', provoking Caroline's more outspoken DJs to voice their resentment on air at this petty piece of politicizing. There

119

were by now clear indications that business initiatives were taking precedence over programming values, and throughout 1967 Radio Caroline continued to shift further towards economic pragmatism. Exposure for records released on the Major Minor label, restricted to one plug per half hour during the early part of the year, had increased considerably by the summer, with an audible effect on programming.

At this juncture of the mid-1960s Caroline's gesture of rebellion and resistance was faltering in the face of commercial demands. By 1967 only the residue of the programming ideals which Tom Lodge had begun to put into practice remained: a tantalizing reminder of what could have been. The plug records proliferated, the money men were in charge, Caroline's benign *laissez-faire* was at their mercy. On the political front formidable forces were now relentlessly mobilizing against the flotilla of so-called floating juke-boxes, and whereas all of the other pirates offered little but capitulation Caroline was about to adopt the unlikely mantle of David against the Corporate Goliath.

There were many working in the BBC at the time who were sympathetic to an expansion of the Corporation's popular music output, and clearly saw in Radio London a blueprint for the future. They were impressed with the station's consistency and professionalism. Recruitment of ex-London personnel towards the end of 1966 began to confirm this. There were, though, early indications that the BBC would be refining the aggressive marketing that was synonymous with the Big L approach.

It assumed that people listened to Radio London in a vacuum. The public are not as keen on proving the things that people working inside radio, music radio in particular, often are. There is an enormous obsession with certain people in radio saying 'you heard it first here'. My own belief is that the public don't actually give a damn. You can create a feel that things are faster, newer, brighter, smoother, slicker, but in reality listeners don't actually want to hear that.

(Tim Blackmore)[42]

Radio London's overriding objective was slick professionalism and a full advertiser's log, but there was more to the station than mere platitudes and hard sell. Caroline and London's respective images of rebelliousness and conformity were never entirely inflexible, despite their apparent rivalry. For instance, the two stations' disc jockeys frequently visited each other's ships, indiscretions for which they remained doggedly unrepentant despite being censured by a constant flow of management memos. The distinction became particularly blurred on the programming front during the final months of offshore broadcasting. Caroline's commitment to freewheeling spontaneity and improvisation was being curtailed by the business commitments of its directors, while London, despite constant management directives to the contrary, was now nurturing some of the most innovative programmes to come out of the pirate era; it was certainly responsible for two of the most innovative disc jockeys of that time: Kenny Everett and John Peel.

Despite being one of Radio London's original team Everett was always a maverick talent, idiosyncratic, and difficult to confine to the 'time and temperature' restrictions of format radio. His relationship with the station was at times an abrasive one. In October 1965 he was sacked for making irreverent comments on air about one of Radio London's religious sponsors, the evangelist Garner Ted Armstrong, whose syndicated programme *The World Tomorrow* was broadcast daily during Everett's show. The sponsor happened to be in Britain at the time, and the following directive from Philip Birch duly found its way out to the ship: 'Client complains of snide remarks about *The World Tomorrow*. What are these remarks? Please make sure they are not repeated. Reply today imperative.'[43]

After a suitable period of penance (spent making taped programmes of record-company-sponsored product for Radio Luxembourg) Everett returned to Radio London in June 1966, but there was little on-air evidence to suggest that the sacking had curbed his natural idiosyncrasies. These continued to thrive despite the constraints of professionalism. Soon after his return the memos began to fly again as Radio London's management showed they were no more adept than before at curbing his individuality, which by now was starting to absorb some of the psychedelic excesses of the period.[44] Heavy drinking was the norm among Everett's colleagues but such behaviour was acceptable, all part of the boys' dorm camaraderie promoted on Big L (even though the slurred utterances of certain notorious disc jockeys were frequently to be heard on air). Everett's own brand of hedonism inevitably spilled over into his programmes. The cryptic clues and innuendoes were there in abundance. 'I've been up all night starving myself in order to bring you new concepts in radio', was not the kind of obscure comment that listeners were used to hearing on a breakfast show.

John Peel's *Perfumed Garden* has acquired a legendary aura out of all proportion to the brevity of its existence. The show which is rightly credited with having introduced the British radio audience to the underground had a life span of approximately three months. The earliest known use of *The Perfumed Garden* as a programme title was in mid-May 1967. It ran for possibly four, certainly no more than five, two-week shifts. Its colossal legacy therefore derives from little more than 100 hours of airtime, but it was the innovative way in which this airtime was utilized which made the programme such an influential force.

Arriving back in England after a spell of four years on American radio in Texas and California, John Ravenscroft (the name Peel was suggested by a secretary in the Radio London office) was employed by Radio London in March 1967 as a regular Top 40 disc jockey. Suitably impressed with his American experience (which had included a spell with KLIF Dallas) Radio London management did not insist on either an audition or a demonstration tape. Peel himself regarded this as a blessing as, in his own estimation, he had neither the style nor voice of a Top 40 DJ. In fact he initially performed his duties to format radio as competently as anybody else, but even the most casual listener would have noticed that Peel did not take the process entirely seriously; sending up advertisements and records became his forte. In this respect he was not as much of a lone maverick as the mythology suggests. There were several other DJs on the station, Kenny Everett and Keith Skues among them, who had a genuinely eccentric approach to Top 40 radio, and Peel's own humorous approach sounded far from out of place in this context.

As one of the most recent station recruits he was also occasionally expected to 'double up' on the midnight to 2 a.m. programme. There was a time-honoured institutional resistance on several of the pirate stations to this slot and Peel soon found that no one else was very willing to volunteer his services. More gradually came the realization that not only was nobody else interested in hosting the 'graveyard shift', as it was commonly known, but also no one on the ship or in the Radio London office was listening to its output. The after midnight slot on Radio London had always been an area of scheduling indecisiveness. In stark contrast to the station's extremely professional daytime output nocturnal programming had always seemed like a managerial afterthought. Owing to the strong interference from foreign stations that Radio London suffered during the hours of darkness the night-time listenership had always been a fraction of what it was during the peak daytime period, and there was a corresponding lack of interest from advertisers.

The slot was initially filled by a show called *London after midnight*, which played light music, and had less emphasis on a rigid Top 40 format. Throughout 1966 the programme was subject to the whims and musical preferences of individual DJs who seized the opportunity to be self-indulgent at a time when audiences could in all probability be measured in five figures rather than seven. One school of thought, dictated by senior announcers such as Paul Kaye and Duncan Johnson, was that the programme should adhere to its original light music brief. Junior announcers were often less faithful to this policy. Tony Blackburn, for instance, initiated a weekend soul music programme. It was this haphazard scheduling inheritance that enabled John Peel to develop his programming ideas without resistance. He started playing the kind of music which was emerging, predominantly but not exclusively, from the west coast of America, and from the burgeoning underground scene in London, which had up to this point received virtually no exposure in the UK.

In 1966 the Federal Communications Commission in the USA had introduced regulations which prohibited radio stations from 'simulcasting' the same programmes on both their AM and FM facilities. In the large conurbations on the west coast

– San Francisco, Los Angeles, and Seattle – the FCC decision effectively gave birth to underground radio. Using its infinitely better sound quality stations began using FM to cater for a growing scene that was ill-served by mainstream pop programming. FM radio became part of the subcultural grapevine, nurturing a sense of community and shared sensations, and keeping all the disparate elements of the counter-culture in touch with each other. It was this approach to broadcasting, still very much in its infancy even in America, that John Peel brought back to England.

> Just before I left California two of the other DJs and myself, on the station I was working on in San Bernadino, thought that what we ought to be doing, as the station's share of the market was slipping, was what subsequently became FM radio. We were playing LP tracks and just broadening the scope of the station, and just generally doing what ended up as the substance of *The Perfumed Garden*. And when I left California I just brought that idea back with me.
>
> (John Peel)[45]

Once Peel began to realize the full extent of staff apathy towards the after midnight slot he started to give fuller exposure to the kind of music that was developing out of this embryonic scene. Rather than use the medium of pop radio as just another distribution facility for the promotion machine, Peel began to drop the regular features normally associated with format radio. He dispensed with the news bulletins almost immediately; more gradually he stopped running the few scheduled advertisements. Weather forecasts and time checks remained but chiefly as a vehicle for Peel's irreverent humour, as he began wryly to mock the assumption that his listeners would desire to know the barometer reading at 1.30 in the morning, or indeed that it was 1.30 in the morning.

Peel soon established a genuine cultural rapport with his listeners, and found that within the English underground scene there was a willing audience for this type of radio, collectively picking up on the programme's reference points and the wider values and ideals they reflected. The evolution of *The Perfumed Garden*, where nightly the underground communicated with itself, mirrored a corresponding stage in the evolution of a whole subculture. Some underground publications even took to advertising on Radio London ('Girls, earn sixpence a minute selling *Oz* magazine!'). By the summer of 1967 the more commercial aspects of what the media was calling 'flower power' were already being exploited. The English underground was still a relatively self-contained community but it was attracting unwelcome attention from those who wished to suppress it. Police raided the offices of *International Times*, the underground's house magazine, and on the pretext of searching for obscene material smashed up property and took away subscription lists from the files, thereby halting the flow of revenue necessary for the paper's survival. The owner of the UFO club in London's Tottenham Court Road, John 'Hoppy' Hopkins was gaoled for possession of a small amount of drugs. Rolling Stones Mick Jagger and Keith Richard also received gaol sentences for minor drug offences. These events prompted William Rees Mogg's epochal 'Who breaks a butterfly with a wheel' editorial for *The Times*, which added the paper's weighty support to the outrage being generally expressed at these exemplary sentences, and played its part in the Rolling Stones' subsequent release on appeal. There was a nightly forum for such opinions in *The Perfumed Garden*; Peel's allegiances were unmistakably supportive.

The English underground in 1967 was a patchwork of issues and causes. Political activists, influenced by situationism, Mao, or anarcho-syndicalism, brought their playpower gestures of contempt to bear upon the institutional kindergartens of the western world. Seekers of mystical truths took the path of passive resistance, Tolkien, Blake, Tarot, or I Ching in their pursuit of wisdom. All tendencies were represented in *The Perfumed Garden*, which became a kind of audio bulletin board for the counter-culture and all the self-indulgent juxtapositions contained therein. When he wasn't running alternative poet laureate competitions (nominations were received in roughly equal proportion for Donovan, Roger McGough, Allen Ginsberg, Paul Simon, Bob Dylan, and Christopher Logue) he might be parodying the formula of commercial radio by running absurdist 'anti-competitions'; in one, a 'competitor' was a listener who wrote in to say that he was refusing to enter (and was therefore automatically disqualified for revealing the fact). Peel was also just as likely to be imploring his audience to remind London Zoo of its ecological duty to protect rare species. Convincing listeners (many of whom didn't seem to need convincing) that he, and maybe they, had been small furry creatures in previous incarnations was just another side of the coin.

None of these initiatives, serious or otherwise (and there was a fair degree of otherwise) was a conscious campaign as such, merely indications of possibilities. Because the prevailing mood was one of tolerance and magnanimity *The Perfumed Garden* galvanized the underground, and allowed it to speak as if with one voice. So all those essential elements, the profound and the profane, the cynical and the naïve, coexisted side by side. In trying to give equal access both to those who were trying to change the world and to those who were just trying to change themselves Peel too naturally embodied many of the attendant contradictions and flaws. His own stance was rarely confrontational, it was merely a plea for tolerance and was against perceived injustice. He was however quick to voice dismay at the way 'flower power' was packaged as part of what the situationists called 'the Spectacle'. He unequivocally dismissed the Alexandra Park love-in as a 'commercial hoax', and had particular reservations about the high degree of musical snobbery that was being engendered and the elitist principles of appreciation already endemic among listeners. He played a lot of blues music on *The Perfumed Garden*, and frequently had to defend the likes of Albert King, Lightnin' Hopkins, and Jimmy Reed against the kind of prejudice masquerading as purism that would soon find a ready niche in the shrewdly marketed progressive rock movement of the late 1960s.

> I certainly didn't see myself as spearheading a movement or being a leader of anything at all, more of a kind of functionary. I've always seen myself, especially then, as linking things and enabling people whose interests were similar to have a common voice. So it was almost like an editorial function, letting people know that they weren't on their own.
>
> (John Peel)[46]

Although *The Perfumed Garden* was essentially free-form radio, with Peel improvising almost every facet, the programme was built around a nucleus of 30 or 40 groups and solo artists. The debut LPs by Frank Zappa, Captain Beefheart, Tim Buckley, Country Joe and the Fish, the Seeds, the Velvet Underground, the Blues Project, the Incredible String Band, Pink Floyd, and the Liverpool Scene, received particular emphasis, as did Peel's personal favourites such as Donovan, the Byrds, Simon and Garfunkel, and the Beatles.

Peel naturally found himself working in a cultural vacuum for much of the time on Radio London. Many of the station's DJs were indifferent to his nocturnal programming habits and were surprised when the kaftan-wearing hippie started to receive far more mail than they did. Peel did not have a bigger audience than the daytime DJs; on the contrary, night-time audiences for the station were a fraction of the estimated 12 million who listened during the day, but a far higher percentage of those who listened to *The Perfumed Garden* wrote in. Unlike daytime programming, where audience participation meant little more than an occasional 'namecheck' or 'dedication', Peel's programme was a catalyst for debate; the kind of letters received actively encouraged genuine dialogue. Peel's popularity became an obvious source of antagonism to fellow announcers. On one occasion the playing of Scott McKenzie's 'summer of love' anthem 'San Francisco' prompted the following on-air outburst from the Canadian DJ Mike Lennox:

I suppose you've read this bit about flower power and everybody being lovely and meeting everyone you see with a smile. John Peel told me an interesting thing. There's a woman called Suzi Creamcheese, who is an American I believe, who believes in this flower power. John Peel was in hospital and all of a sudden this character Creamcheese came into the hospital wearing all white robes, danced around the hospital bed throwing sweet peas at John, and then danced out again. I guess that was supposed to cure him and make him feel much better. And he said it did. But I've yet to believe in that sort of thing. I really don't believe in it. I think it's a good idea passing out flowers and being nice to everyone but I think it's a rather apathetic way of going about things. *(change of tone)* Oh, I've done it now, haven't I? I've angered people who believe in it, and John respects it because he's a firm believer in love and beautiful friendships which seem to be taking over from the west coast of America. I'm not going to talk about it any more. Ten minutes until 7 o'clock . . . *(jingle:* 'Radio a-go-go')[47]

Lennox's tone varied from the incredulous to the disdainful, but even allowing for the fanciful source of the Suzi Creamcheese anecdote, adulterated and embellished no doubt by the prevailing stimuli of the times, it is still a remarkable piece of public resentment. However, after playing the next record Lennox returned to his theme, this time in the more recognizably commercial-radio role of salesman and diplomat, promoting *The Perfumed Garden* in exactly the same tones used for endorsing Vitalis haircream or John Cotton Cigarellos (whose campaign shrewdly utilized the slogan 'join the smoking revolution').

Five minutes and thirty seconds before 7 o'clock on the Mike Lennox show. Of course with all those things I've been saying about John Peel people might get the impression I don't like his programme. This is not true because I listen to John Peel every night between 12 and 2 o'clock. I really do. Try it. It's an experience.[48]

Although Kenny Everett's and John Peel's tenures on Radio London only overlapped by about a month, during February and March 1967, the two shared many mutual interests, ranging from similar musical tastes to a love of their native Liverpool (described by Allen Ginsberg at the time on the liner notes of the first Liverpool Scene LP as 'the centre of the conscious universe'). Months after Everett had left the station to join the BBC – and at a time when both Peel's future employment and the future of *The Perfumed Garden* seemed in doubt – listeners to the show were continually advised to keep listening to Kenny 'because Kenny knows', (although it was never exactly revealed what Kenny knew). Russ Tollerfield, Radio London's studio engineer and one of the few people with whom Peel actually socialized on the ship, was another kindred spirit. While other DJs spent their spare time answering fan mail Peel and Tollerfield made tape loops of the two of them talking backwards. These experiments were often broadcast on *The Perfumed Garden*. On one notable occasion listeners were treated to a doctored version of Engelbert Humperdinck's number one record 'Last Waltz', utilizing the phasing or flanging effect made famous by the Beatles, and later featured, in the true spirit of overkill, on many post-Sgt. Pepper psychedelic recordings.

Pete Drummond also became an afficionado of the programme towards the end of Radio London's existence. Hosting the popular morning show for Radio London's final few weeks, Drummond was not content to use the programme's traditional 11.00 a.m. coffee break for the usual 'put your feet up and have a cuppa' sentiments favoured by most DJs. He programmed the slot adventurously, and frequently featured Peel as his studio guest. The ensuing dialogue was usually far removed from the kind of pleasantries normally aired during the morning break. Peel and Drummond were more likely to discuss the films of Andy Warhol than they were the relative merits of coffee brands. The featured LP of the morning, normally the likes of Vince Hill or Vikki Carr, was just as likely to be the Velvet Underground's debut LP when Peel was the guest, thus enabling listeners to be treated to songs about drug dealing, sado-masochism, paranoia, and street violence, as they took their elevenses.

Peel's other kindred spirit on the station was Tommy Vance. Vance had a similar radio background to both Peel and Drummond, having been the sole English DJ on a top-rated US station. KHJ Los Angeles had been one of the first stations to make creative use of its FM facility after the FCC ruling on simulcasting. Vance had left KHJ in 1965 to avoid being drafted into the armed forces. Upon arrival in England he worked for a few months on Radio Caroline South before leaving to join Radio Luxembourg. Returning to England in December 1966 he again spent some time with Radio Caroline before joining Radio London just three weeks before its close-down. His American experiences left their mark not just on his radio style, which was modelled on the 'speak fast and modulate low' style of the influential Big Dan Ingram at WABC New York, but also on his politics. He frequently voiced pacifist sentiments on the air on Radio Caroline, and on one occasion played Joan Regan and the Squadronnaires' 'Ricochet', and Anne Shelton's World War Two rallying call 'Send all the boys back home', before launching into a personal condemnation of the Vietnam war. During the final days of *The Perfumed Garden* he was usually to be found in the studio conversing on air with Peel about any topic from star signs to the relative merits of west coast rock groups.

Radio London was by no means blind to the new subculture. Despite the predominant trend for making experimental LPs psychedelic groups cut singles too, and London's play-list reflected this, giving a high profile to those underground artists who had already shown distinct signs of doing quite well in the 'overground'. By the summer of 1967 Jefferson Airplane, Love, the Doors, the Strawberry Alarm Clock, the Electric Prunes, and Buffalo Springfield, had all had American Top 10 hits. Their British single releases usually found their way on to the Radio London rota. British acts, like Pink Floyd, Cream, Traffic, and Jeff Beck, who also found themselves classified as underground artists, released singles too – although Pink Floyd's first single, 'Arnold Layne', a song about a transvestite, was banned by Radio London.

Peel's role was totally at odds with the Radio London mainstream and the established channels of the music industry. He didn't conform to the normal routine expectations of what a disc jockey should do, particularly a disc jockey on the most successful commercial radio station in Britain. He didn't wine and dine record pluggers. He didn't go to record business parties. He wasn't 'showbiz'. He had to rely on like-minded spirits to send him records, or he had to buy or steal them himself. He was helped considerably in the latter department by 'The Firm', a self-styled deviant collective of ex-Mods, who had evolved into psychedelic pranksters at the onset of the counter-culture. Before this their biggest claim to notoriety had been to burn down the Speakeasy, the musicians' establishment drinking club. Hired as unlikely bouncers for the UFO club they used to furnish Peel with record company product and spike his drinks.[49] Others who could be relied upon to supply records were Clive Selwood at Elektra (home of the Doors, Love, and the Incredible String Band) and John Mayall, whose

Bluesbreakers Band at the time contained Eric Clapton and the nucleus of what later became Fleetwood Mac, and was in effect a finishing school for British blues apprentices. Peel was able to air Mayall's new LP 'Crusade' months before release, because Mayall himself had personally loaned the master tapes. *The Perfumed Garden* also introduced British listeners to the Misunderstood, an American band Peel had been managing prior to his return from California. Peel eulogized the group on air; their single 'I can take you to the Sun' became a *Perfumed Garden* anthem, and tracks were even played from their unreleased Fontana LP.

Radio London's notion of exclusivity was, in programming terms, confined to securing access to the product and playing it before anyone else. The entire merchandising process is rendered meaningless if that product is not eventually released; promotion is after all geared towards a saleable commodity. Despite the *ad hoc* nature of their copyright negotiations and their blatant flouting of remuneration for performers, the pirates, with the sole exception of Radio Sutch, hardly ever played unreleased or demo material. The offshore stations showed few signs of transcending their role as distributors of the industry's goods. Peel was not unduly concerned with the market as such. His professed role as 'a functionary' was governed by the audience he was serving and was not hindered by commercial considerations. *The Perfumed Garden* engendered a sense of belonging to a cultural community long before it considered the wider commercial one. This philosophy provided conditions under which the various aspects of the underground might thrive, and therefore the circumstances in which specific social alternatives could take root. The offshore stations on the whole seemed to be largely content with market opportunism, and rarely challenged the legitimacy of music industry practice and procedure. It is significant that ultimately it took an individual DJ acting on his own initiative, rather than a management ethos, to exploit fully the loophole the pirates themselves had exposed.

Chapter 4

Other pirates:
Other possibilities

'This is not the BBC.' *(Radio Sutch)*

27 May 1964 – September 1964

The station that truly encapsulated the spirit of offshore broad-casting transmitted for only four months and was originally conceived as a publicity stunt. Initially transmissions ran from midday to 2.00 p.m., 5.00 p.m. to 8.00 p.m. and midnight to 2.00 a.m., a scheduling policy not so much chosen as dictated by circumstance, since the station's equipment was powered by batteries rather than generators, and these needed to be recharged approximately every two hours. The station's owner, David 'Screaming Lord' Sutch, was an eccentric 24-year-old rocker who first achieved notoriety by standing for Parliament in the constituency vacated by John Profumo after the Christine Keeler scandal. Later, in the 1964 general election he stood against Harold Wilson in his own constituency of Huyton, where on behalf of his self-styled 'Teenage Party' Sutch advocated such unlikely policies as legalized commercial radio, the abolition of the eleven-plus examination, an extension of pub licensing hours, and votes for 18-year-olds.

Radio Sutch was the first pirate to broadcast from the abandoned army forts in the Thames estuary. Because of its extremely low power it is quite likely that the station was never received in London, but while it was transmitting Sutch gave listeners in Essex and Kent a taste of truly improvised pop radio. Programmes were sporadic, ramshackle, and anarchic, often beginning and ending when DJs felt like it. Broadcasting

132

equipment was rudimentary at best: a standard household record player was simply wired up to the battery-powered transmitter, which made it impossible to cue up records. This technicality was sufficient to render the station incapable of providing slick programming, not that Radio Sutch needed an excuse. In addition the unstable power source meant that records occasionally sounded slightly speeded up (ironically this technique was utilized by many leading US stations in the 1960s to give the subtle impression of a 'pacey' sound). The Radio Sutch 'studio', merely the most inhabitable tower in the Shivering Sands fort complex, was not soundproofed, so that 'off mike' noises, ranging from muffled coughs and doors closing, to an unrestrained cacophony of screams and shouts were a feature of most broadcasts. Radio Sutch was probably the only offshore pirate where the sound of someone singing manically at the top of his voice while swinging from a rope ladder outside the studio window was commonplace.

When on air the skeleton staff of David Sutch, Brian Paul, and Reg Calvert, appeared to be having a good time of it all, but the schoolboys-on-holiday atmosphere was dissipated somewhat when supplies ran low, or, as on one occasion in June 1964, when the emergency services had to be called out and a relief DJ taken off with food poisoning. While it lasted Sutch and company provided some very entertaining programmes. Unlike many others who ventured into offshore radio the Sutch crew were not 'playing at' being broadcasters; they had few preconceptions and fewer ground rules. Whole sides of Beatles LPs were played without comment between tracks, and if a DJ liked a particular record he might play it two or three times in succession. This was done neither out of boredom nor inexperience on the disc jockey's part, but because if that was how most people listened to records at home then that was how the DJ thought that they might want to listen to them on the radio. David Sutch often played demo tapes and unreleased recordings of other groups; with a listenership that probably never exceeded 5,000 this hardly constituted payola. He played the tapes because the people in the groups were his mates, which meant that unreleased Cavern Club recordings of Heinz and Dave Berry and the Cruisers were aired frequently. Sutch also gave extensive plugs to the Outlaws, who – like all

133

of the above acts, including Sutch himself – were produced by Joe Meek, the pioneering sound man best known for 'Telstar' by the Tornadoes.

Many of the discs featured were from Sutch's own collection, as nobody took the station seriously enough to furnish it with a comprehensive record library. Sutch's motives were basically charitable, and his programme output amounted to little more than cheerful anarchy. In contrast his manager, fellow announcer, and future station boss, Reg Calvert, ceaselessly plugged the records of all the performers he managed – most notably the Fortunes, who were often heard three or four times in an hour. The following hard sell was typical.

> And now folks I'd like to tell you about the group who we've selected as our top group. Our top new group is the Fortunes, and when I spoke to our London office today before I came over here they told me that the Fortunes have got a special treat in store for all Radio Sutch listeners. I'll tell you exactly what it is. They've just got a new record released, and what the boys have said is that if you'd like to join their fan club – no catch by the way, this is quite genuine – normally it costs 5s. But what they've said is, they'll help everybody on Radio Sutch by doing a special radio fan club membership. It costs you 7s. 6d., but for the 7s. 6d. you'll get their new record of 'I like the look of you', that comes to you free, and also you get a big picture of the Fortunes, personally autographed in your name, and also a story about how the Fortunes started off . . . and how they got together to form what we think is one of Britain's top harmony teams.[1]

Calvert would then go on laboriously to clarify everything from a definition of a personally autographed photo ('if your name is Mandy, the photo will say "To Mandy"') to a complete breakdown of postage costs. A typical promotion of this kind could take anything up to seven minutes of airtime, which would have been sufficient to give the record three successive plays instead. At no point did Calvert make it clear that he was the group's manager.

As even Radio London had shown, pacing of programmes was something few of the pirates instinctively understood in the early days. Radio Invicta, another of the fort-based stations, prolonged the simple act of reading a request *ad nauseam*; address read twice, often three times, inept stabs at authenticity by endless 'rustling' in the mailbag, etc., followed by what became a 'rule' of offshore commercial radio. On no account should the record that had been requested actually be available for transmission.

Radio Sutch only ever appeared to have two advertisers: 'Andy's of Whitstable', who supplied some of the station's records, and 'Cliff Davies Cars of Shepherds Bush', who transported Sutch's group when it was touring. While Reg Calvert's more committed hard sell approach would by September 1964 enable him to take over the station and turn it into Radio City, David Sutch was more intent on having a good time. His broadcasting style was witty, disarming, and totally lacking in pretence. He often sent himself up on air ('This is the station of one star ... Brian Paul') but he was shrewd too; the mere existence of his little station on the Shivering Sands fort was in itself a plug for commercial radio. When he wasn't parodying himself Sutch's other targets were deliberate and well chosen. 'The station of one star', for example, was a send-up of Radio Luxembourg's slogan 'the station of the stars', but Sutch's main target was the BBC. Parodies of the Light Programme style were frequently and drily interjected between the particularly raucous rock and roll and rhythm and blues sounds that the station tended to favour (in the great war of the subcultures Radio Sutch's allegiance was undoubtedly pledged to the rockers). There was something vaguely unsettling about hearing the mocking tones of 'We have an announcement to make – this is not the BBC' or 'Are you sitting comfortably?' half way through a Pretty Things or John Lee Hooker record.

Radio Sutch achieved notoriety for relaying late night extracts from novels such as *Fanny Hill* and *Lady Chatterley's Lover*. It was far from coincidental that the selection also frequently included records by comedian Max Miller, much of whose 'blue' material still remained banned by the BBC, 20 years after it had first been aired in the theatre. These extracts were heard by no more than a handful of listeners, but Sutch always maintained that they were popular with lorry drivers, and it is undoubtedly for the X-rated items that the station is best remembered.

Sutch had a good eye for publicity, and the desire to shock was the chief motivation for these broadcasts. In this respect he seemed to be virtually the only individual of the offshore era who was prepared to take all the swashbuckling rhetoric literally. As a gesture Radio Sutch was as valid as any other and cannot merely be written off as hobbyists playing at radio. Sutch made no pretence about his lack of broadcasting ability, and that in itself was the station's strength. When Sutch, as the press had predicted, finally tired of his toy and returned to touring with his group, he handed over Shivering Sands to his manager (which always appears to have been the intention). Radio Sutch became Radio City, and started trying to act like a professional radio station, but it never quite lost the spontaneity and genuine rapport of its predecessor. Even Calvert recognized ultimately that there were other ways of promoting pop groups – ones which wouldn't have listeners tuning to another station as soon as he launched into one of his hard sells. Radio Sutch recognized no orthodoxy, and unlike many of the minor outfits, which constantly gave the impression of small stations trying to sound like big stations, it had few serious aspirations. Its freewheeling spirit anticipated the situationist politics of the French and Italian pirates of the 1970s.[2]

Your monarch of music (KING Radio)

March 1965–September 1965

In February the short-lived Radio Invicta closed down and was taken over by a fresh consortium of businessmen who renamed the station KING Radio. In December 1964 the owner of Radio Invicta, Tom Pepper, and two of his staff had drowned when their unseaworthy supply boat capsized in misty conditions after dropping supplies at the station. The coroner at the inquest recorded an open verdict, but the affair brought to light for the first time the uneasy alliances being formed in the name of offshore radio. Ex-Radio City disc jockey Lee Michaels maintains that he was approached during the summer of 1965 by ex-employees of both Invicta and KING to seize the station's

Red Sands base.[3] Amidst all the rumours there were allegations that money was 'owed', and that the capsized boat incident had not been an accident.

KING Radio came on the air in March 1965, its new owners having invested in new broadcasting equipment in an attempt to get a better signal into the strategically important London area. Some indication of the haste with which pirate operations tended to be put together and alliances hurriedly forged could be gained from listening to KING's pre-recorded test transmissions, which gave the station's location as 'the Nore'. another of the ex-Army forts lying in the Thames estuary. KING was originally envisaged as a separate project, independent of Radio Invicta, but when it did eventually broadcast it came not from the Nore, which had in any case been uninhabitable since the mid-1950s, but from the adjacent Red Sands fort from which Invicta had broadcast. The pre-recorded tests also included announcements for forthcoming programmes called *Fiesta, South East Special, Candlelight and Wine,* and *Mardi Gras.* None of these was ever heard on the station.

KING announced itself as 'London's most wanted and listened-to radio station', which was wishful thinking taken to extremes. When, only six months later, the station closed its audience was generously estimated at 20,000, mostly clustered around the Kent and Essex coasts. KING attempted to continue the middle-of-the-road format favoured by the GBLN project in 1962 and concentrated on established quality artists and light orchestral music. It also tried, unsuccessfully, to engender a new approach to presentation, moving away from the stilted Light Programme pastiche of Radio Invicta towards what could best be described as a kind of populist lyricism. The emphasis on quality alluded to in the station's name, was complemented by syrupy call signs such as 'your monarch of music for the metropolis', and 'the most melodic delicatessen on the medium wave'. Folksiness was emphasized in slogans like 'whether driving in the car or drying those dishes KING Radio fulfils all your wishes'. Despite this overwhelming sentimentality the approach was tempered by a more homely and intimate style than that being practised on the BBC Light Programme, where scripts and forced jollity were still very much the norm. Although admittedly never very successful KING did begin to pave the way for the broadcasting style that Radio 390 was later to bring to fruition on the same fort. Treading a very thin line between twee and pithy, announcers on KING used to read out short poetic couplets between tunes. These ranged from birthday card verse and Patience Strong-inspired homilies to Shakespearian sonnets.

With its 'wonderful words: wonderful artists', KING gave an early demonstration of a growing listenership who didn't just want to be fed a staple diet of pop. Despite its tiny audience there were also signs that the record companies, covertly or otherwise, were going to take a keen interest in this new medium of promotion. In the early days of Radio Invicta all written inquiries to the station had been answered by the A & R Exploitations Department of Polydor Records. Polydor artists such as Bert Kampfert were plugged incessantly on KING, and 'that was a Polydor hi-fi presentation' became as familiar as the fireside chat and chocolate box verse. Earlier it had been widely reported in the press that the Bachelors pop group was set to take over Radio Invicta. Nothing came of this, although Bachelors records and tours were plugged extensively. Stories of this kind clearly illustrated the music industry's growing awareness of the promotional potential held by even the smallest of the pirates.

All the lonely people (Radio 390)

September 1965–July 1967

> What I was concerned with was that I felt that adults were sick of hearing so called DJs waffle on – not so much about the records they played, because they probably did know something about those – but I didn't think the grown-up audience wanted little lads' views on abortion, sex, marriage, and so on. I didn't want little boys talking about things they had no experience of.
>
> (Ted Allbeury)[4]

Radio 390 was the antithesis of everything the other pirates stood for. It was labelled as a sweet music station (although such a narrow definition does not do the station justice) and managed to build a large and loyal audience by playing hardly any pop music. Its success was built on the fact that it catered for a substantially under-represented section of the population.

> 390 wasn't based on any particular radio programme. I suppose if anything it was based on a rather negative thing. It was based on not being Caroline or London. I did feel at the time that non-pop listeners were being very badly served, so it was really designed to be a radio station that I would want to listen to. I recognized that a lot of other people would be of a same mind but I didn't realize quite how many it would be.
>
> (Ted Allbeury)[5]

The newspapers described Radio 390 as 'dignified', 'respectable', 'sober', and 'unashamedly square'. Some critics said it sounded like the Light Programme of the mid-1950s, simultaneously pointing out that this was a compliment and that the Light had never adequately served an audience of this kind. The quality press welcomed Radio 390 with open arms; the *Sunday Times* even sponsored a series of 26 one-hour jazz programmes on the station, presented by its jazz critic Derek Jewel. To those journalists who were disdainful towards what they saw as the candy floss world of commercial radio the soothing sound of 390 was a welcome reprieve. John Woodforde of the *Sunday Telegraph* was a firm opponent of the BBC's attempts to get chummy and informal, and his regular weekly column represented the voice of the archetypal 'Disgusted of Tunbridge Wells' whenever the Corporation announced a new programming initiative. He had been particularly acerbic in January 1965 when the Light Programme revealed that its new early morning programme, *Breakfast Special*, was going to be 'presented' by 'hosts' rather than the 'announcers' of old. With the advent of the pirates the Light Programme had been taking tentative steps towards gaining some sort of pop audience, but it was perceived by some to be doing this at the expense of the core of its listenership. Its attempts to be all things to all people were anathema to those who resisted change of any kind. 'While the BBC struggles to be like Caroline and London, Radio 390 reproduces with ease something of the BBC's former pleasant dignity' (John Woodforde).[6]

But Radio 390 was more than a surrogate Light Programme and the term 'sweet music' which was used to describe its programming policy (as if everything adults listen to which isn't pop is somehow 'sweet music') does little to describe its breadth and variety. Although the station had undeniable nostalgic leanings, with a substantial proportion of music from the 1940s and the prewar era, it also included swing and Dixieland jazz, military bands, pipe organ music, and more contemporary forms of light entertainment. There was plainly more to the station than the popular stereotype of marching, waltzing, and Mantovani would suggest. Somewhat incongruously 390 even featured a specialist rhythm and blues programme, chiefly because the station had inherited black music afficionado Mike Raven from the former Radio Invicta –KING Radio concern. The programme was disliked by 390's shareholders but highly praised by everyone else (including the BBC and Radio Luxembourg who both later hired Raven). In 1966, shortly after leaving 390 Raven wrote a sensationalist account of the Red Sands fort's previous occupants for the *News of the World*. Although acknowledging these less than savoury origins Radio 390 cultivated an image of respectability and integrity.

> There were some people concerned with pirate radio who had a natural instinct for working outside of the law, and I wasn't one of them. I was determined right from the start that we would pay everything that was to be paid, and meet all the requirements of the law. I was always prepared to do something that was unauthorized, but I was not prepared to do something that was illegal. So everything was paid. We paid PRS on the dot every month. We paid income tax. We were a properly run legal company in every way.
>
> (Ted Allbeury)[7]

Radio 390 also revealed a far wider understanding of the possibilities of commercial radio than any of the pop-oriented

140

pirates by running a twice daily half-hour magazine programme called *Voice of Business*. The series ran from July 1966 until 390 closed down and was aimed at specialized industries. Mondays featured civil engineering, building, and the construction industry; Tuesdays featured the manufacturing industry; Wednesdays, advertising and marketing; Thursdays, retailing, grocers, chemists, and general stores; and Fridays, agriculture. The programme was predominantly concerned with promotion rather than analysis and arose in response to those in the business community who felt that many aspects of commerce were not adequately covered by the BBC. The programme's brief included sales stories, research campaigns, prices, distribution, servicing, and even *vox pop* on customer reaction. It was a move which anticipated many of the functions later allocated to independent local radio.

Programme presentation on 390 complemented the station's music policy. Living up to its square image 390 deliberately employed announcers, not disc jockeys, who were expected to be articulate but succinct in their announcements. Station staff were discouraged from developing the merest hint of personality, let alone the kind of rampant egos being displayed on other stations. This was in deference to a programming ethos which recognized that the music was more important than they were and that the audience was more important than both. The formality was a little over-emphasized at times, and some of 390's less than loyal employees often took poetic licence and indulged in bouts of irreverent self-parody. Nevertheless the station was held in high esteem by its competitors. Radio 390 developed its own recruitment hierarchy, independent of those who only wanted jobs on London and Caroline, and frequently attracted broadcasters from the other 'second division' stations. Ted Allbeury intended to start a northern service from the *Cheetah II*, the vessel which Radio Caroline South had leased when the *Mi Amigo* ran aground in January 1966. Indeed, plans for this move were so well advanced that Radio 390 had publicity material and rate cards distributed which carried full information on the proposed Radio 390 North. The threat of legislation and boardroom squabbles ultimately halted the venture.

Allbeury had originally intended to call his station 'Eve, the

Women's Magazine of the Air', but suspecting that newspapers might be reluctant to publicize a potential competitor, and that even if they did listeners still wouldn't be aware of the station's wavelength, he decided on Radio 390. But the station retained its magazine format and was aimed predominantly at the female audience, making few concessions to a male listenership in its daytime schedules. Programmes had quaint titles such as *Melody Fair*, *Tea-Time Tunes*, and *Keyboard Cavalcade*, and in the finest tradition of the popular press the station even had horoscopes made up, in time-honoured fashion, by the staff. Radio 390 also ran a daily ten-minute programme for the under-fives called *Playtime*, and a five-minute radio cartoon called *Moonmice*, which started when the BBC's *Listen with Mother* finished at 2.00 p.m. each day. The station even had its own radio soap opera, *Dr Paul*, which audaciously, and somewhat optimistically, competed directly in the schedules with the Light Programme's long-running *Mrs Dale's Diary*. *Dr Paul* was imported from Australian commercial radio where it had been running for 13 years, and its downmarket leanings contrasted sharply with the upper-middle-class world of Mrs Dale. *Dr Paul* was more in the melodramatic mode of ITV's long running *Emergency Ward Ten* than the folksy BBC alternative *Dr Finlay's Casebook*. Television and radio shared an obsession with serials set in hospitals in the 1960s and 390's soap was very much a part of this tradition. Best exemplified by the American import *Dr Kildare* the genre served chiefly as a projection for stereotypical female romantic fantasies, a function which 390 itself fulfilled, albeit in a more sedate fashion. A sign allegedly used to hang in the Red Sands fort studio which read 'If you've wondered who you are talking to you're talking to your mother.'

We aimed specifically at middle-aged, middle-class house mums, who are, or were then, the loneliest people in the world – so lonely that this voice coming from the speaker meant something to them ... It meant something to them I suppose because it wasn't the BBC, which at that time was still very much under the wing of John Reith and was operated by university-educated home counties voices.

(John Ridley)[8]

The station's style, with polite and unobtrusive male announcers, was built upon a recognition of this dependency. Radio 390 was meant to be perceived as a friend alleviating loneliness. Its captive audience consisted of the house-bound elderly and the stereotypical housewives tied to the kitchen sink, except for the occasional visit to the shops. Allbeury described his station as 'a surrogate husband', providing 'companionship on tap', and found, when he started his own Sunday evening programme *Red Sands Rendezvous,* that he had tapped into a great well of social inadequacy and frustration.

Concerned chiefly with providing refuge and relaxation, 390 may not have suggested any answers other than continued dependency. Ironically, notwithstanding the quality press's support, 390 offered radio as a palliative as much as any other pirate, but in the general clamour to make pirate radio synonymous with pop music radio the questions raised by 390's existence were written out of the broadcasting agenda. Its style of presentation, the audience it catered for, indeed its entire œuvre, were not adequately addressed during the 1960s. Unlike listeners to the other offshore stations, who at least found a substitute of sorts in Radio One, the listeners to 390 were not properly recompensed by Radio Two. This was not just a demographic issue. As the pirates discovered, there was a certain amount of institutional prestige to be gained from running charity appeals, but apart from the revenue from commercials for headache remedies, soothing bedtime drinks, and pension schemes there wasn't a lot of demographic mileage in social insecurity, or in campaigning to eradicate its forms and causes. Teenage angst has always been more marketable. Middle-aged loneliness, and the dependency of the elderly are not such glamorous commodities.

'The boss jocks' (Radio England)

3 May 1966–11 November 1966

Although Don Peirson and the splinter shareholders Tom Danaher and Bill Vick ceased to play a significant role in the Radio London project during the planning stage, they remained convinced that they could establish an uncompromising radio station off the British coast which would transmit the brash authentic sound of American commercial radio. In contrast to Radio London, which offered British listeners a considerably watered-down interpretation of Top 40 radio, Danaher and Peirson intended to import the American approach wholesale. (Peirson had been the chief instigator of the idea that Radio London should relay the unadulterated output of KLIF Dallas for 12 hours a day.)

When the latest addition to the offshore armada finally arrived off the Essex coast in April 1966 its broadcasting vessel, the *Laissez-Faire* contained two radio stations. Radio England was to compete with Caroline and London in the pop market, while Britain Radio intended to offer listeners quality easy-listening music in a style very different from that of its only potential competitor, Radio 390. These were the promises; the reality was somewhat different.

American pop radio in 1966 was undergoing significant changes. When the Federal Communications Commission outlawed the practice of stations simulcasting the same programmes on both their AM and FM facilities it made conditions favourable for a hitherto unseen degree of experimentation. The first major subcultural force to emerge was 'underground' radio, which had an immediate effect on the pace and tempo of programming – it slowed down. The frenzy previously associated with American pop radio became confined to the Top 40 stations on AM and even here it became more subdued. In 1965 the ratings war between the top New York stations WABC, with its 'all Americans', WMCA, with its 'good guys', and WNBC and WINS, had reached its peak. Promotion and competition were at an intensity never experienced before in American radio. At one point WABC reduced its play-list from 70 records to 14 while playing its own promo jingles 48 times an hour.[9] Some American stations got their entire play-lists down to between 8 and 10 records which were on constant rotation. Gradually during 1966 the fervour began to wear off and pop programming slipped back into relative sanity. Within two years of the FCC ruling both WINS and WMCA had become all-news stations. For those chasing the buck it was obvious that the buck had moved on, away from the teenage audience towards more lucrative demographic options. Precisely at the moment when Radio England was trying to sell the American style to Britain that style began to change.

The station's management company, Peir Vick Ltd, consisted of Managing Director Bill Vick, project co-ordinator and Britain Radio General Manager Jack Curtis, and project overseer Don Peirson. Early in 1966 these three took up permanent residence at the London Hilton Hotel and set about recruiting British disc jockeys to complement the full quota of American staff already on the ship waiting to broadcast. The bulk of the American DJs had been recruited from a nucleus of Top 40 stations in Moultrie, Georgia. The programme director Ron O'Quinn, and the DJs Larry Dean, Jerry Smithwick, and Rick Randell, despite being in their early twenties already had six or seven years of experience working in American radio. In retrospect many of the English DJs who were subsequently hired felt that the Americans had been sold a dream package by the station's management: all they had to do was turn up and the British listeners would be hooked on their brash style. This suspicion was borne out by the way Radio England went about recruiting British staff; several were hired on the strength of having 'cute' English accents, the station managers failing to realize that such a commodity was not exactly in short supply in Britain.

The British beat invasion of the USA during 1964–5 presented a similar notion of stereotypical quaintness to American audiences. The phenomenal success of groups such as Freddie and the Dreamers, the Dave Clark Five, and Herman's Hermits, was at the time indistinguishable from the hysteria surrounding the Beatles. Freddie and the Dreamers gave their name to a dance craze, the Dave Clark Five had a 'cute' drummer (and for a while outsold the Beatles), Herman's Hermits featured a repertoire of novelty vaudeville songs such as 'Mrs Brown, you've got a lovely daughter' and 'I'm 'Enery the Eighth I am'. The American pop audience indiscriminately consumed this patchwork of English imagery, while disc jockeys who had never stepped over the county line took to calling themselves James Bond and claiming that Ringo (most Americans' favourite Beatle) was their cousin. By 1966 the boom was over but it was this outmoded notion of Englishness that Peir Vick

Ltd imported regardless. They even brought with them a set of jingles eulogizing the Batman craze, the television series having arrived on British television (to a generally lukewarm response) in March 1966.

They also imported the Moultrie, Georgia school of Top 40 broadcasting, which at the time of DJ recruitment was still very New York influenced, very 'up', and very frenetic, a blurring montage of motor skills and corporate ego. A feature of Top 40 radio's promotional hysteria at this time was the degree of irreverence DJs brought to their job. Big Dan Ingram at WABC and Larry Lujack at KHJ Los Angeles, among others, made it their trade mark to send up both sponsors and records. It was this style that Radio England attempted to approximate.

As well as being the most publicized arrival on the offshore scene since pirate broadcasting had begun, and allegedly the most heavily funded, Radio England also attempted to poach Radio London's staff with offers of massive salaries. Caroline South also had good reason to fear fresh competition as it had only just recommenced regular broadcasts after running aground. Much of that initial fear was dispelled by an incident which illustrated both the ruthless cut and thrust of many pirate operations and the incompetence of the Peir Vick organization in failing to be prepared for it.

Whereas Radio London had merely superimposed their own station IDs on existing KLIF ones, Radio England and Britain Radio brought with them custom-made station jingles. When the two stations began their test transmissions on 3 May 1966 the non-stop music was interspersed with a brand-new high quality station identification package from PAMS of Dallas, previously unheard in Britain. The jingles were distinctive, they were expensive, and within 24 hours of their first airing they had been pirated by Radios Caroline and London, who immediately re-broadcast them with 'Swinging Radio England' edited out and their own station identity dubbed in. While the American DJs spent initial test transmissions hesitantly getting to grips with the finer points of marine broadcasting, using an unfamiliar and crudely wired operating panel, they were inadvertently leaving silent gaps between music and jingles. Normal practice was to talk over station identifications so that unscrupulous rivals couldn't poach them. Radio London was much criticized for doing this when it exclusively previewed the Beatles' 'Sgt Pepper' LP in April 1967, even though it was standard practice in the highly competitive American radio market. The DJ staff on Caroline South tuned in to the first test transmissions from their competitor expecting to hear a brash, slick, and confident station. Instead they heard tentative and faltering announcements complete with enough 'dead air' to make simple and rapid editing a formality. The immediate effect of the jingle poaching was that the would-be innovator sounded merely derivative. Radio England was even accused of stealing Caroline's jingles!

Despite this blunder Radio England did introduce listeners to many of the gimmicks and techniques familiar to American audiences. Radio England didn't have DJs, it had 'boss jocks' (which despite the station's general leaning towards a New York style was actually west coast terminology borrowed from KHJ Los Angeles). Echo and reverberation effects took the station into the realms of the avant garde, for these were not just used to enhance announcements but were used selectively on records too. The gimmickry transformed news bulletins into pure theatre. Radio England didn't just 'report', it presented 'space news hotline' or 'bannerline'. The state of the art technology was utilized at every available opportunity, and it soon became clear that despite the stolen jingles débâcle Radio England had brought with it a sophisticated array of equipment, including the first automation units ever used on British radio. These were specifically designed for extended non-stop music programmes. Despite being very quick to dismiss the threat of Radio England, every offshore station was plagiarizing its terminology and over-using the gimmickry of voice echo within months. By the end of the year every pirate worthy of the name had copied for itself a set of the original stolen PAMS jingles.

Radio England also instigated another programming feature already familiar to American listeners, the playing of non-stop 'oldies' at weekends. This was something that American Top 40 radio was beginning to phase out by 1966, but Radio England's regular weekend 'great gathering of golden goodies' gave high profile to hits from the past. For British listeners it was the first time that the pop music heritage had been packaged in this way. Radio England also programmed current US chart hits which hadn't been successful, or sometimes even released, in Britain. To make the New York connection explicit the top DJ Gary Stevens was hired from WMCA to present a daily show. His programmes were taped in New York and made few concessions to an English audience. Unlike the previous WMCA 'good guy' heard on offshore radio, Jack Spector on Radio Caroline, who to some extent tailored his reference points to suit his new audience, Stevens relayed his brash and abrasive New York style without compromise or change of pace. WMCA had always featured a high proportion of rhythm and blues and Radio England constantly scooped its rivals by being the first station to play new Detroit soul product. Radio London prided itself on being weeks ahead of the pack with its prediction chart, but Radio England's own play-list was so far ahead of the *Fab 40*, that from a strictly marketing point of view it made no programming sense whatsoever.

A kind of programming schizophrenia was achieved on Radio England by putting all the 'cute' English voices on at night and the brash American ones during the day. The thinking had been to train the inexperienced British announcers in the American house style, even though it had never been satisfactorily decided what that house style was. The results were embarrassingly derivative. Young DJs from Birmingham, England, such as Johnnie Walker and Roger Day, had to do their radio apprenticeship while masquerading with accents nearer to Birmingham, Alabama, without being able to develop their own personalities. In fact neither Day nor Walker were known by those names until they joined Radio England; the extent to which Peirson *et al.* would go to mould their DJs in the American image was shown by the fact that both new recruits were given their on-air identities because there was already a convenient jingle package with the names Johnnie Walker and Roger Day on. This was common practice in the USA where there was a proliferation of 'Shadows', 'Moondogs', and 'Johnny Darks' in every state. When one moved on another was simply brought in to replace him. The individual was expendable. The brand name was indispensable.

It was during the summer of 1966 that the storm broke over John Lennon's 'more popular than Jesus Christ' comments. The

Beatles were touring in the USA, playing what were to be their last ever live dates, when fundamentalist and extremist groups in the South began to pick up Lennon's remarks, made in an interview with Maureen Cleave for the London *Evening Standard*. The article entitled 'How does a Beatle live? John Lennon lives like this',[10] was a thoughtful piece capturing the star in an introspective mood during his post-Beatlemania ennui. Lennon's remarks, albeit casually conveyed, were carefully considered, but the Ku Klux Klan and other racist groups seized on the issue and exploited it to further their own cause. Beatles records and associated merchandise were burned in public demonstrations and the Beatles received anonymous death threats during the tour. Radio England, as well as having the DJ Jerry Smithwick covering the tour, also ran a 'Beatles booster' campaign highlighting the bigoted nature of the protests and inviting listeners to write in and pledge their support by becoming a 'Radio England Beatles buddy'. A shrewder station would have made a profit out of such sentiments. All Radio England offered was its well-intentioned moral support, with the playing of non-stop Beatles music during its oldies weekends. Gary Stevens was characteristically outspoken on his syndicated show, outlining for the British audience the racial divide which existed in the southern states and lambasting the publicity-minded motives of the Bible-belt stations which had first latched on to the story. On a land-based station with the immediacy of telephone support and instant listener feedback, a campaign like this might have had some effect. On the North Sea it didn't have the same impact but it did graphically illustrate the flexible agenda-setting which was possible on the pirates and the degree to which a station like Radio England could respond to issues with much more fluidity than the BBC's cumbersome structure would allow at that time.

Radio England was never able to simulate the flow of American Top 40 radio simply because it didn't possess the necessary components to ensure that flow. Advertisements failed to materialize in sufficient quantities to satisfy the station's backers. There was some sponsorship initially but few accounts were renewed. Mutual animosity existed between the English and American staff; the Americans were contemptuous of what they perceived as the English DJs' rank amateurism, and the

English were intimidated by ego battles and personality rivalry on a scale they had never witnessed before. The rivalry was further fuelled by Radio England's spectacularly unsuccessful pop package tour featuring the Small Faces, Dave Berry, and Neil Christian. Despite all of these being Top Ten acts at the time the tour was badly promoted and often played to half-empty houses. The American DJs chosen to compère the tour were dismissed half way through the itinerary when it became plain that they had no rapport with the English audiences. Shortly after this the 'Moultrie Four' resigned and returned to the USA.

The station's incessant New York terminology undoubtedly came as a culture shock to large sectors of the British audience, but the station's failure ultimately had more to do with managerial inexperience than the fact that it called its DJs boss jocks. Undoubtedly some intriguing ambiguities did arise from the different usage the two countries have for phrases like 'fanny' or 'bang up', and some effort was eventually made by Radio England's management to 'Anglicize' the station. This merely resulted in the appointment of a few less abrasive Americans with the kind of mid-Atlantic accent familiar on the other stations, plus a second generation of mild-mannered English disc jockeys who still had to keep up the practice of having names like 'Boss Cat Bruce Wayne' and 'Johnny Dark' even if their accents were more reminiscent of Southend, Essex than South Side, Chicago.

In early October 1966 it was announced that Radio England was to close and that the broadcasting facility was to be leased to a Dutch operation, Radio Dolfijn. As with Radio Caroline's brief period of 'method' spontaneity (which coincided almost exactly with Radio England's life span) the experiment had not been allowed fully to develop. Radio England had been broadcasting a full programming schedule for little more than four months. In the only opinion poll carried out during that time, by NOP, Radio England's July audience was estimated as 2,274,000. Even allowing for a large margin of error these figures still compare favourably with those of Radio London, which in a far less competitive market claimed a 2 million listenership during its first three months of broadcasting. But Radio England's management had banked on quick success.

The station was extremely popular among teenagers, – arguably it was the only pirate apart from Radio Sutch which catered solely for them – but as usual it was the commercial sponsors (or lack of them) who had the last word. Radio England closed on 11 November 1966. Its final programme was a shambles. Unlike several of the later pirate close-downs which were often done with dignity, and in some cases provided an excellent forum for discussion about what the pirates had achieved, Radio England's indulgent finale was merely filled with the voices of those who couldn't wait to cash their latest pay-cheques before they bounced.

'Hallmark of quality' (Britain Radio)

3 May 1966–22 February 1967 (as Britain Radio)

February 1967–6 August 1967 (as Radio 355)

While Radio England was getting all the media attention Britain Radio had been given a much lower profile, and had been much less successful with listeners. In the NOP poll of July 1966 its audience was estimated at 718,000 compared with Radio 390's 2,633,000, but it had at least attracted a modicum of advertising. In fact its first campaign had seen the unprecedented launch of a product on offshore radio. Sunbake Bakeware took out a series of 30-second spots which were broadcast in English, French, Dutch, and German, in what was a tentative step towards pan-European advertising on the station. The fact that no further European advertising was forthcoming should have given early warning to those stations who believed they could defy British anti-pirate legislation with such tactics.

Unlike Radio 390's 15- and 30-minute programmes Britain Radio favoured standard 'strips' of three or four hours. Its quality easy listening approach tried to bridge the demographic gap between the softer end of pop and the sharper end of middle-of-the road music, using a primitive format clock which simply rotated four categories; male singer, female singer, instrumental, group. Britain Radio's jingle package, 'The Smart Set', which announced the easy listening station as the 'hallmark of quality' was re-used, legitimately, by BBC Radio Two in the early 1970s. Britain Radio outlasted its more flamboyant twin station by four months, and continued sharing broadcasting facilities with the unsuccessful Radio Dolfijn until March 1967, when Peir Vick Ltd finally went into liquidation.

My perception of things was that Jack Curtis had no notion of the country he was broadcasting to. He didn't have a clue about British radio ... I used to see the Radio England jocks hanging around the Curzon Street office in their striped blazers, eating ice cream and burgers and looking very American and I remember thinking 'Jesus, these guys are from another planet. They don't know where they've landed.' The same attitude prevailed at both stations. They were calamitous failures because the people appointed to run the programming had no notion of who they were broadcasting to. They presumably thought that they were broadcasting to Philadelphia, or downtown Houston. They certain were not broadcasting to London and the suburbs.

(Alan West)[11]

Considerable resentment was expressed by several of those like Alan West and Ed Moreno who joined towards the end. Unlike the original English DJs they had some previous broadcasting experience and were therefore not automatically prepared to defer to the Americans' better judgement.

There are men in radio at the helm (so to speak) who had never seen the inside of a studio a year ago and these people set the pattern of programming. How many times have I laughed inwardly as I have had to literally explain a technique or simple procedure to an alleged programme controller.

(Ed Moreno)[12]

Disenchantment came to a head just before Peir Vick Ltd went into liquidation when Ted Allbeury was brought in from Radio 390 to boost the listenership of what had previously been his chief rival. Allbeury had been ousted from 390 after a boardroom coup, when, seeing the legislative writing on the wall, he had recommended moving the 390 operation from a fort to a ship. When the 390 board was not prepared to entertain this Allbeury accepted a position with the American organization as Managing Director, and set about re-creating the 390 format on Britain Radio. The immediate response of the General Manager, Jack Curtis, was to resign. Allbeury had previously referred to the Britain Radio sound as 'a lucky dip'. Curtis in turn called 390 'Stone Age radio' and defined Allbeury's programming philosophy as 'a series of segmented dirges stitched together by sterile announcements'. As if the point needed further elaboration Curtis added, 'I believe we hold each other's formats in equal contempt.'[13]

Allbeury's first task as head of Britain Radio was to go to Holland to supervise repairs to the *Laissez-Faire*, which had been severely damaged during a North Sea gale. During this time changes were made to programming policy and there was a complete overhaul of the whole operation. The affairs of the two stations were taken over by Carstead Advertising Ltd, managed by Allbeury and directed by John Withers, brother of Tony Withers (better known as former Radio London senior disc jockey Tony Windsor). Windsor, recently retired from London for 'health reasons' was brought in to be programme director of the English service. Britain Radio returned as Radio 355. Radio Dolfijn, having been unsuccessful in capturing the long-established Radio Veronica's audience, returned as Radio 227 and reintroduced an exact Dutch replica of the former Radio England format. Most of the remaining American staff were dismissed.

The intended transformation of 355's slick 'hallmark of quality' style into 390's cosy fireside chat and carpet slippers image didn't work. Despite taking many of his broadcasting staff with him after the 390 boardroom coup Allbeury found that few managed to make the transition from a relatively inhabitable and stable fort structure to a rusty, under-funded, and ill-equipped ship. There was also a great deal of professional animosity between the staff of the two former rivals, particularly over the issue of specialist programming. David Allen had established a very successful country music show on 390 but he was rapidly ejected from 355's own *Country Style*. Similar fates awaited those former 390 announcers who hosted specialist rhythm and blues and light orchestral shows. Finally, in a harsh scheduling ultimatum, instigated by Tony Windsor, those deemed to be incapable of holding down three- or four-hour shows were dismissed. Most of the ex-390 announcers immediately returned to their old station. So after a brief experimentation with the 390 'series of segmented dirges' style, berated by Jack Curtis, 355 reverted back to the old Britain Radio format until its close-down.

Little market research was done by any of the offshore stations during the last few months of the pirate era. Unsubstantiated figures suggested that Radio 355 had a 2.25 million listenership at the time of the station's demise. Both 355 and 227 closed a few days before anti-pirate legislation came into force. The ships' contracts and insurance had come up for renewal and it was not thought worth the necessary administrative expense to continue broadcasting for just one more week.

Cash and carry (Radio 270)

July 1966–14 August 1967

> Radio 270 was the most pragmatic of all the stations because it was serving an area which wasn't radio conscious in any sense of the word. It was run 100 per cent by people who had no radio experience whatsoever.
>
> (Alan West)[14]

The Managing Director of Radio 270 was Wilf Proudfoot. He had served as an RAF sergeant in India from 1941 to 1946, and as a town councillor for Scarborough between 1950 and 1958. He became Conservative Member of Parliament for Cleveland in the 1959 election, a seat which he lost in 1964. A confirmed free-marketeer, Proudfoot first served office as a Parliamentary Private Secretary to the minister of state at the Board of Trade. Between April and July 1962 he served as a Parliamentary Private Secretary to the Minister of Housing and Local Government. During his time as an MP and as a councillor he was a firm advocate of rent differentials, opposing rent freezes and tenants' rights. After failing to get re-elected after one term of office he opened a chain of grocery stores and newsagents in the Scarborough area. These were plugged extensively on his radio station alongside promotions for forthcoming local charity functions, and annual dinner and dances. There were frequent advertisements for hunt balls, banquets given by the mayor and mayoress of Beverley, and dinners in aid of the local Round Table.

Radio 270 carried localized advertising which rarely extended outside the Yorkshire area, and the station's syndicate of shareholders, Ellambar Investments Ltd, was made up almost entirely of local businessmen. The chairman of Ellambar was Leonard Dale, Managing Director of the Dale Group of Companies, manufacturers of electrical goods. The Dale group fitted out the Radio 270 ship with its own Dale marine generators, and like Proudfoot, Dale used Radio 270 as a vehicle for promoting his own products. Dale Electrics advertising was largely aimed at industrial manufacturers and contractors rather than the general public. Proudfoot also targeted wholesalers and contract purchasers; his advertising emphasized bulk buying and catering-size measures of instant food and were aimed at industry as much as the housewife.

The Managing Director of Ellambar was Don Robinson, a wrestling promoter, who also had a financial interest in Flamingo Park Zoo, Morecombe Marine Land, and various other leisure and tourism concerns. Radio 270 was registered in Panama as 'Progresiva Compania Commercial SA', and the station's broadcasting vessel was registered in Honduras. The British agent for PCC was the Australian Noel Millar, who was also 270's first programme director. PCC's Company Director was Jack Lamont, an American film producer.

Technically Radio 270 was poorly maintained. Faulty generators, crudely edited jingles and makeshift cartridge machines were a constant impediment to smooth programming. An erratic power supply caused records and tapes to speed up and slow down, and the station was frequently off the air for 'essential maintenance'. Apparently lacking a sense of irony, Radio 270 had initially intended to go on air on 1 April 1966, but constant technical problems kept the station silent until June. Explaining the delay to readers of *Ad Weekly* on 29 April Leonard

Dale stated 'We are taking the extra time to recheck and double check every aspect of the station. Wherever a failure seems even a remote possibility we are planning additional precautions.' Once on air the station continued to break down regularly.

On the programming side Radio 270's original DJ team was dominated by the usual assortment of young Australians, who, on the strength of a few months' radio experience back home, had rapidly risen through the unskilled ranks of British pirate radio to positions of prominence. In its programming style Radio 270 was the classic case of the small localized station trying to sound like the national networked one. This confusion over regional identity brought with it inevitable problems:

> There was a tendency among us all in those days to try and sound like Big Dan Ingram, and WABC, WMCA, or WINS New York. There were a lot of phoney accents. You had New York Queens blended in with broadest Leeds. It sounded weird and it showed on 270 more than anywhere else because of this funny dichotomy of backgrounds.
>
> (Alan West)[15]

A Yorkshireman exhorting his audience to buy tinned potatoes in a pseudo-American accent was clearly no more absurd than someone from Essex adopting the same strategy, but it was arguably not the best way to build a sense of intimacy or local identity. During 1967 Radio 270 was joined by several of the DJs who had left the now outlawed fort-based stations, and began to adopt a more ethnocentric approach, with a firmer idea of where it was broadcasting to. This was the nearest it came to offering any kind of localized service, but while the station undoubtedly did establish an audience in a catchment area largely unserved by the other pirates, what its listeners actually heard bore little resemblance to what was originally promised.

> 270, when it was launched, had the same kind of trumpeting that you now get with ILR stations, in that the actual programming bears little relationship to what is laid out in the original application document. 270 did that, they launched

off with a whole string of absurd ideas. They were going to be like 390 but playing Top 40 music instead of Mantovani. We were going to have a vicar on Sundays with a church service. And I don't recall them ever doing any of it.

(Alan West)[16]

Like all the pirates, 270 did start to carry charity appeals in order to convey community involvement. The station also allowed direct political campaigning on air. Radio 270's opening coincided with the first parliamentary murmurings of anti-pirate legislation; pro-commercial radio sentiments, unmistakably Conservative in tone, were broadcast right from the beginning.

Progress relies on competition. Television proved this. With the introduction of ITV in 1955 television rapidly improved. Britain is the only democratic country in the world tolerating a monopoly in broadcasting. There is no reason why the BBC and independent commercial radio stations cannot work side by side to provide a service common to other countries in the free world.[17]

The promotion ended on a note of pluralism and listeners were invited to write to their MP. As with all later broadcasts the key notions fuelling the debate were crude stereotypes of 'democracy' and 'free world'. The statement was also inaccurate: in Europe alone a whole range of countries had broadcasting monopolies, France, Sweden, and Luxembourg among them. But such inaccuracies set the tone for the coming campaign. As with other pirates, 270's broadcasts reached a peak in frequency during the period leading to the passing of the Marine Offences Bill.

Regionalist rhetoric (Radio Scotland)

31 December 1965–14 August 1967

Another pirate attempting to define local identity in terms of local product promotion was Radio Scotland. BBC Scotland's regional coverage amounted at this time to a few hours' 'opt-out' a day from the London bias of Home Service transmissions, and there was undoubtedly a genuine case for media devolution in the form of localized broadcasting. Unfortunately Radio Scotland was not a very convincing role model. The company which owned the station, City and County Commercial Radio (Scotland) Ltd, was formed in October 1964. It originally claimed that it was going to apply for local radio franchises for Glasgow, Edinburgh, Aberdeen, and Dundee. The fact that the company was registered in the Bahamas hardly supported its claims to be representing local interests. By the summer of 1965 the shareholders were looking for a ship.

The station manager was Tommy V. Shields, an ex-D. C. Thomson employee with a background in public relations; he became owner of Radio Scotland's advertising operation, TVS Publicity. Managing Director of TVS was Shields's son Tommy Shields Jnr. Deputy Managing Director was Alex Brown, formerly Advertising Manager of the Thompson publication *Golf Monthly*. Managing Director of Radio Scotland itself was James Donald, a theatre manager in Dundee. The original Sales Director for the operation was Maurice Jephson, formerly a salesman with Calor Gas. He left before the station's launch and was replaced by Ian Yates from STV (Scottish Television). The senior sales executive was Antony Meehan who came from Carreras–Rothmans Cigarettes. Other backers were the former Edinburgh Lord Provost and Vice-Chairman of the Scottish Liberal Party, Sir Andrew Murray, and Andrew Lewis Carr and Stanley Jackson, directors of the Equitable Industrial Company (which had interests in greyhound racetracks, gambling casinos and real estate).

Radio Scotland's initial programme policy indicated that the station was to offer a service consisting of 60 per cent pop music and 40 per cent Scottish news plus special minority programming. Soon after coming on air the station began to concentrate almost entirely on the Top 40. The only concessions to local interest were the occasional programme of Scottish dance music and traditional Irish and Scottish ballads. For the rest of the time the station was content to dish up an unimaginative assortment of American evangelists, and music

158

pitched mainly at the pop audience. Management initiatives made it clear that it wasn't just the American evangelists who were preaching righteousness. Radio Scotland banned anti-war protest songs such as Barry McGuire's 'Eve of Destruction', and any records it considered in 'bad taste', for example Napoleon XIV's 'They're coming to take me away, ha-ha'. Since Shields had worked for D. C. Thomson, another strict Presbyterian who presided over a media empire, parallels between his puritanical streak and the BBC's Reithian legacy were not entirely coincidental. Shields used to present his own programme on Radio Scotland, and utilized an archaic broadcasting style which itself harked back to Reith, 'I'd like now to ask that fine balladeer Andy Stewart to sing', Shields would formally announce, as if Andy Stewart was sitting there in the studio right beside him.

Radio Scotland recruited several DJs disenchanted with the changes in programming policy at Radio Caroline. Several prominent victims of the Caroline South purges worked for the station for a while, but left equally disenchanted with their new habitat. Radio Scotland was already in financial disarray when it began broadcasting on 31 December 1965. The station lacked vital technical equipment, and by not allowing itself adequate time for test transmissions played into the Postmaster-General's hands by interfering with essential services. During 1966 there were several changes of location as the station tried to find a suitable position from which to broadcast. As the former lightship had no engines of its own it was towed round the coast of Scotland, accumulating massive running costs, and losing £1,000 a day in advertising revenue in the process. During this period it broadcast from inside territorial waters, once again attracting the attention of the Postmaster-General.

Broadcasting from the rough waters off the Firth of Clyde was clearly never a viable long-term option and it is extremely doubtful that the station would have survived much longer than it did without some major mishap occurring. Radio Scotland did little to redeem itself during this period; it presented a very poor case for a local Scottish service and in doing so jeopardized those who had a more genuine claim to present. All the regionalist rhetoric in the world couldn't disguise the station's barely concealed and poorly executed opportunism.

Basic training (Radio Essex)

October 1965–August 1966 (as Radio Essex)

August 1966–January 1967 (as BBMS)

The spurious identity claimed by Radio Essex was built on little more than the fact that the station carried local advertising. The reason it carried local advertisements was simply that it couldn't attract any national ones, and, as with other pirates, a local audience meant little more than local consumers. Good reception was only possible in south-east Essex and regional flavour was restricted to the postmarks on the request which came in from the station's tiny catchment area. Radio Essex, like several other stations, operated on a shoe-string, using rudimentary studio equipment, and a prewar 1 kw ex-United States Air Force radio beacon, which had to be converted for radio use. Its DJ staff, all of whom were new to broadcasting, had to endure appalling living and working conditions. Ten-week shifts were the norm and on one occasion a skeleton crew of three disc jockeys were completely marooned on the cramped Knock John fort and had to survive on dehydrated peas and coffee powder until a supply boat could reach them. Radio Essex management traded on the good will of disc jockeys eager to gain radio experience, and cynically operated on voluntarist principles. At best the unskilled announcers were paid very poorly, and while legal wranglings were going on to determine ownership of the Thames estuary forts during the last couple of months of the station's life they were not paid at all. One ex-announcer described the station as an outward bound course for budding young disc jockeys.

Despite this Radio Essex programming was impressively varied, catering not only for pop fans but also for enthusiasts of the big band sound, country and western music, and trad jazz. Almost all the station's young inexperienced DJs were recruited locally, and despite some extremely mediocre presentation (Essex was arguably the most amateurish of all the pirates) several had a specialist knowledge of the music they were playing. At first on Radio Essex, as in the early days of Radio Caroline and Radio Atlanta, there was an emphasis on individual programmes rather than streamlined programming. But when the station was renamed BBMS (Britain's Better Music Station) in October 1966 programme schedules were more strictly formatted in order to demarcate between the station's two perceived audiences. Night-time programming between 9 p.m. and 6 a.m. was aimed predominantly at teenage pop fans, while daytime output was given over to an adult easy-listening format, concentrating on an anodyne mixture of light orchestral music and ballads. Radio Essex was one of three pirates to target this neglected audience, the BBMS easy-listening approach leaning more towards the Britain Radio–Radio 355 style of three-hour strips rather than Radio 390's 15- or 30-minute slots.

Night-time programming was segmented into three equal portions called 'Formula 66'. Part one concentrated on the Top 30, part two on soul and rock and roll 'oldies', and part three on light pop music and new releases. This offered the illusion of variety, although in truth all night-time programming was filled with the sound of young inexperienced announcers learning their trade, and tended very much towards the 'that was . . . that is' time and temperature style favoured by the more American-influenced stations.

Programming on Radio Essex was unfortunately a secondary issue. The station which had begun its days by ousting a rival from its transmission site ended it in the rhetorical acrimony of the law courts, with the 'owner' Roy Bate vainly defending his sovereign and territorial rights against the legislative procedures of the British government. After BBMS had made its final broadcast in January 1967 the whole operation was shifted to the adjacent Roughs Towers, and it was widely believed that BBMS would soon start broadcasting again. As the next chapter will show ensuing events had very little to do with providing a 'Better Music Station', British or otherwise.

'Ha-ha, said the Clown.' (Radio City)

September 1964–8 February 1967

The circumstances surrounding the death of Radio City's owner Reg Calvert (dealt with fully in the next chapter) unfortunately overshadow the station's true worth as a broadcasting operation. Radio City was held in high esteem by its fellow professionals if not by the general public. It was truly the broadcasters' radio station, with a reputation for innovation way beyond its ability to transfer plaudits into assets. City claimed an audience of 2.5 million and Reg Calvert boasted that his station was worth £150,000, but financially the station was not a success and had little regional identity. Although aimed ostensibly at London, as its name suggests, reception in the capital was poor. A reasonably good signal was heard in Kent and Essex and extended into much of East Anglia and the Midlands, but it was noticeable that promotions for Reg Calvert's dances in the provincial towns had a far higher profile than anything that might be happening in 'Swinging London'. There was genuinely local advertising but it was usually sporadic and short-lived. The *Basildon Request Show*, a one-hour programme sponsored by traders in Basildon High Street, Essex, was typical of the station's narrow regional scope.

Most revenue was accumulated from the religious programming which Radio City carried, such as A. A. Allen's *Revival Hour*, *The Voice of Prophecy* ('thirty minutes of inspiration'), and *The Wings of Healing*. These were profitable concerns, fully networked on radio stations world-wide, and they accounted for 80 per cent of City's total income. Unfortunately one of the first effects of the boarding party of June 1966 and the shooting of Reg Calvert was that almost all advertising disappeared. The religious organizations pulled out straight away, and for its last few months Radio City had no revenue coming in at all.

When Reg Calvert inherited the Shivering Sands fort from David Sutch in September 1964 he also inherited much of that station's freewheeling anarchic spirit. It no longer possessed quite the shambolic splendour formerly displayed by Sutch but it did retain a certain uncontrived friendliness. Radio City must have been the only pirate where the boss's daughter made programmes: Candy Calvert presented *Candy's Pop Shop* during her school holidays. There was a completely open house policy on recruitment and anyone who wrote in asking for a job was sent out on a week's trial; many lasted precisely that long and there was a constant turnover of casual labour. Reg Calvert's managerial zeal was given free reign at first, but apart from plugging the Fortunes extensively his only notable success in this department occurred when a few well-placed pound notes succeeded where three months of extensive plugging had failed and he managed to hype 'Mirror Mirror' by Pinkerton's Assorted Colours into the lower end of the Top 50 in February 1966.[18]

By 1966 Radio City had assembled a very good broadcasting team consisting of the usual assortment of Australian emigrés, television continuity men, and those who had drifted in from film and theatre. A genuinely cohesive unit emerged which combined Radio London's professionalism and Radio Caroline's energy, and it was easy to see the appeal of this modest second division outfit to the two major pirates, who both made take-over bids. Radio City had the first, and for a long time the only, programme dedicated specifically to the Beatles and Rolling Stones. The daily *5 x 4 show* was a simple populist reaction to the prevailing mood of the time and was constantly voted among the top ten shows on offshore radio. Radio City also featured what was undoubtedly the most innovative programme to emerge from the pirate era. Launched on little more than the premise that Australian presenter Ian McRae could do a reasonably good Harold Wilson impersonation, the weekly comedy show *The Auntie Mabel Hour* soon developed into a genuinely sharp and satirical platform from which its hosts lampooned contemporary issues. Part scripted but mostly ad-libbed by McRae and co-presenter Alan Clarke, *The Auntie Mabel Hour's* contemporaries were BBC Television's *That Was The Week That Was*, and *Private Eye* magazine, but the programme's cultural peers were the *Round the Horne* radio team, with its mixture of overt camp and impenetrable innuendo.

In an age when the concept of 'with-it-ness' was already becoming decidedly frayed round the edges and English pop music was beginning to reflect on its past in the unlikely guise of a 1920s revival (public school boaters and stripey blazers, admiralty uniforms, the New Vaudeville Band, Bonnie and Clyde, the psychedelic music hall of the Who, Small Faces, Kinks, and Sgt Pepper), *The Auntie Mabel Show* was another unashamed throwback. Its reference points and kindred spirits were the anarchy of the Goons, Hellzapoppin, Spike Jones, Lord Buckley, and the Marx Brothers; its theme tune was the Temperance Seven's trad jazz arrangement of 'You are driving me crazy'. When McRae, Clarke *et al.* attacked targets in the pop world the show resembled *Expresso Bongo* minus the morality clause. Nor did pirate radio escape the show's irreverent perspective. In a sketch called *Swinging Radio Worksop* Radio England was satirized mercilessly for its brash approach and hi-tech pretensions. Radio 390 was affectionately sent up for its archaism, although it is fair to say that Radio 390 announcers were not above intentionally doing this themselves.

During its final weeks City was the first pirate to play the Beatles' new single 'Penny Lane'. This was days before Radio London claimed an exclusive and a full week before the Light Programme preceded its airing of the single with the BBC's own claim to exclusivity and the unfortunately devalued introduction 'brought to you by special arrangement'. City's seasoned eccentricity held out to the end with an impromptu, but not altogether serious, ban on Monkees records. This was based on a more than slightly whimsical objection to 'music made by robots and played by cartoon characters'.

Like Radio Caroline, a projection of Ronan O'Rahilly's attitude and Chelsea set initiative, Radio City inhabited a parallel world, far removed from the corporate pretensions of most of the offshore entrepreneurs. It evolved out of David Sutch's particular brand of shrewd eccentricity, was commandeered by a pop group manager who to all intents and purposes wouldn't have recognized a hit record even if it had the formula of the X factor clearly inscribed on its cover, and was staffed by informed and articulate disc jockeys. This unbalanced triumvirate of anarchic gestures, grandiose schemes, and hip programming won the station respect from its peers, while contributing directly to the death of its owner.

Summary

The paucity of management initiative displayed by many of these outfits was largely offset by the enthusiasm of creative and quick-thinking teams of young and relatively inexperienced announcers. Boardroom friction was a commonplace feature of all the pirates, and disc jockeys were frequently at the mercy of decisions made by people who usually knew far less about radio than they did. As a training ground for new entrants to the profession the smaller pirates undoubtedly served a purpose; 'a blueprint for the future', the self-righteous claim made by some of them, was slightly more dubious.

Despite many of the smaller pirates' proprietors being autocratic and dictatorial in their dealings there was an undeniably folksy aspect to their stations' working practices which made 'corner shop' and 'cottage industry' analogies entirely appropriate. Reg Calvert used to offer relief disc jockeys permanent contracts on the strength of a recommendation from his wife Dorothy, the sole criterion being whether or not she liked the announcer's voice. Jean Bates, the wife of station owner Roy Bates, used to have a similar kitchen sink role at Radio Essex. Radio 270 DJs were paid by cheque when they came off the ship, these then had to be cashed at one of Wilf Proudfoot's grocery stores. One ex-Radio Scotland DJ described his station's programming format as 'basically you went to the cupboard and pulled out whatever the previous DJ hadn't already played'. In the midst of Radio England–Britain Radio's hi-tech array of automation units and facilities for bringing in the news from other solar systems its method of cataloguing records consisted of punching the centres out of 7-inch singles, juke-box style, and hanging them on pegs on the wall. True to its traditionalist image, Radio 390 used to close down each night by playing the national anthem.

Some of the smaller stations seemed intent upon proving the Postmaster-General Tony Benn right in his assessment that they were merely quick buck merchants out to make maximum profits with the minimum of outlay. Radios 270, Scotland, and the Radio England–Britain Radio conglomerate were all considerably underfunded, which had an inevitable, often audible, effect upon programming. Radio Scotland had a cramped and poorly converted studio which was entirely unsuitable for broadcasting. Radio 270, having stolen its jingles from Radio England like everyone else, replaced its rival station's identification with badly edited inserts of its own, often to comical effect. Faulty equipment frequently rendered advertisements unintelligible and caused other promotions to stop mid-sentence as they were snarled up by the machinery. Radio 270 never used a tender boat to deliver supplies, as was normal procedure with the other stations; instead it periodically upped anchor and sailed into Bridlington harbour. Such actions went unannounced on air so that the station could continue broadcasting as it entered territorial waters. Even Radio 390, the most respectable of all the pirates, cut corners; in August 1966 one of its employees, Mrs Maureen Seymour, was apprehended on the beach at Whitstable by GPO investigators and charged with using a walkie-talkie as an illegal land-link to the station on the Red Sands fort.

Living conditions on some of the stations were atrocious. As if trying to run a business from the North Sea wasn't inconvenient enough few of the pirates' owners seemed to make any concessions to the discomfort that these circumstances brought about. Living quarters were often cramped and noisy and only minimal attempts were made to convert marine vessels into suitable working environments for radio stations. The reality of Radio England's spartan living quarters contrasted sharply with the station's extravagant publicity campaign prior to going on air, which claimed that the American-funded outfit was going to replace Caroline and London as number one station in the audience ratings. Even a station as well-funded as Radio London had gone on air originally without its studios being adequately soundproofed. On the sea forts announcers were often expected to provide their own sheets and blankets.

There was a ready supply of staff to work on all of these stations. Many were willing to work for no wages in the hope of furthering their radio careers, and on the smaller stations they often did work for nothing. It was partly out of such constant adversity that some semblance of broadcasting atmosphere developed, but it was also a convenient excuse for exploitation for the less scrupulous station owners. Supply tenders sometimes didn't turn up because of bad weather; this was a natural enough occupational hazard, but supply tenders also didn't turn up because no one from the station's management had bothered to pay the tender company. Sometimes this was because the coffers were empty, more often than not such enforced hardship for staff coincided with the latest publicity extravaganza being made by the radio station.

The smaller stations tended to interpret the brief of the major stations rather literally, while their actions showed that they neither understood the scope and sophistication of that brief, or possessed the infrastructure necessary to make it operative. The worst of these small outfits were undoubtedly the ones who sacrificed local flavour in order to try and emulate the large stations. In the main the smaller stations demonstrated what could sometimes be achieved by talented or unscrupulous people in rusty vessels situated in international waters. The North Sea was not the natural habitat for such ventures despite the romantic claims being made by the more skilful exploiters of public sentiment. However, though work-place and legal juridical circumstances were not typical, in all other respects these were entrepreneurial small businesses aspiring to become entrepreneurial big businesses.

CHAPTER 5

The politics of piracy

Dirty water

David Sutch and Reg Calvert had been the first offshore entrepreneurs to squat the old abandoned wartime forts in the
Thames estuary, but from very early on there was keen competition for the use of these facilities. There were few of
the prohibitive costs and technical hindrances which made
ships so expensive to maintain, and therefore the sea forts, by
whatever means they were acquired, were at a premium. In
February 1965 Reg Calvert announced that he was planning
to expand his network by starting a new station on the as yet
unoccupied Knock John fort. As the fledgling Radio Essex
project also had an interest in this site it turned out to be the
cue for several months of aggressive raids and counter-raids
on the fort. The Radio Essex team eventually won the series
of skirmishes and began broadcasting from Knock John in
November 1965. Both the popular and provincial press tended
to treat all this maritime gazumping as a joke. Calvert and Sutch
had always appealed to Fleet Street's desire for a novelty angle
on the pirates, instigating various publicity schemes and stunts
to keep their small station in the public eye, but the battle
for the forts had its more sinister episodes. Writing after the
apparently accidental death by drowning of the Radio Invicta
boss Tom Pepper, and the subsequent takeover by KING Radio,
the former Radio City DJ Rick Michaels revealed:

> An air of mystery surrounds the operation of Radio King.
> The author was invited to join an elaborate plot to seize
> Radio King during the summer of 1965 by a former member
> of Radio Invicta and Radio King, who claimed the operators
> of the station owed them money, and moreover the station

was about to change hands illegally. They planned to use a chartered helicopter to seize the fort. It was also mentioned in passing that Tom Pepper's death may have been something other than an accident.[1]

After a tentative start clearer patterns of ownership and intent began forming on the offshore stations during 1965. Mergers were frequent and expansion inevitable as the battle of site acquisition and profit accumulation grew more competitive. On the Red Sands fort the uneasy alliance that had existed between the former shareholders of Radio Invicta and its successor KING Radio was eventually secured, not by strong arm tactics, but by a fresh cash injection of £150,000 from a new group of backers. In September 1965 KING became Radio 390. That same month negotiations began between Radio Caroline and Radio City to discuss another possible merger. Under the terms of the amalgamation, which became effective from 1 October, the sales teams of the two stations were combined, and while programming would remain independent Caroline was to provide the smaller station with a news service. This service did in fact operate for a brief period towards the end of 1965, but the joint sales company (never Radio Caroline's strong point) was soon in debt. During this period the company was collecting £2,000 a month on Radio City's behalf. By December, when the deal allegedly fell through, the joint company owed Radio City around £7,000–8,000. Documentation exists which shows that the joint sales company actually delayed the implementation of advertising contracts that City had negotiated before the merger. Statements from the Radio City files also conclusively prove that bills for costs accrued by the station during the period September–December 1965 (customs duties, fort maintenance, new broadcasting equipment and machine parts, etc.) were being forwarded to Project Atlanta Ltd, as was all advertising revenue as contractually agreed. Although the agreement was not formally terminated Radio City resumed responsibility for its own finances from 1 January 1966. Claims for numerous debts, outstanding from the period of agreement, continued to be forwarded to Project Atlanta. Solicitors' letters obtained from the Radio City files indicate that many of these debts had not been settled four months later. It is impossible to ascertain from these documents alone whether the Radio Caroline organization was still in some capacity technically responsible for Radio City's affairs after 1 January 1966, or whether Reg Calvert was merely exploiting a few grey areas of small print with a little creative accountancy of his own.

The Caroline–City deal had taken place against a back-drop of accelerating tension and unease, with the Caroline organization experiencing a few boardroom upheavals of its own at this time. In December 1965 Ronan O'Rahilly's Planet Productions acquired the assets of Project Atlanta and Allan Crawford resigned from Radio Caroline's board of directors, With the take-over it was assumed that Caroline had also severed all connection with Project Atlanta's chairman and largest shareholder, Major Oliver Smedley. In fact Company House records show that Smedley still held stock of 60,000 Project Atlanta shares as late as 1972. During the period of the Caroline–City deal Smedley handed over a radio transmitter to the City organization for possible future use on the proposed new service. Ostensibly the whole argument which was to lead to the fatal shooting of Reg Calvert by Oliver Smedley was over this transmitter. In fact the piece of equipment which arrived at the Shivering Sands fort had seen 25 years' service on station KCUL Fort Worth, Texas and was declared obsolete on inspection by the Radio City engineers. Smedley however claimed that the transmitter was worth £10,000 and eventually took drastic steps to retrieve it, leading a commando-style boarding party out to the Shivering Sands fort on the evening of 19 June 1966, and silencing Radio City.

In April 1966 Calvert began negotiations with the Radio London chief Philip Birch, who was proposing to set up a station called United Kingdom Good Music (or UKGM). Under this deal the two stations would have a servicing agreement and a joint sales company. Radio London would manage the City operation and take 55 per cent of advertising revenue, while Calvert retained ownership of his station. The agreement, finalized in May, was set to commence on 1 June, and to be fully operational by 1 July. Representatives from Radio London (the disc jockeys Duncan Johnson and Keith Skues, and office manager Dennis Maitland) visited the Shivering Sands complex for a preliminary site inspection with the aim of installing new equipment, but were not impressed with the City set-up.

During this period Oliver Smedley had continued to pursue a separate partnership deal with Calvert, instigating a series of convoluted proposals, firstly offering him £10,000 cash for his fort, and then offering shares in a joint stock company. Calvert remained noncommittal, neither confirming nor turning down the proposals, while still continuing negotiations with the Radio London organization. Fearing that he was being double-crossed and would not be remunerated for his transmitter Smedley organized the boarding party. The day news broke about the raid a hastily arranged summit meeting was convened between Calvert, Philip Birch, and four representatives of Project Atlanta, including the shareholder Horace Leggett, and Smedley himself. At this Soho meeting Calvert, in a paranoid state according to one witness, accused all those present of plotting against him, and spoke of using nerve gas to rid his station of its invaders. Smedley in turn made a proposition to Birch that in the event of a take-over by the UKGM team Birch should donate £5,000 and 50 per cent of all advertising revenue to Smedley's own organization. Birch told him that the offer clearly bordered on blackmail, and was quick to disassociate his company from the whole affair.

> I turned it down flat. I told those who made the offer that they had no moral right to offer this, and that I had never heard such a crazy idea ... It may sound like a Hollywood scenario. Two of them came up to me at my garden gate last Monday morning and offered to sell the station to me. They said they had just taken it over and were willing to do business ... I told them the whole thing was ridiculous and that nobody would buy a station after force had been used in this way. *One told me it was a hard world and that you could not always pick the way you did business.*
>
> (emphasis mine)[2]

On 21 June, the day after that stormy meeting, Calvert went to Scotland Yard, where he was refused police assistance. In an increasingly agitated state the City boss was driven down to Smedley's home in Essex, arriving at around 11.00 p.m. The door was opened by Smedley's housekeeper Pamela Thornburn. A violent struggle ensued in the hallway between Calvert and Thornburn during which Oliver Smedley appeared and shot Reg Calvert dead. A gas gun was found on the body. The day after the shooting Essex police visited the Shivering Sands fort, and took statements from the boarders but no arrests were made and no one was taken off the fort. On Sunday evening, 26 June, without incident or explanation, the boarding party left as mysteriously as it had arrived. Radio City resumed broadcasting within the hour using a transmitting crystal which the staff had kept hidden during the entire occupation of the fort. When Oliver Smedley appeared in court on 18 July, the charge of murder was reduced to manslaughter, and the case was referred to Chelmsford Assizes. On 11 October, after a trial lasting just one and a half days, the jury decided that Smedley had acted in self-defence, and without retiring to consider their verdict found him not guilty. The judge awarded costs to Smedley, who walked from court a free man.

In the wake of the trial conspiracy theories thrived. Calvert's widow Dorothy, who took over the day-to-day running of the station after her husband's death, maintains that in the immediate aftermath of the incident her life was threatened, she was followed by private detectives, her phone was tapped, her letters to the Department of Public Prosecutions went unanswered, and government D-notices restricted access to background information to the events of 21 June. As rumours of collusion and cover-up spread unchecked the press had a field day. Those who had taken part in the raid were only too happy to add to the sensationalism: 'What has happened so far at Radio City has only scratched the surface. I can put my finger on the button and break a story which is going to involve interests in Switzerland, Liberia, Panama, and Bermuda.'[3]

Strong rumours circulated in offshore circles that what had happened once could happen again. There were unsubstantiated stories about a second boarding party being planned in January 1967 just weeks before Radio City closed down. A collection of 'persons unknown' did in fact visit the Shivering Sands complex two weeks after the station's demise in February 1967, and stripped the forts of all removable assets right down to the rusty wartime cast iron radiators. According to the author

John Pearson, Paul Elvey, a Radio City engineer and DJ, who was fired by Dorothy Calvert immediately after the June 1966 raid, was later hired by the Kray twins as a contract killer.[4] At the time the Krays were allegedly about to embark upon a gold smuggling venture, and a plethora of uncorroborated theories linked this operation with the Shivering Sands forts.

The death of Reg Calvert initiated a fresh series of legal arguments which concentrated on the extent to which the pirates' supposed property rights had been undermined by their display of blatant gangsterism. Otherwise respectable members of the business community, some with honourable war records and well-publicized military backgrounds, had clearly been seen to be resorting to guerrilla tactics in the acquisition of sites. Some justified their seizing of ex-military property with pragmatic homilies of the 'we were here first', or 'we all have to learn to live together' variety; some then claimed virtual sovereign rights on their squatted marine structures. Most interested parties shrewdly dissociated themselves from the libertarian free-for-all. Radio Caroline, for instance, issued a press release which stated that all connections with Oliver Smedley and Project Atlanta had been severed in December 1965, but despite such disclaimers all the pirates were implicated to some degree, even if it was simply guilt by association. Certainly none were able to remain free of the ultimate legal consequences.

The incidents that took place on the Shivering Sands fort during the summer of 1966, and the bad publicity which ensued were undoubtedly the catalyst for anti-pirate legislation. But although an immediate consequence was the hastening of legal clarification of the rights of the occupants of the forts (they didn't have any) it was claimed in the House of Commons the day after the Reg Calvert shooting that a radio bill to outlaw the pirates was not high on the ministerial agenda. It was indicated that parliamentary priority at this time was being allocated to more mundane matters such as introducing new methods of television licence collecting, improving the techniques for detecting licence evasion, and increasing the penalties for those charged of this offence. Revenue collecting was supposedly more important than chasing up the robber barons of the airwaves. The following week the Postmaster-General Tony Benn indicated in the House of Commons that he had 'no means of ensuring that these [Radio City] broadcasts would not be resumed'. This contrasted sharply with the tone of his diary entry for 22 June 1966 which stated that 'gangsterism has moved into the pirates and the Government's failure to act is now an absolute disgrace'.[5] In an apparent ministerial volte-face the government published its bill to outlaw the offshore stations on 2 July. The next day Tony Benn was moved in a Cabinet reshuffle to the Ministry of Technology, following the resignation of Frank Cousins.

The government acted cynically both in its timing and over the legal position of the forts. Speaking on the BBC Home Service on Friday 24 June, Colonel Gerald Draper, Reader in English Law at King's College London, took exception to the statement in the House of Commons by the army minister, Gerald Reynolds, earlier that day; he had said, 'There is no present or foreseeable defence purpose which would require me to exercise control over these forts.' Draper claimed that this completely neglected the question of whether the Crown still owned or had abandoned the forts. The case for the latter had hardly been backed up by the action of the Port of London Authority, who maintained navigational lights and other maritime installations around the forts throughout the pirates' occupancy. In fact when the forts were first occupied by the pirates the then Conservative government had contacted the PLA to ask what action it was going to take. It emerged that Port of London responsibility for the Thames estuary sea-bed ended one mile from the coastline and from there on any sea-bed installations were the property of the Crown Estate Commissioners, the PLA being responsible only for maintaining warning lights and buoys, to prevent danger to shipping.

Draper also stressed that the issue of 'defence purposes' was a red herring, as the forts were hardly likely to be utilized against an enemy attack in the near future! It was also clearly indicated that the forts were inside territorial waters, and, as fixed structures, were not classifiable as islands. This made a complete mockery of the rhetorical argument which had persisted since David Sutch had first broadcast from Shivering Sands in May 1964 and which had now cost Reg Calvert his life. The Ministry of Defence was usually accused of holding on to land long after it had any use for it (as with ammunition dumps, emergency wartime rail links, artillery ranges on common land etc.). In the case of the Thames estuary forts the reverse was true. The last of the MoD maintenance crews had been withdrawn during the winter of 1958–9. After this time the ministry simply neglected its duties. But even though it had abandoned responsibility the forts remained Crown property.

Reg Calvert maintained a naïve faith in his *de facto* ownership of the fort despite failing to purchase it from the War Office in 1965. This nominal offer to buy was the kind of stunt he could indulge in as a pop group manager. But subsequent events showed that Calvert had got into deeper and dirtier water than he could handle, finally overreaching himself in trying to sell an asset that was not his in the first place. Among his enterprises before becoming involved in offshore radio Calvert had worked as a postwar spiv, selling contraband confectionery during sweet rationing. During the 1950s he was blacklisted by the Musicians' Union because he refused to pay the going rate to entertainers at his dance hall functions. In his history of pop group managers, *Starmakers and Svengalis,*[6] Johnny Rogan portrays Calvert as a lovable eccentric who made good during the rock and roll era, managing and nurturing his stable of artists very much in the Larry Parnes mould (although with none of Parnes's business acumen), while running dances in the Midlands. Rogan displays an ambivalent attitude towards Calvert's 'eccentricity', sensationalizing his penchant for firearms and 'animal experiments'. (One example which combines the two depicts Calvert, in front of witness, shooting a pregnant doe, and then trying to perform a delivery of the dead fawn.) On the other hand great play is made of Calvert's apparent paternal qualities and good nature. 'A jolly guy blown away by a gun', is David Sutch's epitaph on him. Stuart Colman, who was a member of the Calvert-managed Pinkerton's Assorted Colours, offered equally telling comments on pirate radio's unwilling martyr: 'There was a lot that never came to the fore. There was a lot of crookedness going on that was far beyond Reg's capabilities or background.'[7]

The season of political rhetoric

The owners of these stations do not invest millions of pounds' worth of equipment merely to keep the electronics industry happy. The advertisers using the stations, which include some of our largest and most successful companies do not allocate money from their advertising budgets as part of a rash philanthropic gesture or to cock a snook at the Government. The owners of the stations and the advertisers on the programmes are spending their money to meet a demand which has never been satisfied and which has never been recognised by the state monopoly broadcasting service.

(John Cordle, Conservative MP)[8]

I remember being in Caroline House and Ronan telling me about how all the other stations were going to close down. And he made it very clear to me. He said, 'Listen, they're only in it for the money. We are in it for a principle. We are in it for an ideal. We are in it for a philosophy.'

(Tom Lodge)[9]

Government legislation to outlaw the pirates came in the form of a Marine Offences Bill, which proposed to make it illegal for a British citizen or company either to work on, advertise on, or otherwise supply or assist an offshore radio station. The bill, published on 2 July 1966, received its first reading in the House of Commons on 27 July. On 20 December 1966 the government issued its white paper on the future of sound broadcasting, which recommended among other things a popular music service to be run by the BBC and also the setting up of nine BBC local stations. The Marine Offences Bill received its second reading on 16 February 1967. The debate this time included extensive discussion about the local radio proposals and the contentious issue of funding. On 5 April the bill reached the report stage and after a third reading was sent to the House of Lords, where surprisingly Lord Denham successfully moved an amendment forbidding the pirates to be closed down until a suitable replacement programme could be found, a delay which merely gave the pirates a stay of execution. On 14 July 1967 the bill received the royal assent and came into effect at midnight on 14 August.

Shortly after the proposed legislation received its first reading summonses were delivered to the fort-based stations. The government didn't need a Marine Offences Bill for these particular prosecutions; instead it invoked the Wireless Telegraphy Act of 1949 to begin the process of closing down Radios 390, Essex, and City. In rapid succession these stations were served with notice to quit. The owners of Radio 390 received their summons on 21 September 1966 and appeared in court on 26 November. On being fined £100, 390 closed down temporarily pending an appeal, which was subsequently heard and quashed on 12 December. Radio 390 was represented by Sir Peter Rawlinson, QC (later Baron Rawlinson of Ewell) who was at the time Conservative MP for Epsom. The successful prosecution counsel representing the Post Office throughout the case was John Newey, chairman of a Conservative constituency association in Kent. Believing that the Red Sands fort was outside British jurisdiction, Radio 390, upon management instructions, recommenced broadcasts on 19 December. Because of the prolonged legal wranglings over territorial limits the station managed to stay on air until 28 July 1967, closing just two weeks before the introduction of the Marine Offences Bill.

Radio Essex was served with its summons on 28 September, fined £100 on 30 November, and after implausibly contending that the Knock John fort was not inside territorial limits because no one had ever prosecuted the European fisherman who trawled these waters, became the short-lived BBMS before finally closing around Christmas 1966. When Dorothy Calvert was successfully prosecuted on 9 February 1967 she closed Radio City immediately. City's close-down programme offered thoughtful analysis about the future of pop radio: an impromptu DJs' forum stressed the futility of having had to broadcast at sea in the first place, emphasized that this was not simply a party political issue, and claimed that bureaucracy, not socialism, was the enemy.

While the fort-based pirates argued their final futile cases over the question of ownership (which could have been invalidated simply by invoking existing laws applicable to the maintenance of military installations) the government concentrated on the question of position. They applied the Territorial Waters Order which had come into force on 10 September 1964 and made provision for 'low water marks', a crucial technicality whereby a sandbank exposed at low tide could be counted as land and a new territorial line drawn up accordingly. Radio 390's counsel attempted to disprove the validity of the 'low water mark' ruling but to little effect. Six months previously Reg Calvert had asked for police assistance to rid the Shivering Sands fort of its invading boarding party only to be told that the fort lay outside British jurisdiction. It was in this somewhat cynical atmosphere that the last rites of the offshore era were acted out.

The attempt to bring anti-pirate legislation to the statute books set an administrative process into motion which had far-reaching effects. The bill was opposed by many Tories and subsequently the Conservative manifesto for the June 1970 election pledged to bring legal commercial radio to Britain. The Conservative victory in 1970 led to the setting up of independent local radio under a new governing authority, the IBA. The first ILR stations began broadcasting in 1973, establishing the agenda for sound broadcasting's mixed economy for the next decade. The pirates certainly played their part in initiating the debate, but the Marine Offences Bill was only ever superficially concerned with the content of what the pirates communicated. In the lead-up to legislation the squabbling over prized assets and ownership rights completely overshadowed other equally valid arguments about access and representation. Having rejected Tony Benn's proposals for a National Broadcasting Corporation the Labour Party entrusted property rights to the BBC monopoly, and funding to local government, localized trade, educational and religious institutions, and the licence fee. The Conservatives entrusted ownership to the free market, and funding to the commercial enterprise of the business community.

This surface conflict obscured the debate's hidden agenda which was ultimately concerned with which facet of state power was the more convenient option for rationalizing cultural activity and output. There was a paucity of genuine dialogue as all interested parties became embroiled in unceasing rhetorical point-scoring, which reached a peak in the House of

Commons. The Labour Party was cast as the kill-joy protagonist of a repressive bill which would curb expansion of the radio spectrum. The Conservatives in turn were cast as liberators of the populist sentiment and its accompanying electoral vote, a stance which *The Economist* interpreted as patent opportunism, when it spoke of the Tories hiding their interests 'behind bogus arguments of principle'.[10]

The main government players in this political theatre were the Postmaster-General Edward Short, and the Chairman of the Labour Party Communications Committee, Hugh Jenkins. The campaign of vilification waged by Short and Jenkins against the pirates was reciprocated as several offshore stations waged a hostile counter-campaign. The main Conservative opposition to the bill came from Paul Bryan, Shadow front-bench spokesman on broadcasting, and his fellow MPs Ian Gilmour and Eldon Griffiths.

During the fourteen months he presided over the pirates' fate the Postmaster-General Edward Short maintained an aggressive stance, motivating Ted Allbeury at one stage to attempt to sue him for 'wrongfully and maliciously inducing advertisers to break contract with them [Radio 390] and damages for wrongful and malicious intimidation of the company's customers', plus other claims relating to contractual relations between the radio station and its advertisers.

> Whilst I was dealing with Tony Benn as Postmaster-General I found him not only quite charming but perfectly straightforward. His attitude, even to the press, was 'it's a load of rubbish to say these are pirate radios. It's just some businessmen who have found a loophole in the law which they are using and at some stage we shall close it.' Now when Edward Short was brought in with the ex-schoolmaster stuff he started saying we didn't pay PRS and tax, so I decided to have a programme where I could say quite frankly that he was a liar.
>
> (Ted Allbeury)[11]

During the offshore radio debates Short described the pirates as 'squalid'[12] and stated, 'every burglar too would like legalising'.[13] Referring to what he called the 'anarchy' of the pirates'

179

lobby for support he observed, 'The chartists' petition paled into insignificance against the fraudulent nature of this.'[14] The spectre of moral panic surfaced again in statements such as, 'Controls and restraints in certain fields of public concern become more and more imperative.'[15] Speaking to the Media Executive Circle in June 1967, on the eve of legislation, Short resolutely declared that 'the government is not prepared to authorize privately owned homeform radio'. Hugh Jenkins, Labour MP for Putney, aired his distrust of the offshore entrepreneurs in November 1966 on BBC TV's *The Frost Programme*, where facing representatives from most of his adversaries in a heated debate he accused Radio 270 owner, and former Conservative MP, Wilf Proudfoot of 'stacking away [his] loot at [his] West Indies hideout'. Proudfoot proved to be a formidable debating opponent, holding up his belief in freedom of choice against the Labour government's pro-monopoly stance. Jenkins, having called the offshore stations 'outlaws', was asked by Frost to define his terms. In a moment of treasurable lucidity the Labour MP replied in exasperation, 'because they simply refuse to conform!' Proudfoot drily observed that if they were already outlaws what was the purpose of a bill to outlaw them?

In the House of Commons Jenkins made similarly emotive references to 'the dark stench of gangsterism'.[16] He later elaborated upon this analogy when debating with the Conservative Paul Bryan, stating 'it is extraordinary that the Honourable Gentleman's definition of setting the people free is setting the gangsters free.'[17] Bryan had previously admitted to having met representatives from most of the pirate stations, 'thus forfeiting a chance to join the PMG in heaven'[18] and was a prominent opponent of the bill's second reading, frequently leading his party into the division lobby. He was particularly scathing about the Labour government's indecisiveness and prolonged delay in formulating and presenting legislation.

For two and a half years we have had sanctimonious little lectures from him and his predecessor about the evils of pirates . . . we have been told that no self-respecting government could tolerate these outlaws, that they must be expunged very soon, that this was very squalid picture of which none of us should be proud. We suggested, perhaps unworthily that the Government were waiting until after the election, but we were told that the only reason was the impossibility of fitting this great measure into the parliamentary programme. Hundreds of bills were pushed through the machine, but there was still no room for this massive reform. We imagined that for some reason it must be necessitating some enormous 100 clause bill but now the great moment has arrived and what do we see? A little seven-page affair for which we were offered half a day for the Second Reading debate. This is what could not be fitted into the programme over all these years. This is the great bill for which no time could be found before the election. And the Government hoped to polish it off in half a day.[19]

A similarly provocative role was played by Eldon Griffiths when the bill received its final reading. He made political capital out of the repressive terminology which both Short and Jenkins had used throughout the bill's passage through Parliament, and claimed that the Marine Offences Act was based on 'envy, spite ... and a compound of technical ignorance, financial ignorance, and ignorance of the consumer'. After being called to order by the Speaker of the House for straying into an unrelated attack on the telephone service Griffiths delivered a forceful eulogy to populism characteristic of the Tory campaign.

I hope that the Postmaster-General will not imagine that all those who listen to the pirates are irresponsible teenagers. On the contrary they are large numbers of our fellow citizens in all walks of life, men and women, rich and poor, country folk and town dwellers ... behind [this Bill] lurks the notion ... that the people are not to be trusted, that they must hear only what he believes they should listen to.[20]

These debates frequently degenerated into farce as MPs tried to score populist points from each other. The Conservative MP John Cordle accused Labour MPs of being 'not with it and out of touch with the young'. The Labour MP Christopher Rowland,

181

after comparing the pirates' popularity to the landlord who keeps an illicit tavern open without a licence, embarked upon a content analysis exercise in order to assess what he called 'the cultural problem'.

> On Britain Radio I heard a song called 'Where my little girl is smiling'. I turned to Radio London where I heard 'Baby I need your love all the time'. When I switched to Caroline South it was 'Let me cry on your shoulder'. Back to Britain Radio where I heard 'It takes two baby'. On to Radio London to hear 'Hey there Georgie girl', and then to Caroline South where I heard 'Please release me and let me love again', followed by 'I'm losing you'. Back to London to hear 'I've been a bad bad boy'. By this time I began to think that perhaps I had been.[21]

There seemed little purpose to such observations, beyond revealing that most pop songs are about love. Only a few of the song titles bore more than a passing resemblance to records from the time. The rest were a composite of the misheard and the approximate. Rowland indicated unashamedly that accuracy was hardly important when dealing with 'impoverished programmes . . . for the ill-educated masses'.[22] Rowland labelled the pirates 'Trojan horses . . . for commercial radio in this country', and ended his speech on a note which strongly echoed Mervyn Griffiths Jones's legendary 'Is this a book you would wish your wife or servant to read?' speech made during the *Lady Chatterley's Lover* trial, when he stated 'I would take as much notice of my valet, if I had one, as of petitions organized by the pirate stations.'[23]

Such utterances were typical of the cultural divide which existed between the majority of MPs and the subject matter of which they spoke, pop radio in general being held in very low esteem by most members. Hugh Jenkins drew a distinction between material necessities 'like coal or steel' and 'an ephemeral article like . . . the sound of music'. The comments of Dr Winstanley, Liberal Party spokesman on broadcasting, typified those of the House, when after running through a brief guide to twentieth-century mass communications which illustrated how each successive development had been seen as a threat to existing media, he stated that 'it would be folly to suggest that pop music ranks with these various media and that it should be given corresponding thought or a corresponding place'.[24] Dr Winstanley did concede, though, that if the natives liked this sort of thing they should be allowed a portion of it. *The Economist* echoed this begrudging tone in its own editorial sentiments on the issue: 'Rubbishy as they undoubtedly are they do serve a market.'[25]

The pirates' own political campaign began during the summer of 1966, as soon as the proposed legislation was announced. Few of the offshore stations gave any indication that they thought that the legislation would succeed and the initial response to the bill was resolute and optimistic. However, as parliamentary procedure began to take its inevitable course the pirates lost their initial buoyancy and the mood hardened. Both London and Caroline management insisted that they would continue broadcasting after legislation came into effect, relying on foreign advertising and most probably using Holland as a supply base. London had even aired a few Dutch and Belgian advertisements, and late in 1966 had talked of starting a continental service. The fort-based stations had entered this final chapter with the same degree of caustic pragmatism they had displayed in the initial battle for site possession. 'We all have to learn to live together' was replaced by a resigned 'you can't fight city hall'. Others chose at the death indignantly to claim citizenship and employment rights in hyperbolic terms which took little account of existing political realities. 'Free radio' entered the pirates' glossary of rhetorical shorthand, which simply meant free from government control rather than shareholder or payola control.

The commercial radio lobby was spearheaded by the right-wing Institute of Economic Affairs, and a smattering of free radio pressure groups set up during late 1966. The Commercial Radio Listeners' Association, which later became the Free Radio Association, and the Broadside Free Radio Campaign both gained the support of Radio Caroline. Radio London, despite regular plugs exhorting its listeners to 'support free radio' and write to their MP, refused to give official backing to the free radio activists' crudely run campaign. These pressure groups had negligible influence (the FRA recruited less than

2,000 members) and offered little genuine analysis. The general consensus even among would-be supporters was that they did too little, too badly, too late.

Radios Caroline and London really only entered the political campaign in earnest around the time of the local council elections of 13 April 1967. A hundred seats were being contested by the major parties in London as well as in 23 county councils throughout England and Wales. Radio London held its own private poll, with questions of the 'When did you stop beating your wife?' variety, which asked which local candidates were in favour of 'free radio'. Of Tory candidates polled 98 per cent were in favour, 82 per cent of Liberals, and only 20 per cent of Labour (or 'the Socialists' as they were by now being pejoratively called). By pledging to close the pirates down, Labour by inference, was leading the electorate down a totalitarian road. In an increasingly hysterical campaign, the words 'police state' also began to enter the vocabulary of abuse.

The results of the poll were featured extensively by both Caroline and London during the period leading up to the elections. On polling day this coverage reached saturation point, with news bulletins making great play of the newly released monthly trade figures, which showed an overall deficit of £29 million. Caroline's campaign was particularly efficient. Its coverage of the election results began at midnight, as soon as the first results came in, and continued throughout the night. The Conservatives swept to victory with a landslide majority in London, and elsewhere the general trend was a swing to the right by anything up to 12 per cent. By 9 o'clock the following morning Radio Caroline was running fresh promotional material claiming that it may have had some influence on the results. There were several mentions of 'blue rosettes' being worn and DJs and newsreaders could hardly contain their glee on air.

On Sunday 6 August, just days before legislation came into force, listeners to Radio London's 11.00 a.m. coffee break slot heard the senior announcer Paul Kaye chatting to the newly elected Tory councillor for Hillingdon, André Proteau. Proteau was ostensibly on board the ship on a 'fact-finding mission', but it was obvious from the tone of the interview that he had come to sing the praises of commercial radio. The pirates rarely directly advocated voting for the Conservatives, preferring to present information heavily weighted in the Tories' favour and leaving listeners to act accordingly. Direct political sentiments were never wholly absent from the DJs' repertoire though. Several, including Rosko on Radio Caroline South and Kenny Everett on Radio London, frequently encouraged listeners to 'support the young Conservatives', and there were constant reminders of the allegiances of the political parties on the issue of offshore radio. In September 1966 Gordon Wilson, secretary of the Scottish Nationalist Party, announced that his party would be advertising on Radio Scotland, but nothing ever came of this. A similar intention by Radio Scotland's Managing Director Tommy Shields to stand in a parliamentary by-election in the Labour-held marginal Glasgow Pollock also came to nothing. On Radio 270, though, a tape was broadcast of York University Conservative Association's Monday Club, interviewing the Tory MP Patrick Wall. Shortly afterwards there was a follow-up broadcast featuring Wall and his fellow Tory MP John Biggs Davidson. Wilf Proudfoot claimed at the time that he was willing to broadcast speeches 'even from the Communist Party' if they wanted to make use of the facility. Shareholders of Ellambar Investments, unhappy with the way Proudfoot was running the station, called an emergency meeting in March 1967 and several of 270's original team of announcers left the station.

Radio Scotland's business practices also came under the microscope during February when Hugh Jenkins revealed that the brother of one of the station's shareholders had once been imprisoned for 'carrying Conservative principles to their logical conclusion'. Clearly it was not an offence to be related to someone who had commited a crime, but the Labour MP's characteristic vitriol did have the unexpected effect of revealing much of the sharp practice that lay behind Radio Scotland's claim to legitimacy. First it was revealed that Sir Andrew Murray, one of Radio Scotland's most prestigious shareholders, had in fact relinquished all ties with the station after only a few weeks. Then in May 1967, after the sacking of the station controller Brian Holden, the entire sales team and senior disc jockey staff also resigned. It was later revealed in the

House of Commons that Radio Scotland had narrowly avoided becoming the first pirate to be seized by the British Navy. It was only saved by the complexity of the legal procedure which would have arisen from having to take the issue to the Scottish Procurator Fiscal.

During this period Radio Caroline began to promote on air two musicians from Rhyl in Wales, who refuted the claim that unregulated non-stop pop music would put live musicians out of work. They argued quite reasonably that there was a reverse side to this argument and suggested that the radio pirates had in fact given many unknown acts and artists their first break. The case might have had more credibility if demo tapes of unreleased material by unknown artists hadn't been so conspicuously absent from Radio Caroline's programmes at this time, and if the station hadn't been pursuing its 'pay to play' policy so rigorously.

The poet Ronald Duncan, who offered his services to Radio Caroline as a writer, had been a founder member of the English Stage Company and had recently began to embrace the philosophy and the ideals of the American beat writers' community centred on the City Lights bookshop in San Francisco. Caroline frequently aired Duncan's sentiments on 'the writer's right to write'; his only direct contribution to the campaign was a series of blimpish patriotic promotions aired during the spring and summer of 1967. These were designed to counteract what Caroline DJs deferred to as the 'tissue of lies and Labour propaganda'. To the mawkish strains of a Glen Miller serenade one of the more sophisticated examples ran as follows:

INTERVIEWER: Tell us about your grandfather.

INTERVIEWEE: (with curious hybrid of West Country and Suffolk accents): My grandfather died on the Somme in 1915. They gave him the Military Cross, sir.

INTERVIEWER: I'm sorry. What about your father then?

INTERVIEWEE: Father? He was born just a couple of streets from grandfather sir. Died fighting for freedom at Dunkirk in 1940. They gave him the DSO, sir.

INTERVIEWER: Well, what about you Mr Jones?

INTERVIEWEE: Well I was born down in Taunton sir. Then moved up here. Had a little shop just outside Felixstowe as a

matter of fact. Used to supply that there Radio Caroline
with all sorts of odds and ends like. They gave me three
months, sir.

INTERVIEWER: Do you think you got a raw deal?

INTERVIEWEE: Not so much me, mate. It was Dad and Grandad
what was conned, wasn't it?

Elsewhere the rhetoric was equally fanciful (and in the case
of one or two promotions aired on Caroline and Radio 355
very anti-Semitic too, as those in power were invariably given
stereotypical Jewish accents). Radio 270 kept up its fervent
campaign with a promotion which took the form of a letter
to a local MP.

Sir, in enforcing a state controlled alternative to commercial
radio in Britain has it occurred to you that the people
don't want to be forced to listen to an alternative, but they
want the real thing and freedom of choice? Before offshore
commercial radio in Britain, radio was dying. Are you going
to hand it back to its executioner – the monopoly? Think,
more than half the population listens to commercial radio.
It must be what the people want. Is Britain a free country?
(*Vox pop* voices off; 'Yes of course it is', 'Don't ask me mate,
my name's not Wilson.') Well why doesn't it act like one? It's
up to you to fight for free Conservative radio in Britain. Do
not tolerate state controlled radio.

Write to your Member of Parliament today.

As it became obvious that the Marine Offences Bill would
be passed attention turned to interpreting the small print.
Loopholes had already been exposed during the bill's second
reading by a Member who doubted whether the legislation
would rule out the possibility of international advertising.

Suppose there is an international company which has a
British subsidiary and an office in New York outside the
scope of the European Convention. What is the situation
if the New York office or the New York parent decides to
place advertising on a pirate station, which is clearly of
benefit to the UK subsidiary, without the UK subsidiary itself

placing the advertising or being charged for the account? I would like an assurance that this could not be a loophole in the Bill.

(Christopher Rowland)[26]

On this issue Rowland was reassured that any such tactic would be 'a miserable loophole' and 'whistling in the dark'. His fellow Labour MP Stratton Mills commented, astutely as it turned out, that there was 'probably not enough advertising for more than one pirate ship or so to operate', but was equally keen to point out that the Postmaster-General would 'find himself a laughing stock if a coach and horses could be driven through the Bill'. What the pirates were about to discover were the limits of multinational cooperation when it came to subsidizing illegal ventures. On the issue of citizenship, though, free reign was given to further rhetorical flight of fancy. The renowned government opponent Paul Bryan put forward the following hypothetical scenario:

We were told in committee that even the ardent evangelist who allowed his sermon to be reproduced was liable to be put in prison. We were told that a parson who thanked Radio X for giving the date of his church bazaar could be thrown into chains. None of this nonsense have we been successful in removing, either by ridicule or argument.[27]

The spectacle of church ministers becoming common criminals was eagerly taken on board, particularly by Radio Caroline. Ronan O'Rahilly cited the Archbishop of Canterbury and Cardinal Heenan in his defence and made it clear that he was prepared to offer them both airtime as a matter of principle, even though it had clearly never occurred to Caroline's shareholders to put the station's facilities to such use during the previous four years. Reaction from the various religious organizations who had been advertising on the pirates indicated that none was prepared to take up the offer. The largest of these, Herbert W. Armstrong's Radio Church of God, spent an estimated £850,000 a year to present its syndicated programme, *The World Tomorrow*, on over 300 outlets world-wide, including Radios Luxembourg, London, and Caroline. But when the proposed legislation became a certainty they pulled out, as did the Evangelical Alliance, who declared that it would not seek to circumnavigate the law by placing programmes through its American offices. The Lutheran Hour which had been broadcast on Radio 390 and Caroline North expressed similar sentiments. The Seventh Day Adventists' *Voice of Prophecy* programme, aired on both Caroline networks, was discontinued in March 1967.

Ronan O'Rahilly had declared in December 1965 that he was prepared to take his case to the Court of Human Rights in Strasbourg, but it would have been futile. Article 10 of the European Convention for the Protection of Human Rights and Freedoms (Rome 1950) clearly states that the principle of freedom of expression in broadcasting is entirely subject to permitted licensing of what individual governments, and not the Court, regard as legitimate broadcasting systems. When it actually came to putting these notions of citizenship and freedom of expression to the test Caroline's own initiatives fell into familiar rough water.

Early in 1967 representatives from Radio Caroline began converting yet another of the unoccupied sea forts, Rough Towers, into what was allegedly to be a heliport and health resort. It was suspected that the proposed health resort was a smoke-screen and that Rough Towers, which unlike the other forts did indisputably lie outside British territorial waters, was going to be used as a supply base for Radio Caroline after the Marine Offences Bill came into force. An estimated £15,000 had already been spent on the project when Roy Bates, of the recently closed Radio Essex, seized the fort. With the pirate drama approaching its conclusion another familiar scene was about to be enacted in public.

Ronan's concept of owning that tower was very interesting. It was not for a radio station, contrary to what everyone believed. Ronan had a lot of philosophies and one of them was that one of the biggest problems in the world was nationalism, and that nations were a fiction of man's mind. If you can diffuse the power of nationalism it is a step towards world peace. This was Ronan's concept. So he had a team of international lawyers look into the definition of what is a nation. He found that you need a constitution, a name, and a whole list of stuff – then you can become recognized as a nation. The moment you start to be recognized as a nation then you become a nation. So what Ronan wanted to do was create a nation on that tower for the sole purpose of 'if he can create a nation then anyone can create a nation'. So you can have unlimited amounts of new nations and the existing ones would have less meaning.

(Tom Lodge)[28]

This fanciful fusion of situationism, anarchy, and spectacularly unsuccessful passive resistance anticipated many later counter-culture initiatives, such as John Lennon's purchasing of an island off the coast of Eire for the Diggers' community. Unfortunately O'Rahilly's gesture met with considerable resistance. Allegedly the Caroline organization and the Radio Essex team cooperated in the initial stages of the venture, but as in the past cooperation among offshore rivals turned out to be a rather nebulous concept, to be revoked at any stage. After the familiar charade of coup and counter-coup, as previously illustrated by the Essex and Radio City organizations on a neighbouring fort, O'Rahilly saw his ideals of nationhood degenerate into a pitched battle, with firearms and flame throwers.

In order to effect the offshore stations' imminent demise the government embarked upon a concerted press campaign to clarify the full implications of the Marine Offences Bill. The prime targets of this campaign were those who supplied the pirates, not those who listened. Full page advertisements were placed in *The Times* and *Financial Times, Lloyds' List, Merchant Shipper*, many East Anglian papers, and other regional publications close to the pirates' nearest port of call, such as *The Isle of Man Examiner* (Radio Caroline North), *The Scarborough Mercury* (Radio 270), and *The Edinburgh Evening News* (Radio Scotland). Advertisements were also placed in various music trade papers, plus appropriate audio, electronics, and related technical publications. The advertisements carried the crest of the GPO, who also footed an advertising bill which amounted to £17,754. As the death sentence was announced most of the pirates still in existence grudgingly accepted their fate. At one point Radio 355–Radio 227 looked set to join Caroline and

London in defying the legislation, but Ted Allbeury conceded that the option of using Holland as a neutral supply base was going to carry more risks than it was worth.

> Regarding the pressures that were put on, I think it would be wise of me not to be too specific about that. As I ran an operation into Holland [Radio 227] that meant going to Holland very frequently. This very draconian Marine Offences Bill stated that any British subject who operated on a pirate ship could be arrested, tried, and summonsed. It really was a preposterous law. It even had a clause that applied to any form of broadcasting, even those that had not yet been invented. It really was a great piece of spite. And it was made clear to me, let us say, to put it fairly euphemistically, that I would not be immune from the rigour of the law.
>
> (Ted Allbeury)[29]

Allbeury hinted that he had been 'warned off' at the highest political level, but it was Radio London which sounded the most ominous note when, after giving every indication of continuing, the station's newscasts suddenly announced on 29 July that it would, after all, be closing down. The official line from Radio London management was that if there had been any conceivable way of continuing after the Bill then it would have done so. It was obvious, though, that pan-European advertising was not forthcoming and that the larger pirates' multinational friends were not prepared to stretch their allegiance beyond the boundary of the law.

Radio Caroline alone seemed oblivious to this, and even though it was noticeable that most major advertisers (including the prestigious Caroline 'Cash Casino' campaign) were already winding down their contractual obligations well before the date of the bill was finalized, Caroline announced that it was prepared to defy the law and continue broadcasting after 14 August. Plans were hastily put into practice to move Caroline's centre of operation from London to Amsterdam. Naturally disc jockeys and crew on the two stations were among those most affected by the changes and were put under considerable pressure to weigh up their personal options:

Gradually we heard that more and more people, especially from Radio London, were getting signed up by the BBC and we got left with a nucleus of DJs who said they would stay. And Robbie [Dale] and I thought they would ... We were on leave that week prior to the close-down and we'd had a fantastic week of encouragement and support. But the fellows who'd been out on the boat hadn't had any of that and were getting worried, and they were out there next to Radio London, who they knew were going to turn off. And they started to think about what life was going to be like. It's a big thing knowing that you can't go back home. And because it all went round and one said I'm not going to stay because it's too risky, so the seed of fear and negativity was sown and spread around the ship, and they were all there with their bags packed when we arrived back.

(Johnnie Walker)[30]

Among the first to leave were many of those who had been most vocal in the free radio campaign, indicating that allegiance and conviction had their limits. It was clearly conviction of a different kind that most British disc jockeys had on their mind when weighing up the options. The possibility of two years in prison or a £400 fine was an effective deterrent to most of them. Nobody was sure how the new measures would affect non-British subjects. Although the Caroline organization stated that it was going to rely chiefly on North American staff, and early indications from the BBC strongly suggested that it would not be employing many Americans, many of the non-British subjects still working with the pirates as 14 August drew closer clearly did not think they would be immune from the new legislation. Some announced on air literally hours before the Act came into effect that they were reluctantly leaving.

The situation on Caroline North, supplied mainly from Ramsey, Isle of Man, was made more complex by the fact that the Manx parliament initially refused to operate the new legislation and shrewdly used it as political leverage for its own Manx Radio. Opponents in the Manx parliament invoked everything from possible entry into the Common Market to sonic booms by British aircrafts in Manx airspace in order to display their displeasure. A constitutional conflict, with decidedly racist overtones, temporarily split the Tynwald. Obtaining support from the United Nations Petitions Committee was rejected on the grounds that it would have meant forming allegiance with 'undesirable' Arab nations. The Caroline organization temporarily aligned itself with the Isle of Man's defiance, carrying a series of characteristically melodramatic features about the mighty Manx man standing up to the oppressive British government, but Manx opposition was short-lived. The question of constitutionality ultimately hinged on whether or not the issue was strictly a domestic matter for the Isle of Man (like its tax laws, for instance) or an issue which transcended the frontiers of the island. As the radio waves themselves transcended the frontiers of the island the result was a foregone conclusion. The very principles and technical conveniences which had allowed the pirates to thrive in the first place were now being utilized against them. The effect of the Manx conflict was simply to delay legislation until 30 August. Until this time Caroline North was supplied from Ramsey as usual.

Uncertainty about how effective the Act would be gave rise to an atmosphere of rumour and hearsay; it was even hinted that listeners might be prosecuted for tuning into the stations. Technically this had always been feasible under the existing Wireless Telegraphy legislation, but the Postmaster-General Edward Short had indicated during the Bill's second reading that although the measure appealed to him it was not legislatively convenient. Despite this the music paper *Disc and Music Echo* resurrected the myth a week before the Act came into force, and quoted the official GPO stentorian line on the issue. '*Disc* readers beware! If you support the continuing pirate stations by sending in record requests that are read over the air you will leave yourself technically liable to prosecution under the Marine Offences Act.'[31]

Most of the other music papers were clearly glad to see the back of the pirates: the impending legislation warranted no more than a few brief lines in the respectable *New Musical Express* and the Musicians' Union-supported *Melody Maker*. In contrast *Disc*, along with *Record Mirror* had always been broadly sympathetic to, and a keen publicist for, the pirates' cause. The Liverpool-based *Music Echo* in particular, before it had been merged with *Disc*, carried regular guest features by popular pirate DJs such as Tom Lodge and Mike Ahern. But now even this power-base was being eroded. A conspiracy of silence enveloped the pirate issue. Publications ranging from *Advertisers' Weekly* to *Time and Tide*, who had consistently publicized the pirates' activities, suddenly banished all mention of offshore broadcasting from their pages.

The *Laissez-Faire*, the ship which had begun its pirate life with promises of market supremacy for Radio England, and ended up as a floating clearing house for viable going concerns, concluded its buccaneering days with indecent haste. The Dutch operation, Radio 227, closed down prematurely and without any formal farewells, on 21 July 1967. Its final hours consisted of pre-recorded programmes which made no mention of the station's demise. In contrast, just over two weeks later, on 6 August, Radio 355 managed to address its final messages to its audience with some degree of professional composure. Radio 390 closed suddenly at 5.10 p.m. on 28 July, following the failure of its final appeal in the courts. As soon as the original court ruling, confirming that the Red Sands fort was indeed inside British territorial waters, had been upheld a hastily arranged close-down message was rushed out to the station and a muted and formal farewell was read out over the air by the senior announcer, Edward Cole. The station closed down as it always had done, with the national anthem.

August 14, the last day of permitted broadcasting before legislation came into force, saw the close-down of Radios 270, Scotland, and London. Scotland and 270 chose to broadcast right up until the midnight deadline, but Radio London's management, shrewd publicists right to the end, wisely closed the station at 3 p.m., thus ensuring maximum coverage on the evening radio and television news, and a vast crowd of well-wishers and mourners to greet them at Liverpool Street station on their well-publicized return to dry land.

Ever since Radio London had announced its surprise decision to comply with the new legislation plans had been put into operation to close down with a sense of occasion. The final *Fab 40*, broadcast on Sunday 6 August contained 18 records not even on general release, record companies having queued up for one last chance to use the station's prestigious promotional facilities. Sponsors too clamoured to have their products aired during the station's last few days, even though advertising rates for the finale went through the roof. Radio London's final day's programming was a superb piece of stage-managed professionalism and consistency. Throughout the day messages of thanks from leading figures in the world of entertainment were read out by the DJs. Many of the station's former presenters were also on hand to pay tribute. The final hour, hosted by Paul Kaye, the first voice ever heard on the station and the last remaining original staff member was pre-recorded to ensure no last minute slips. Only the 2.30 p.m. news bulletin was read out live and inserted into the official close-down programme. Many of the records played in this final show carried an added poignancy; the Rolling Stones' 'The last time', the Walker Brothers' 'The sun ain't gonna shine any more', Cliff Richard's 'It's all over', all added to the sense of loss felt by those who had played a part in this, indisputably the most successful of all the pirates. The last record played was the Beatles' wearily psychedelic 'A day in the life'. This was followed by the voice of Paul Kaye saying 'Big L time is three o'clock. Radio London is now closing down.' After a final rendition of the station's theme music the signal on 266 metres crackled and went dead. Listeners who instinctively retuned to Caroline South on 259 metres heard its senior disc jockey Robbie Dale read out an emotional eulogy to Radio London, followed by one minute's silence.

Radio 270's final day of broadcasting was chiefly memorable for one incident. An air–sea rescue helicopter from the local RAF base at Leconfield flew out to the station during rough weather to drop a package containing farewell messages from those DJs who were unable to get out to the ship for the final broadcast. The mission carried a strict instruction not to mention the drop, but the package missed the 270 vessel and landed in the sea. The station's listeners were given extensive coverage of the events on air without realizing that an official inquiry was being mounted into the incident the moment it was mentioned.

Radio 270 had achieved some cohesion in its programming during its closing months, with the occasional magazine programme (one feature came from one of the station's ex-announcers working at Expo 67 in Toronto) reminding listeners that there was life beyond Top 40 radio. But only three DJs remained on board for the final day's programming, each having to do roughly seven hours of broadcasting. The close-down programme was a shambles, with a DJ plainly nerve-wracked by the importance of the occasion stumbling his way through the closing announcements. Wilf Proudfoot appeared briefly on tape to give his best Rotary Club after-dinner address to the audience and to remind them once again that free radio would inevitably come, once the socialists had been drummed out of office. The following day the 270 vessel was moored in Whitby Bay and put up for sale.

While the more astute disc jockeys and staff of the various stations stored away souvenirs and mementos of this unique chapter in British sound broadcasting history, pillaging a microphone here, liberating a cartridge machine there, Radio Scotland DJs celebrated their final day's broadcasting by throwing the station's record collection overboard. They also relayed the usual messages of parting sorrow on their final day, and individual DJs thanked the station's management for giving them their first break in radio. Station management repayed the favour by leaving the disc jockeys out at sea for another three days before having them taken off, during which time the marooned DJs considered switching on the transmitter again, thus risking the first prison sentences under the new legislation.

Evening news broadcasts on television and radio gave extensive coverage to the final day's events. The headlines were predictably reserved for Radio London's departure, scepticism was expressed regarding Radio Caroline's intention to continue in the face of adversity, and editorial attention turned to the new BBC pop network Radio One, due to open on 30 September. Radio 270 was referred to on ITN's *News At Ten* bulletin as Radio Yorkshire, and other pirates, past and present, received equally scant and inaccurate coverage. The end had clearly come too soon for most to make the profits they had envisaged at the outset. Even Radio London claimed that it had only started to receive a return on its original investment during the last few months. Radio Scotland announced a loss of £100,000 at its demise, claiming that the station would have been in the black given another six months, although given another winter off the Scottish coast it would in all probability have ended its days at the bottom of the Clyde estuary. Radio 270 claimed to have taken in £100,000 worth of advertising in 14 months, just covering its initial outlay of £75,000. Management claimed that no salaries were paid to the station's directors and no dividend to its shareholders. How much of the £100,000 worth of advertising consisted of in-house promotions for Proudfoot grocery stores and Dale generators was not revealed. As was typical of the whole offshore venture hard facts about cash transactions were not easy to come by, when investors banked in Bermuda and registered their property in Panama or Liberia. It was left to Ted Allbeury, speaking on the Home Service 5.00 p.m. news, to offer some characteristically sober reflections:

They will have cleared their costs and made a little bit of money. I don't think that offshore radio has been a great money-maker for anybody. I think perhaps what's more important for people inside the business is that I've not seen any evidence that it's brought them a great deal of happiness.[32]

CHAPTER 6

If you want to sell in England

The pirates and promotion

> If you want to sell in England,
> if you want to tell everybody what you got
> radio's the way to do it
> and Radio London is the very spot . . . (*backing music*)
> (*product name here*)
> >   (Radio London jingle and promotional
> >   package for potential advertisers)

The fact that pirate radio is used by advertising is largely due to the efforts of agencies. Despite the considerable publicity obtained by the ships, down to earth advertising time selling, backed up by good research has been noticeable by its absence. It is remarkable that the people who invested considerable sums of money into these enterprises have failed to realise that they only have one lifeline of income, namely advertising . . . the case for commercial radio would have been so much better made if the main business approach had been to advertisers and their agencies, instead of to press agents of national newspapers.

>   (C. Higham, Director, J. Walter Thompson)[1]

Different pirates approached promotion in different ways and not all were able to emulate the success or sophistication of the Radio London operation. Reg Calvert of Radio City initially wanted a promotional vehicle for the groups he managed, although ironically he neglected his thriving dance hall business for his less lucrative broadcasting facility. Proudfoot and Dale used Radio 270 to bring the existence of their respective merchandise to the notice of a wider public. Tommy Shields erected a banner for separatist regional rights for Scotland, although as it turned out there was nothing separatist about his station's format. Roy Bates of Radio Essex adopted a robust strategy to attain sovereignty rights over his small rusting island at Rough Towers. Ted Allbeury of Radio 390, one of the few with a sense of altruism, campaigned for the rights of a neglected section of the population to continue listening to what they had listened to 20 years previously. Radio Caroline carried most of offshore radio's symbolic and emblematic baggage. Only Radio London was able to sustain a workable and consistent model of commercial pop radio, thus proving that 'if you want to sell in England' the way to do so was by bolstering the operation with multinational finance and a watertight corporate management structure.

The enduring mythology of the offshore stations suggests that their main appeal was to the teenage audience; this contrasted sharply with the interests of the bulk of advertising clients, who aimed predominantly at housewives. However, radio advertising had improved very little since the early days of commercial radio: market research for the pirates was poorly sponsored, and selling techniques remained primitive. The offshore stations, like many before them, merely tried to re-create the prerequisites of another medium. Early television advertising, both in Britain and the USA clumsily emulated the formal requirements of print, and was therefore heavy on detail but low on visual impact. Such advertisements were often fronted by white-coated 'scientific experts', stereotypical housewives gaping wide-eyed in amazement at technological progress, or, using an approach particularly favoured in the early days of ITV, the physical presence or voice-over of an ageing British thespian endorsing the product.

The early radio advertisements on the offshore stations continued to follow the received formula as handed down by television and the printed word. Not surprisingly many of those involved in the sales side of the pirates had gained previous experience with the ITV companies. Advertisements were either read 'dry' by announcers straight from scripts, which were often poorly adapted to the requirements of the different medium. Worse still, the pirates bought in advertisements from agencies which used an overamplified television sound, singularly unsuited to radio transmission. Some of the big agencies simply rejected offshore radio as a viable medium. In 1967 the Erwin Wassey agency on behalf of Gallaher Ltd undertook market research to find the most suitable strategy to widen the appeal of its client's 'Park Drive' brand of cigarettes. With a total working budget of £112,000 for the months July to December 1967 they rejected advertising on the pirates for the following reasons:

> The two stations covered in the Park Drive areas are Radio Caroline North and Radio 270. This medium is not recommended as a very low coverage is obtainable and profile of the audience is opposed to the Park Drive Target Market.[2]

The pirates' limited regional coverage and their courting of the teenage audience were factors that frequently worked against them. Initially, though, there were more pragmatic reasons that potential clients rejected advertising on the pirates:

> Unless they had previous experience with Luxembourg or Normandie they knew nothing about it and distrusted it, and above all they disliked it because rates were very low compared to TV so their commission was accordingly low.
>
> (John Ridley)[3]

During his time as Sales Director with Radios Atlanta and 390 Ridley had to convince clients that it was not necessarily in their best interest to use financially prohibitive facilities such as vast symphonic bands, copyrighted music, or the voice of a celebrity, in order to sell the product. He also advised them to take account of the medium's technological limitations.

> They could make very little on production costs because one thing they did not realise . . . was that it is not necessary to spend an enormous amount of money to produce a thirty second radio commercial. They tried to insist that we used the most expensive studios possible with thousands of pounds' worth of mixers and very complicated microphones and vast technical staff and all the rest of it, forgetting the fact that the vast majority of the listeners to the commercial were hearing it on [a] clapped out old radio covered in dust, jarring and

vibrating and babbling away to itself like an elderly relation in the corner of the kitchen.

(John Ridley)[4]

Ted Allbeury shared this perception and emphasized another aspect of radio advertising's shaky heritage: the reciprocal nature of much of his station's sponsorship. Like Gordon McLendon before him he knew the value of the mealticket.

John Ridley had held a very senior position at Grundig, but we [Radio 390] didn't know how to sell radio, and as he quite rightly says people didn't know how to buy it either. But that also applied to TV in the beginning. It wasn't until the American advertising agencies like Young & Rubicon came waltzing on to the television scene that they put anything right. We were giving away time. We were selling anything we could for anything we could, and that, I later found, was how Roy Thomson used to operate when he had his own radio station in Canada. If he needed a new valve for a transmitter he went to the local manufacturer and offered him ads in exchange for the valve. We were very much like that.

(Ted Allbeury)[5]

Radio 390 relied on mail order advertising for much of its revenue, selling everything from garden bulbs to silk stockings by post. For such purposes clients were never allowed to rent less than three weeks of airtime. The reasoning behind this requirement was very much in keeping with Radio 390's perception of its audience and its overall programming philosophy. Anecdotal rather than empirical, its folksy reasoning eschewed sophisticated market research.

As we gained experience we were able to tell our potential customers that at the end of the first week they would try and cancel their contract. They would say, 'We want to try for a week and see how it goes.' We would tell them that was no good – it's three weeks or nothing. They would say, 'Why three weeks?' and after a while we were able to say 'I'll tell you what's going to happen. At the end of the first week you will want to cancel because you've had nothing at all. After two weeks things will start to come in. Half way through the third week you will reach your peak, and you will be delighted, and from then on it will tail down to half way through the fourth week when nothing will happen. But for the next six months you will continue to receive these little bits of paper with postal orders for your silk stocking offer or your bulb offer or your wrist watches or whatever.' And they would ask why and we would say, 'Because Mum writes down that name and address on the back of an envelope, puts it behind the clock on the mantelpiece and doesn't come across it until the next time she dusts, and then she says "oh, I'd like those bulbs" and she sends off her money.'

(John Ridley)[6]

There are no accurate figures available by which to calculate offshore radio's overall share of media advertising during the 1960s. In 1964 the general trend was for advertisement sales to decline on television and marginally to rise in the press. But from early 1966 the Labour government's recessionary policies ensured that the newspapers' temporary rise in fortunes was halted. *Ad Weekly* reported on 25 June 1965 that overall advertising expenditure for the first quarter of 1965 was up only 2 per cent, compared with 13 per cent for the first quarter of 1964. The American trade periodical *Advertising Age* published figures for the years 1964–5 which showed that while all other outlets for British advertising (the press, television, cinema, and outdoor billboards and displays) remained relatively static, the annual figure for commercial radio revenue increased from $14,700,000 to $47,000,000. Out of total figures of $1.48 (US) billion and $1.56 billion respectively this was still a relatively insignificant percentage of the overall media revenue from advertising. Furthermore, as the totals also include Radio Luxembourg figures the percentage which can be attributed to the pirates remains unclear. *The Economist* of 23 April 1966 estimated that the pirates' own figure for 1965 was 2.5 million with one third of that going to Radio London. *The Sunday Times* figures from September 1966 reported the pirates' own estimates: Radio Scotland claimed a monthly revenue of £30,000; Radio 270 claimed £7,000; Radio 390, the only station to estimate net profit rather than net income claimed monthly profits of £14,000.

Although the pirates had to rely on a continuous flow of cigarette advertising and sponsorship from American religious organizations, programme output was also influenced by economic trends within the record industry. By 1966, with record companies eager to prolong the beat group boom, 75 singles, on average, were being released every week. Even the largest record companies' promotional techniques at this time were very crudely formulated, but dealing with low cost units such as 45 rpm records they could afford to invest with impunity, sustained by the knowledge that one major success would recoup the money invested in a multitude of failures. One star act with a run of chart records was a vital asset in an industry where short-term profits were the norm and the shelf life of the product was estimated to be six to eight weeks. Failing to recognize that Beatlemania was a temporary blip on the cultural seismograph rather than the norm, the record companies continued to pursue what was literally a hit and miss strategy, even though a high proportion of those records released every week stood no chance of becoming big sellers. The pirates undoubtedly benefited from this high level of production; indeed it is questionable whether some of the smaller stations would have been able to exist without it. Outfits such as Invicta, City, and Essex were grateful for everything that came their way, and featured a high proportion of new product from unknown groups in their programme output. Radio City, for example, ran a new releases programme at 1.00 p.m. every day.

Consequently one of the main accusations levelled at the pirates was that they had an adverse effect on record sales. Apart from the sheer hypocrisy of this argument, with record companies lining up to condemn the pirates while their paid representatives made sure that new product regularly reached the stations, there are three other crucial factors to consider:

Firstly, after the initial hysteria of the Merseybeat phenomenon had died down there was a levelling off of sales, as singles consumption returned to pre-Beatlemania levels (which were relatively low anyway, following a similar tailing off after the introduction of 45 rpm records during the rock and roll explosion of the 1950s). In fact singles sales were down 23 per cent in the first half of 1965 compared with the previous year. This decline certainly coincides with the appearance of the pirates, but while singles sales dropped the number of singles manufactured actually increased, as record companies continued optimistically to swamp the market, believing each new act to be the next Beatles or Rolling Stones. One result of over-production was to increase costs and cut record company profits. It wasn't until 1966, for instance, that EMI cut its weekly quota of singles releases from 21 to 15.

Secondly, while singles showed a decrease in sales, total record sales remained fairly static. Board of Trade figures for 1965 showed that the total number of records pressed (94 million) was 7 per cent down on 1964 but that revenue from sales remained around the £25 million mark. Profits accumulated from exports accounted for £3.5 million of this sum, the highest figures since 1959. Beatlemania aside, the sustained buoyancy of the market was almost totally due to a marked rise in both LP production and sales. Production in 1965 rose 13 per cent over the previous year, overall production of LPs having doubled since 1959. There was a massive campaign during 1965 to promote LP buying. Promotional strategy to launch EMI's cheap budget label 'Music for Pleasure' involved increased distribution to retailers previously not associated with record selling – newsagents for example, as well as the more traditional large chain outlets such as W. H. Smith and Boots. By the end of 1965 the MFP label was selling 120,000 a week. Pye Records instigated a similar campaign with its 'Marble Arch' and revamped the 21s. 'Golden Guinea' series. At the same time the record companies introduced new restrictive practices which severely curtailed the growth of the singles market, far more than the pirates had ever done. Because they were deemed to be no longer cost effective, a levy was introduced on small orders (10 per cent on orders of less than £5) which hit the small retailer and stimulated sales from the larger chain stores.

Thirdly, the whole issue of damaged sales hinges on the

accusation that the offshore stations only played pop singles. This was clearly untrue. From the very earliest days of Radio Caroline and Atlanta there was a concentrated effort to cater for fans of light music, Latin-American style music, blues, folk, and jazz. There was a genuine breadth and variety of programming on many of the smaller pirates too. So what were the real motives behind the record companies' opposition to the pirates?

Two prominent critics of offshore radio were Sir Joseph Lockwood, head of EMI and Bill Townsey, in charge at Decca. In 1961 these two companies accounted for 84 per cent of all Top Ten record sales in Britain. By 1966 this share had dropped to 57 per cent and by 1970, long after the demise of the pirates, their share had dropped to 38 per cent. In 1961, EMI and Decca, along with Philips and Pye, completely monopolized the buying of airtime on Radio Luxembourg. By 1966 there were 12 other options open to those who couldn't get on to the Luxembourg play-list. The level of EMI and Decca's official venom, and their desire to make the pirates a scapegoat could be measured in direct proportion to their correspondingly reduced share of record sales.

A counter claim made for the pirates was that it was they who broke down the 'big four' monopoly by stimulating the growth and sales of small record labels and therefore expanding the market. Yet there were very few genuinely independent labels at this time. Almost all the small labels still relied on the major companies for financing, manufacturing, and distribution. What actually happened was that the large companies spread their assets, reflecting patterns of diversification in the corporate structure of other media conglomerates. Decca, for instance, launched the Deram label, which had immediate success with the Move, Cat Stevens, Procol Harum, Amen Corner, and the Moody Blues. Soon after this EMI relaunched its long dormant Regal Zonophone label, taking the Move and Procol Harum from Deram in the process. (Rivalry to secure the services of those perceived to be in the vanguard of the underground scene was still notably confined to the top two companies.)

Also, companies previously not associated with the UK market increased their British outlets. Until 1962, for instance,

Columbia Broadcasting System product was distributed in the UK by Oriole. When this arrangement ended the CBS label was launched with independent distribution. CBS can hardly be classified as a small label even if it was encroaching upon the 'big four' monopoly! Similarly the German company Polydor, part-owned by Philips, had, through its joint distribution arrangement with its Dutch partner, previously concentrated on the European market, with light orchestral and easy listening music from the likes of Bert Kampfert and James Last. In 1967 Polydor began independent distribution to Britain and had quick success with Jimi Hendrix, Cream, and the Bee Gees. There were similar initiatives during the late 1960s from such unlikely 'small labels' as MGM and RCA (previously distributed by Decca), Warner Brothers and Reprise (previously distributed by Pye), and Liberty and United Artists (distributed by EMI). United Artists, like several others, was slow to move from music publishing into record production and the label didn't begin to make its influence felt until the late 1960s.

In accordance with the *laissez-faire* initiatives of the times the young mavericks in promotion and management were given their heads and were allowed new creative offshoots. With distribution provided by Polydor, Kit Lambert and Chris Stamp started the Track label, which built its initial success on groups from the Polydor stable such as the Jimi Hendrix Experience and the Who. Also distributed by Polydor was Georgio Gomelsky's Marmalade label. Among its first releases was the infamous 'We love the pirate stations' by the Roaring Sixties. The Rolling Stones manager Andrew Oldham formed Immediate, which was distributed by Brian Epstein's NEMS. Oldham's chart successes included number one records by Chris Farlowe, the Small Faces, and the McCoys (the latters' 'Hang on Sloopy' was leased on a no-profit basis from the USA). These labels allowed their owners to indulge their anarchic whims to their arts' content, until they or the label burnt out. Leasing fashionable but often obscure material from the USA eventually proved to be Immediate's and Track's undoing. Both went into liquidation in the early 1970s. The path to hip capitalism is strewn with such failed initiatives, as the Beatles' financially disastrous Apple label was spectacularly to prove. Marketing rationalization only began to appear with the systematic packaging of progressive rock. By the early 1970s every major record company had its resident 'house hippie' working as A and R talent scout, while major groups such as the Rolling Stones, the Moody Blues, and the Beach Boys developed their own short-lived record labels.

Track, Immediate, and Marmalade were all launched too late to allow accurate assessment of the influence offshore radio might have had on their sales. The related questions regarding what influence the pirates had on individual, rather than overall record purchases, and to what extent they were able to manipulate the charts are equally contentious. Because of the crude methods used by the trade papers and the BBC to collate their hit parades, records were frequently hyped into the lower reaches of the Top 50, whereupon the ensuing extra promotion and airplay could normally guarantee a hit. The Small Faces, Pinkerton's Assorted Colours, and the Jimi Hendrix Experience are just three groups who are indebted to the skilful art of payola.[7] To what extent the pirates were able to make a hit purely by their own powers of promotion is more debatable. Radios London and Caroline undoubtedly played their part in helping the careers of many unknown acts. The Moody Blues' 'Go now', the Byrds' 'Mr Tambourine Man', Tom Jones's 'It's not unusual', and Procol Harum's 'A whiter shade of pale', and the early recordings of Simon and Garfunkel all owed their initial exposure to the offshore stations.

The pirates also took advantage of strict BBC procedures when giving airplay to records which would otherwise have been denied promotion. The practice of playing an English cover of an American original, for example, resulted in the Light Programme concentrating on Cilla Black's version of 'You've lost that loving feeling', while the pirates persisted with the Righteous Brothers' original, which eventually went to number one. Numerous records which received the BBC's equivalent to the X certificate – 'restricted airplay' – were also plugged by the pirates, but the offshore stations by no means fully exploited this situation. For a variety of pragmatic, political, and moral reasons the pirates frequently banned records themselves. Barry McGuire's anti-war song 'Eve of Destruction', 'restricted' by the BBC, was another of the pirates' promotional successes, but even this record was banned by

Radio Scotland, and payola allegations aside there is evidence to suggest that Radio London played a gatekeeper role every bit as selectively and severely as the BBC.

A record's high profile on the pirates never automatically assured a hit. Reg Calvert's only chart acts among the plethora of groups he managed were Pinkerton's Assorted Colours and the Fortunes. Ronan O'Rahilly promoted the English soul singer Barry St John for three years without success. Even Georgie Fame, who enjoyed an almost symbiotic relationship with Radio Caroline owed most of his success to his unceasing club work and a particularly prestigious support slot on the 1965 Tamla Motown package tour of the UK. Radio London gave extensive exposure to artists they had a vested interest in, like Episode Six and Val McKenna, without ever denting the BBC charts. As befitted Radio 390's general *modus operandi* the sweet music station was almost entirely free of sharp practice. One of its DJs was allegedly so besotted with Anita Harris that the station played the 'Anniversary Waltz' to excess but that was about the extent of 390's vice and corruption.

The pirates' influence was restricted to the lower end of the Top 50, where they were able to give a record an initial push. Their effect on the Top 20 was negligible. Indeed a sobering counter argument contends that family entertainers such as Ken Dodd, Vince Hill, Vikki Carr, Engelbert Humperdinck, and Harry Secombe, who received little exposure on the pirate stations and gave such an incongruous look to the pop charts during the supposedly psychedelic summer of 1967, owed their success to that old faithful, the BBC Light Programme.

So what did the programming initiatives of the offshore stations ultimately achieve? There seem to be three overlapping schools of thought among broadcasters involved with the venture. One school suggests that the pirates proved the demand for legal commercial radio in the UK. Questioning whether this was the desire of the listeners or merely the need of the advertisers, another school of thought offers the variant that listeners didn't so much want commercial radio *per se*: what they wanted was format radio, of the kind best exemplified by Radio London and the juke-box rota which had inspired Gordon McLendon and the rest of the Top 40 pioneers back in the early 1950s. A third school of thought suggests an even simpler conclusion: listeners just wanted non-stop music radio on tap.

Unfortunately the crude factionalism of the pirate' final struggle, when supporters romantically depicted the offshore populists fighting a noble battle against the elements and authorities, while opponents painted them as squalid entrepreneurs peddling the unacceptable face of pop culture, in no way addressed the full complexity of what the pirates initiated and accomplished. The parliamentary rhetoric, the inexpert and half-hearted campaign to save the pirates, the rapidity with which the majority of listeners supposedly forgot them, and, it has to be said, the readiness of many ex-pirates to play down their buccaneering past, all conspire against accurate definitions of the pirates' true worth. In the immediate aftermath of legislation there was an attempt in some quarters to eradicate the pirates from the history books, or otherwise denigrate their broadcasting legacy. How the BBC chose to interpret the pirates' broadcasting initiatives – what they accommodated and what they selectively excluded – will be the subject of this book's final chapter. What the official channels of pop provision chose to ignore altogether is the subject of the concluding section of this chapter; the offshore pirates' last lingering defiant postscript was provided, fittingly, by Radio Caroline.

Major to minor

Once I thought life was going my way
It was just like a beautiful song
When you came well I thought you would stay
Now it seems everything has gone wrong.

Major to minor – all the dreams that I planned were so big and so grand
They burst like a toy balloon
Major to minor – it's the wrong harmony and we can't find the key
We're so far apart I can't even start the tune.

Once our love had original words
Well I've heard them again and again
Same old song you can sell to the birds
And it turns to a bitter refrain.

Major to minor . . .

('Major to Minor', the Settlers, (written by Jackie Trent and Tony Hatch), © Welbeck, 1967)

Legislation altered everything. It changed the nature of DJ recruitment, inconvenienced previously smooth-running staffing rotas, and further threatened already fragile business networks, as grapevines had to be uprooted and relocated. Legislation changed the nature of advertising and the volume of funding *per se*. It influenced everything from the tendering of essential supplies to the acquisition of the pirates' real bread and butter – new records. Because it changed strategies in such a fundamental way the business of running an offshore operation was completely transformed. Radio Caroline underwent such a transformation after 14 August 1967. It was no longer a mere legislative inconvenience, flaunting its rebelliousness, leap-frogging over long-established copyright procedures, or squatting unwelcomed in international waters or unauthorized and supposedly clogged wavelengths. After 14 August 1967 Radio Caroline was a true outsider.

Radio Caroline's continued presence in the post-Marine Offences Act period represented a two-fingered gesture of defiance, aimed directly at the Prime Minister, Harold Wilson. At midnight on 14 August listeners to Radio Caroline heard Pete Seeger's protest anthem 'We shall overcome', followed by a prepared speech read by the DJ Johnnie Walker, who thanked the Prime Minister 'for recognizing Caroline's right to exist'. To the Caroline organization the station's legality had been tacitly acknowledged by the government's not outlawing the ships but merely the British subjects who worked on them. Walker's speech was followed by the 'global village' fanfare of the Beatles' 'All you need is love', and then Radio Caroline's British staff entered illegality.

Ronan O'Rahilly had announced just before legislation that

he intended to broadcast a taped programme called 'The private life of Harold Wilson', which would reveal hitherto unknown 'facts' about the Prime Minister. Whether the programme ever existed is a matter for conjecture. Like so much concerning Radio Caroline after 14 August 1967 the gesture was made in an atmosphere of bluff and double-bluff. Station management had also declared that it intended to continue as Radio Caroline International, with offices in New York, Paris, Toronto, and Amsterdam. Caroline House in Chesterfield Gardens officially closed for business on 8 August and most of the office equipment was promptly shipped to Amsterdam. A Dutch office had been in operation since April, run by the South African Basil von Rensburg. But in the first week of defiant broadcasting after 14 August there was still no address for listeners to send requests to. They could though, it seems, still write to Caroline House for Caroline Club transistor radios and T-shirts. O'Rahilly himself, as an Irish passport holder, was exempt from the new laws, and continued to operate warily from the office in Dean Street, London, originally the headquarters of Project Atlanta.

The proposed New York office turned out to be a Madison Avenue contact address and yielded nothing in the way of advertising. The Toronto office was the headquarters of Terry Bate's company, Marich Associates, but there is no evidence to suggest that any sponsorship was forthcoming from Canada. Pan-European clients did not appear to be queueing to use the Paris facility either. It was also announced that offices were to open in Tokyo and Germany but nothing ever came of this.

What Caroline listeners heard instead after 14 August was a continuous series of 'dummy' advertisements aired to confuse the authorities, while disguising the identity of real sponsors. Of 28 promotions logged in a typical 24-hour period in August 1967 none was genuine. A spokesman for Beecham, one of the companies whose promotions continued to be aired, pointed out that all contracts with Caroline Sales had ended in November 1966. Representatives for the Swiss watch manufacturers Bulova, and the cigarette firms Du Maurier, Peter Stuyvesant, and Consulate, also stated that Caroline was merely broadcasting old tapes that had been used in campaigns preceding legislation. Other firms being promoted expressed uniform dissatisfaction at this unwanted publicity. One such sponsor, the photographic dealer Derek Gardener, even went to Amsterdam, with press photographers in tow, to deliver his indignant protest personally. Advertisements for Gardener's photographic business broadcast prior to legislation had mentioned special offers running until 30 September. In this instance Radio Caroline was gleefully fulfilling outstanding contractual obligations to its unwilling client. Similarly, advertisements which appeared for Vidor batteries were the residue of a three-month agreement which that company had signed with both Caroline and London in June, two months before legislation. The confectionery firm Rowntrees (whose Spangles, Kit-Kat, and Smarties advertisements also began to appear on the station) claimed that it had never arranged to advertise on Radio Caroline. Even Nabisco, who just months earlier had been an integral part of the Caroline 'Cash Casino' campaign now strongly disclaimed responsibility for the advertisements still being used.

In fact most of the advertisements aired on Radio Caroline for Rowntree and Nabisco products were taped from children's television (hence a sudden predominance of promotions for 'Twiglets', 'Jelly Tots', and 'Smarties'). All these bogus advertisements were characterized by over-amplified and substandard television sound quality. Those which appeared for Norwood Cars of Norwich were part of a reciprocal deal the firm had had with certain Caroline DJs. During the winter regular promotions for a product of dubious origin called 'Alco-kill' began to appear. 'Alco-kill', although not able to reduce the amount of alcohol in the body, did claim to be able to disguise the smell of liquor on the motorist's breath, and had been devised to beat detection by the newly introduced breathalyser. Although widely available on the Continent it was illegal in Britain. By endorsing such an unethical product Caroline gave early indication that it was desperate for funds.

If people were in any doubt about where the real funding was coming from after 14 August they only had to listen to programmes on both Caroline stations, where product from the Major Minor record label continued to receive saturation exposure. Some Major Minor promotions lasted as long as seven minutes; two played in succession seemed to constitute programmes in their own right. Foremost among the label's new promotions was a campaign to launch the Irish singer and songwriter David McWilliams, a promising although slightly derivative talent in the Dylan–Donovan mould. McWilliams received considerable hard sell on Radio Caroline, but neither this nor the regular full page advertisements in the music press convinced the public or record reviewers. In any case the music press couldn't be seen to endorse McWilliams in the nervous post-legislation period. It was feared that such a move might be interpreted as a discreet plug for Radio Caroline. As exposure on Radio One was never going to be an option the momentum of McWilliams's career was halted by the backwash from the Marine Offences Act.

Major Minor's real bread and butter was Irish folk and country ballads; on Caroline South these continued to be programmed incongruously among the Wilson Picketts and Otis Reddings. The label also specialized in light classical music by outfits such as the Roberto Mann Singers and the Raymond Lefevre Orchestra. Lefevre, whose stock-in-trade was lush instrumental versions of popular hits of the day, like 'Release me' and 'Whiter shade of pale', enjoyed considerable success on the Continent and even had a Top 10 hit in the USA with 'Soul coaxing'. Major Minor also had a penchant for novelty records; their intrusion into the programming of a pop and soul oriented radio station was contentious and gave rise to considerable friction among Caroline DJs.

Most media observers were surprised that Caroline actually continued at all after 14 August. Many believed that O'Rahilly would keep his stations on air for one extra day as a token gesture. Even the Caroline DJs kept a wary watch on the horizon immediately after pirate radio's Black Monday, half expecting to see an approaching naval destroyer. Their worst fears looked like being confirmed on Monday 21 August when the Sunk Head tower, indisputably outside territorial waters and therefore, in the eyes of the authorities, ripe for pirate exploitation, was demolished with the aid of several tons of gelignite in front of a specially invited audience of television and press reporters. The explosion, which received front page coverage in several newspapers including *The Times*, could be seen from the *Mi Amigo* and Caroline South DJs commented with a flippancy which belied their worries on 'those doing Mr Wilson's dirty work'. The fear was short-lived and when the threat of provocation passed the initial jubilation and defiance gave way to a general feeling of anti-climax.

In August and September both Caroline North and South ran on skeleton crews. The daily supply service and the pre-Marine Offences Act luxury of two-week shifts on the boat followed by one week off disappeared. The tender journey to the South ship, a relatively calm two- or three-hour trip from Frinton or Felixstowe, became an 18- to 24-hour endurance test from Ijmuiden in Holland. Reaching the North ship now involved crossing the Irish Sea from Dublin rather than cruising across Ramsey Bay. The DJs who jubilantly broadcast on Radio Caroline South at midnight on 14 August were still there a month later. The initial bravado had soon given way to a subdued atmosphere, and programming grew correspondingly jaded and repetitive as DJs rotated the six-hour programming shifts. Although there had been immediate on-air evidence that within days of the Act somebody was delivering British daily papers to the Caroline South ship, it also became apparent that new records were not getting to the ships as easily as before. There was no lack of record company co-operation. Before legislation official condemnation had gone hand-in-hand with unofficial compliance, and a plentiful supply of willing agents, independent distributors, and opportunist pluggers and promoters still ensured that their product continued to reach the ships, come hell or high water (usually the latter). On the surface it was business as usual – provided the weather held. The problem was that Caroline now lacked the internal organization for getting new product with anything like its old efficiency.

Chart programmes were the first noticeable casualty and the Caroline Top 50 was quietly dropped from the schedules. The station continued to allude to the existence of a hit parade format within programming, and records were still allocated chart positions in what was essentially a non-existent chart, but these were just hollow gestures to pad out the format of 'time–temperature–artist–record–chart position'. It also became apparent that in the pre-Marine Offences Act period more energy had been spent on rhetoric than maintenance. Within days of the Act coming into force essential items were in short supply, and in the none-too-subtle guise of 'engineers' requests' the following 'coded' message was read out at 10.20 a.m. on the Robbie Dale show on the morning of Saturday, 19 August: 'This morning our puzzle comes from Mr Joe Bloggs who says "can a 50 kw transmitter be put back on the air if you have 120 semi-conductor diodes of number IN 1222?"' The follow-up to this transparently bogus inquiry came after the next record: 'After consulting a panel of experts we have decided that it *is* possible to fix a 50 kw transmitter with 120 semi-conductor diodes, number IN 1222 . . . it would mean reconstructing the rectifier panel'.

Such coded communiqués were nothing new to offshore radio. Even during pre-legislation days stations used varying makeshift methods to relay messages to shore. Cryptically appropriate records were often played to indicate that something was amiss; 'Rescue me' by Fontella Bass was a favourite! After the boarding party incident Radio City used the Fortunes' 1965 hit 'You've got your troubles' in emergencies. David Sutch and crew had previously used a characteristically less refined method, invariably relaying the vital information that they were running out of bread, tea, etc. over the air between discs. Even Radio London occasionally slipped in a discreet message for head office during twilight hours, but no one had previously used the practice during prime time. By 2 September 1967 Johnnie Walker was openly declaring on air that the station needed new needles for the record decks. On 30 September, the day that Radio One began broadcasting, Caroline South DJs were unable to announce records at all because of continued technical problems with microphone and panel, and could only relay non-stop music.

Soon after 14 August Johnnie Walker began airing an impassioned promotion that he had assembled, called 'Man's fight for freedom'. To the strains of military marching music (the instrumental 'B' side of S.Sgt. Barry Sadler's 'Ballad of the green berets') it melodramatically depicted the plight of those DJs who had forsaken 'their families and loved ones' to pursue a principle. Although Caroline management was initially dubious about its propaganda value Walker took unilateral action to air the promotion regularly. Its concluding scenario fancifully depicted the *Mi Amigo* sailing gloriously up the Thames in victory celebration.

215

I got really demoralized. That promo I made, 'Man's Fight for freedom' was an attempt to keep our, and our listeners', morale alive. The worst thing that got us was the publicity. The newspapers weren't allowed to write about us, and when Radio One came on air in September there was nothing but Tony Blackburn centre page spreads in all the tabloids.

(Johnnie Walker)[8]

An overlooked but arguably more significant promotion, also initiated by Walker, was aired briefly during early October 1967 to counteract the massive publicity Radio One's opening had received. Acting as the libertarian David to the BBC's corporate Goliath. Walker selected and collated the less favourable portions of the national press reaction to the new network. The promotion's 'us and them' sentiments pitted 'They have Robin Scott aged 47' against 'We have Ronan O'Rahilly aged 27', and contrasted Radio One's 46 DJs with Caroline South's five. It continued in a similarly crude but effective vein, although the line 'The BBC has raised its transmitting power. Don't you think we have done the same?' strained credibility somewhat in the light of the frequent transmitter breakdowns and coded messages going out over the air. Defiance was undermined further on 26 September, when owing to the cumulative effect of staff shortages Caroline's skeleton crew conceded that it could no longer maintain a 24-hour service. From this date transmissions closed at 2.00 a.m. and recommenced at 5.30 a.m.

During October Caroline courted further controversy by broadcasting an edition of Radio Two's daily soap opera 'Mrs Dale's Diary'. The BBC understandably gave the gesture a cool reception – particularly since Johnnie Walker had jokingly thanked the Corporation for providing a 'special link' arrangement between the two stations, thus allowing the Corporation to resurrect old accusations about flouted copyright. The prank was also greeted with dismay by many in the industry who deemed it to be unprofessional. On another occasion Walker presented an entire show from his cabin bunk, readily admitting that these increasingly provocative gestures were largely born out of frustration. The isolation of Caroline's small nucleus of DJs was compounded further by a policy of virtual exclusion

216

by the media. With the newspapers concentrating on Radio One, Caroline only seemed to warrant a mention when its advertising accounts and methods of funding came under scrutiny. Even the music papers, previously full of publicity for the pirates, only made tentative and discreet references to offshore radio's last survivor while they tested the legislative waters. The one exception to this was Granada TV's *World in Action* team, who had made the original investigative foray into the pirates' territory in April 1964, and now returned to the *Mi Amigo* to film an edition called 'The O'Rahilly file'. The first time the seven-man team tried to visit the Caroline boat, on 12 September 1967, they were instructed not to board by coast guards acting on instructions from GPO officials. The *World in Action* team made a second, successful, attempt three days later by travelling to the *Mi Amigo* via Holland. The team members went on board to film on condition that their presence was not mentioned on air.

When the programme was aired in late September viewers saw a very different Ronan O'Rahilly from the one who had appeared in the previous *World in Action* broadcast. Gone was the tongue-tied youth seated at the right hand of Jocelyn Stevens. Now, in a dramatized opening sequence, viewers saw a determined O'Rahilly, his stark features framed in close-up while an authoritative 'voice off' demanded personal details in the clichéd manner of a 'name, rank and number' inter-rogation. To 'occupation' the Caroline boss wryly answered 'marine broadcasting'. To 'politics' he replied 'I suppose I'm an anarchist'. Pacing up and down on a bare studio set, and visibly warming to his theme, O'Rahilly espoused his liber-tarian philosophy and hammered home his twin obsessions of persecution and injustice.

Johnnie Walker and Robbie Dale both toyed with the idea of challenging the validity of the Marine Offences Act in the Court of Human Rights by flying into Heathrow, having pre-warned the press of their intentions, and daring the authorities to arrest them. But such stunts proved to be unnecessary. In the anti-climatic aftermath of 14 August it had been shrewdly suspected that with the GPO's work effectively done not a single DJ would be arrested. Such suspicions were confirmed during the following months when new presenters not only

217

started to filter through to the stations with apparent ease but also began to slip confidently back into Britain without any real attempt to hide their identities. The story confirming this broke in *Disc and Music Echo* on 11 November 1967, to an indifferent response from the authorities. Knowledge of Caroline's troubled finances was by now an open secret and the GPO was clearly content to play a waiting game. When Walker dared to return to England to see his family he claims he was asked for his autograph by a customs official!

Caroline's post-14 August recruits were, on the surface, an unlikely group of rebels. The ex-Radio Scotland DJ Stevie Merike assessed the station's motives at this time as being basically fiscal rather than revolutionary. His own motives were recognizably pragmatic, and far removed from the desire to cock a snook at authority.

> I wasn't interested in all that. All that I was interested in was the fact that I was on Radio Caroline. Caroline was the one station I wanted to be on. I never wanted to be on Radio London. I felt it was very plastic and very non-communicative. The only thing that was communicative on that ship was Kenny Everett, and that was only in passing wit occasionally. All I was interested in was just being there.
>
> (Stevie Merike)[9]

Like many of his contemporaries Merike had gained his initial radio experience in the familiar late 1950s ennui of Forces Radio, not with the prestigious BFN network, but on a local closed circuit station at the RAF college in Hereford.

> I did breakfast programmes all the time I was at college ... which was great because it excused you all the duties you have to do at RAF college like bedmaking and all that garbage. It was supposed to build the man in you. It just built the boredom in me.
>
> (Stevie Merike)[10]

Andy Archer, who joined the station in December 1967, also had an RAF radio background. He had previously worked with Radio City, and like Merike was conversant with the

pirate recruitment grapevine. Indeed Archer's employment
illustrated the ease with which Caroline was operating a British base during its period of supposed exile. Along with the
American recruit Howard Castle (known on air as Bud Ballou)
he was sent to 'Mid-Atlantic Films' in Dean Street, Soho, which
was used by Radio Caroline as a makeshift mainland base. There
was also a well-entrenched community of ex-pirates in Holland
providing a steady supply of DJs. Both Merike and Archer attest
to the considerable hardship which had to be endured during
the winter months of 1967–8. Andy Archer's initial impression
upon arrival shortly before Christmas 1967 was that there was
far more internal organization on the ship than on land. Merike
verifies this, and gives a graphic account of the Caroline crew's
isolation:

It was chaotic. Tenders turned up when they weren't meant
to, then they never turned up at all. I remember we were all
out there for four weeks at one point without anything. Or
a ship would turn up with records and the mail but not to
take anybody off. There was a period when we were down
to the last twenty five gallons of drinking water, and we were
running out of food and all sorts.

(Stevie Merike)[11]

A sporadic supply service and the prospect of a sea crossing
to Holland every few weeks had a cumulative effect on morale.
Less was heard about 'Man's fight for freedom', less still about
cocking a snook at the authorities. A crisis point was reached
in early December 1967.

Every time I did that journey it was terrible. I've been over
the North Sea in a force 12 when you were just hanging on
for dear life. And you are retching for 24 hours non-stop, and
with sea sickness you just don't stop when your stomach's
empty, you keep going but you just wanna die. There were
times when I contemplated . . . I mean I just thought if I open
the door and go over the side that would be it, and would
end all this bloody torture. What was really bizarre though
was the nightmare 22- to 24-hour journey across the North
Sea, getting a train to Amsterdam to recover, and next day

219

going to the airport and flying back across that same North Sea and within 40 minutes being in London.

(Johnnie Walker)[12]

During this period, which marked the beginning of a notably severe winter, Walker was audibly at the end of his tether. He expressed on air his frustration with supply shortages and continually prolonged periods of duty without leave, and left the ship shortly afterwards. The senior DJ Robbie Dale, who was on leave at the time of the incident, told a *Daily Telegraph* reporter that Walker had washed his clothes in left-over celebration champagne as a protest against the continual water shortage. For the duration of this short-lived protest three DJs were left to operate a makeshift service. While Walker sat in his hotel in Amsterdam contemplating his future he heard that his idol, the musical linchpin of his radio programmes, Otis Redding, had been killed in a plane crash. Walker returned to Caroline South on 19 December, beginning an emotional return programme with an unbroken sequence of appropriate records; P. J. Proby's 'I Apologise' ('I don't expect you to take me back, after I caused you so much pain'), the Beatles' 'You really got a hold on me', and 'Wait' ('It's been a long time/now I'm/coming back home'), and Manfred Mann's 'There's no living without your loving', before explaining the context of his previous outburst to listeners. Later in the programme, in an extended impromptu chat Walker, in faltering tones, paid a moving tribute to Otis Redding.

This frank emotional commitment bonded Walker to his audience, but his honesty was not always so welcome. One November night on the after midnight programme Robbie Dale and Walker informally discussed music policy. Initially light hearted, the argument became increasingly heated. Even allowing for the relaxed conventions of late night programming it was a little raw. At one point Dale half jokingly made a verbal disclaimer, dissociating himself from the controversy which Walker was generating. What began as harmless speculation on the relative merits of soul singers and quality balladeers eventually led to a consideration of the kind of music Radio Caroline should be playing. Dale argued for stricter demarcation between 'middle of the road' items for the housewives and more up-tempo music for the night-time audience. Walker advocated more soul music and complained incessantly about 'the list', the infamous catalogue of plug records, which had by now become an inseparable component of the station's daytime output. The encounter between Radio Caroline's two senior disc jockeys was pointedly interspersed with a stream of Major Minor product which did little to appease Walker, and the squabble continued long into the night. Animosity towards 'the list' had by now become rife among the station's staff. The more daring Caroline DJs carried out their own unauthorized quality control.

> Johnnie Walker got so fed up with the Major Minor plug records one morning that he just played the Bachelors for an hour and a half solidly and called it everything he should have played from the plug list. We just fell about laughing on the ship that day. We were all fed up with the plug records.
>
> (Stevie Merike)[13]

Plug product as a rule dictated music policy on the station, and sometimes as many as 14 to 18 records an hour came from 'the list'. A secretary in the Major Minor office meticulously logged the playing of all plug records including non-Major Minor product, which also made up a sizeable portion of programming. The pay-to-play issue brought barely concealed internal conflicts to a head. One faction, spearheaded by Walker, advocated music that was relevant to Caroline's audience while the company line was that the plug records were essential for the station's survival.

> To have given up what I did – which was as I later discovered a definite job on Radio One – putting up with all these terrible tender journeys, and not a very great living situation in Amsterdam on leave – to go through all that to play this shit music just did me in. And Robbie used to say 'yeah but if we didn't have it – that's what's keeping the station on the air'. But of course it wasn't. It was lining businessmen's pockets. And money that was due to the Wijsmullers to keep Caroline on the air wasn't being paid.
>
> (Johnnie Walker)[14]

As Caroline entered 1968 staff from both stations were under no illusions about the precariousness of their situation. The customary station identity jingle on the South ship which stated 'with offices in Amsterdam, Paris, New York, and Toronto', was abbreviated by Johnnie Walker to 'controlled from absolutely nowhere'. There were still occasional glimmers of hope on the programming front; the station's supply of records had been re-routed sufficiently for Caroline to recommence an American 'Hot 100' chart programme in January 1968, but this was thanks largely to the initiative of a discreet Atlantic Records representative. The station also relaunched the 'Caroline Countdown' Top 50. But because of its potential lack of credibility – resulting from the inclusion of plug records – it was broadcast at the incongruous time of 12.30 a.m. on Monday mornings, making it the least publicized chart programme in the history of pirate radio! It was privately acknowledged that a chart programme on a station riddled with payola was not a feasible option, hence the token nature of the initiative and the lateness of its hour.

Despite such fresh programming impetus station morale had audibly dropped to an all-time low. Disc jockeys could frequently be heard complaining about the lack of a supply tender and homesickness was a common topic of conversation. Ronan O'Rahilly began to admit openly that the financial position was far from healthy; breaking even now seemed to constitute the limit of Caroline's ambition. Caroline disc jockeys had not had a pay rise since the Marine Offences Act had been passed, Walker and Dale were still earning £25 a week; the others received £17 (still less than half the salary of Radio London DJs 12 months previously). Some consolation was derived from the fact that paypackets were still being received fairly regularly. What Caroline DJs didn't know was that bills were not being paid and debts to the station's tendering company were mounting.

On Saturday 2 March 1968 Johnnie Walker's regular 9.00 p.m. to midnight programme contained all its usual features. Walker played his prescribed mixture of Motown and Major Minor, responded to lengthy letters from listeners with their underlying sub-texts of loneliness, and answered specific inquiries about the forthcoming Stax tour of the UK, which he hoped to be compèring. During the programme he hinted that the station might be going off the air at some time in the near future for essential maintenance in dry dock (the *Mi Amigo* not having been overhauled since running aground in January 1966). It was an innocuous remark that was to backfire with telling irony.

The same evening Radio Caroline North closed as normal at the slightly earlier time of 10.00 p.m. Having suffered constantly from staff shortages, the station had audibly lacked momentum for months. Several of the station's DJs had begun to think that some kind of drastic organizational overhaul would be essential if the venture were to survive. It had been mooted that the North ship might be sold off and the whole operation transferred to the South station.

During the evening of 2 March a Dutch tug anchored in the foggy outer reaches of Ramsey Bay, about a mile from Caroline North. It refused to state its business or destination when Isle of Man coastal authorities tried to establish radio contact. In a well co-ordinated pre-planned operation, which shrewdly played on the lack of communication between the two stations, both ships were boarded in the space of a few hours early on Sunday 3 March and were forcibly seized by seamen acting on behalf of Wijsmuller Ltd. The North ship was boarded at 2.00 a.m. Acting on strict instructions from his employers a spokesman for the tendering company read a short message to DJ staff and crew members, ordering a complete close-down of the station. At 6.00 p.m. on Sunday the silenced vessel began the slow haul back to Holland. The South ship was hijacked equally abruptly at 5.20 a.m. just as Roger Day was about to go on air to commence the day's programmes. A sealed letter was presented to the captain and, like Caroline North, the South ship was put under tow and taken back to Holland.

It was the most bizarre sensation really. To have done your show the night before and closed down, never to come back. You can't nip back. That's the magic thing about radio, that connection, that one to one contact. Each person gets from it what they want, and so it's horrible when it suddenly goes, and when you don't know why that's even worse.

(Johnnie Walker)[15]

223

Piratical rhetoric was laid to rest the moment Caroline was repossessed by the marine baillifs. Johnnie Walker's previous suspicion that the authorities did not want to have to arrest a single DJ was finally confirmed. The GPO had summed up the situation correctly, placing faith in Caroline's inability to sustain an operation while hindered by legislation. When the two remaining pirate ships finally received the 'midnight knock' there was a sense of inevitability. In the initial confusion nobody, including the press, knew whether the ships were being taken back to Holland for the long overdue servicing which had been hinted at on air, or for more drastic reasons. Only when the south ship's anchor chain was severed and dropped into the sea were Johnnie Walker's worst fears confirmed. The disc jockeys, forbidden from entering the studios, busied themselves on the sea crossing by discreetly disposing of potentially incriminating paper work, including the plug records list! In the days following the seizure considerable mystery surrounded the silencing of Caroline and the national press was full of conflicting reports. Ultimately, though, there was nothing mysterious about the real reasons. The franchise holder had not been paying the rent to the landlord, and nobody had thought to tell the sitting tenants.

> That was the tragedy of it. The tragic irony that the money was there to keep the ships afloat. So it wasn't the Marine Offences Act or the government that caused Caroline to go off the air. It was the bloody greedy business brains.
>
> (Johnnie Walker)[16]

When the ships arrived back in Holland it emerged that Wijsmuller's directors were divided over the tactics which had been used to bring matters to a head. One faction had favoured negotiation, the other drastic action. Phil Solomon insisted that the ships be put back out to sea before unpaid debts were met, the Wijsmullers insisted on payments first and continued to hold on to the ships for security. During this prolonged débâcle the DJs were paid off. Some remained in Holland to see what would develop, others slipped quietly back to England. No police state awaited them. There was no grand finale and no martyrdom. Not one DJ returning from exile was arrested, and the GPO, content in the knowledge that the Marine Offences Act was now fully effective, did not attempt to prosecute anyone. A broadcasting revolution that had begun with idealism and romantic fervour had ended in acrimony and the squalid spectacle of shareholders arguing over their prized asset.

I came back to London after about four days, thoroughly depressed and dejected. It was such a bring down really. If we were going to go off the air I wanted to go off in a blaze of glory. It wasn't the way I wanted the thing to end, after putting so much into it. When I found out the reasons that really annoyed me. The money had been made. That Raymond Lefevre LP I did the promotional ad for was in the Top Ten. That did it as far as I was concerned. Not only had the listeners been done over but so had we.

(Johnnie Walker)[17]

CHAPTER 7

British Broadcasting Incorporation

'We'll gather lilacs'

> SIR R. THOMSON: Will the Right Honourable gentleman firmly resist all pressure from vested interests to deprive the British public of a very good and amusing programme? Would he regard it [the pirates] as a spur to 'gee up' the BBC to provide something like it?
>
> MR BENN: No sir, I shall not keep that particular consideration in mind.[1]

One thought that something would have to happen eventually. There would have to be some sort of legislation of commercial radio. But I didn't suspect the government would, as they did, say that the pirates would have to be closed down by legal methods and the BBC would be instructed to provide an alternative service. But I think most of the people on the popular side at the time saw it as a very good opportunity for us to make a mark and show that we could do it given anything like the resources the pirates had.

(Teddy Warrick)[2]

The Labour administration of 1964–70 steadfastly refused to acknowledge the direct link between the closing down of the pirate stations and the opening of the BBC's first ever pop music network. The BBC's own policy document *Local radio in the public interest*, issued in February 1966, was solely concerned with extending the public service principle to the local sector.

Not until 12 December 1966, when the government white paper on the future of broadcasting was published, was it suggested that the BBC would be obliged to provide a continuous pop music programme. On 30 June 1967 Edward Short announced to Parliament that the BBC would officially open its new pop service on 30 September. On the same day, in the debate on the Lords' Amendments to the Marine Broadcasting Bill, the Conservative MP Paul Bryan taunted the Postmaster-General about its timing: 'The Right Honourable Gentleman has doggedly continued to assert that this programme has nothing to do with the replacement, and it is by pure chance that it will come on air at about the same time as the pirates leave the scene.'[3]

On 27 July the BBC Director of Radio, Frank Gillard, unveiled sweeping changes to the entire national radio system that would kill off, in name at least, the Light, Third, and Home services. From 30 September these would be known respectively as Radios Two, Three, and Four. The new pop network, tentatively referred to in the past as Radio 247, was given a new title, Radio One. Concurrent with this the down-turn in the economic climate and the government's subsequent recessionary measures had a marked effect on BBC finances. The Corporation was not allowed to raise the licence fee, and it soon became clear that Radio One had been conceived during a period in which resources were restricted and growth severely curtailed.

Radio One was therefore the product of prolonged political indecision, followed by sudden legislative obligation, and hasty internal reorganization. With the reforms the Corporation was once again confronting a crisis of accommodation. Attempts to redefine the role of light entertainment had been evident both during and immediately after the Second World War, as well as during the early years of rock and roll. Now, as a direct result of the existence of the offshore stations, similar ethical and administrative issues were confronting the BBC. In considering the BBC's willingness to take on such obligations the following questions of interpretation and emphasis have to be considered: What overall influence did the pirates (like Luxembourg and Normandie before them) have on network reorganization? To what extent did the offshore stations hasten

Radio One's arrival? Was it actually in the BBC's interest to acknowledge the pirates' legacy, and if so which aspects would be accorded legitimacy and which aspects would be ignored or marginalized? To what extent, for instance, did the BBC desire to imitate the pirates, indeed to what extent could they actually duplicate the more freewheeling aspects of pirate programming? Was the kind of experience made available by recruiting from the pirates going to be appropriate to the BBC? To what extent would the pirates' programming initiatives be subservient to existing production values? How would concessions to Top 40 formatting be reconciled with the former 'all things to all people' legacy of the Light Programme? These issues form the basis of this concluding chapter.

Radio One's initial mandate did not extend beyond providing a popular music service. It was not clear what kind of popular music service the new network was going to carry. At the planning stage there was little sense of cohesion or corporate unity and no generally agreed purpose other than the vague brief from the government. Production staff simply wanted to get on with the job of providing the best programmes possible with the best resources possible and were in no doubt as to the role the pirates had played in initiating the new situation.

> I was grateful to the pirates, not commending them for breaking the law, but for doing something which had to be done, because the status quo wasn't going to change . . . I suspect that if the pirates had not come along and done what they did we would not have developed anything like as well as we did.
>
> (Tim Blackmore)[4]

When asked on the Home Service in January 1967 'if the pirates had aroused some unsatisfied need in the public', Donald McLean of the BBC's Popular Music Department replied, 'Unequivocally, I think, yes they have'. His initial affirmation was qualified by a cautious assessment of the wider context:

> Not a particularly hard thing to do if you consider the circumstances, that we have a limited number of wavelengths

and limited resources, or prescribed resources, and an awful lot of needs to cater for. *One could choose any of the kinds of product that the BBC broadcasts, which has a large and wide appeal,* and pinch other people's wavelengths, other people's copyright, and so on and you would certainly build a need for that product.

(emphasis mine)[5]

The populist image created by the press was of 'Auntie BBC adjusting her hemline', and the Light Programme 'letting its hair down'. Yet McLean spoke the familiar language of administrative reform. Phrases like 'better use of resources', 'redeploying finance', 'optimum ways of utilizing resources', 'juggling with wavelengths', dominated his account, and clearly indicated that an increase in pop music provision was not the only option open to the BBC. In this he echoed the preferences expressed by the Postmaster-General during the second reading of the Marine Offences Bill.

My colleagues and I are in no doubt that there is a wide demand for continuous light music and that it would be right to meet this demand. If there is a demand of this kind I think it should be met. I do not think it is a demand for non-stop pop. Clearly the housewife who is at home during the day – and some still are – like to hear something like 'We'll gather lilacs' and that sort of nostalgic music.[6]

Like Radio London before it the BBC constructed a notion of institutional prestige and responsibility by playing down the importance of teenage appeal. Financial stringency and a consideration of the type of audiences to be served were reflected in the eventual publication of Radio One's initial schedules. These indicated that the new network, far from being a separate entity with its own distinct image, was in fact going to simulcast with Radio Two for much of the day. From 7.30 p.m. to 10.00 p.m. Radio One would effectively close down, relaying only Radio Two's evening output of familiar Light Programme fare, thus ignoring the teenage audience. It was also announced that Radio One would have an allocation of only 'around' seven hours of needle-time per day, so clearly non-stop pop records were out of the question.

Recruitment

> The BBC at the time obviously was, some people would say still is, a stuffy organization, and would find it difficult to come to terms with replacing pirate radio stations so it did need a man who was prepared to fight in the BBC corridors of power for what he thought was right. Robin Scott was the man put in charge and he was largely responsible for the choice of DJs. It would be discussed with people like myself and Johnny Beerling and we would be asked what we thought of various people.
>
> (Teddy Warrick)[7]

Teddy Warrick was later assigned the position of programme organizer at Radio One but initially both he and Johnny Beerling were producers in the gramophone department. Robin Scott was Radio One's first Controller. Given the choice between hiring disc jockeys from Radio Caroline, a station which had chosen to continue broadcasting in defiance of the Marine Offences Act, and Radio London, a successful commercial outfit, run by men with a proven track record in industry and commerce, the BBC took the less controversial option.

> I remember having a conversation with Tony Blackburn when he was on shore leave from Radio London. We met at a record company reception and I asked what plans he had for the eventual close-down of the pirates. He said he had no plans and was proposing to see it out with Big L. I said – as a piece of personal advice – 'if you think they will be able to survive after the MOA comes in you may find you'll miss the boat. We are making plans for what will start in September, and if you're saying you don't wish to be part of those plans then I think you are making a mistake, because I would say it's quite likely you will be one of the people we would consider employing.'
>
> (Teddy Warrick)[8]

Radio London disc jockeys were actively sought out by senior producers. Discreet visits were even made to the Radio London ship during the period when Radio One programme policy was still being formulated. Those already integrated into the career structure of the showbusiness mainstream, such as disc jockeys whose affairs were managed by an agent, were particularly well placed. The Harold Davidson agency, for instance, had the ex-Radio London disc jockeys Tony Blackburn, Kenny Everett, Dave Cash, and Ed Stewart on its books. When the first line-up of Radio One disc jockeys was announced on 4 September 1967, 11 of the 17 ex-pirates recruited came from Radio London. Of those 11, Chris Denning, Keith Skues, Kenny Everett, Tony Blackburn, Duncan Johnson, Pete Brady, and Dave Cash, had already broadcast on the Light Programme prior to the announcement. Among a second batch of recruits, Mike Lennox, John Peel, Pete Drummond, and Ed Stewart had all belonged to the team which had closed down Radio London on 14 August.

Radio Caroline was represented by just four names: Simon Dee, Rosko, Rick Dane, and Mike Ahern. Simon Dee had been an ex-pirate for two and a half years by the time Radio One opened. Having been the first offshore announcer to 'go legit' Dee had joined the 'big four' DJ monopoly of David Jacobs, Alan Freeman, Pete Murray, and Jimmy Savile, and hardly fitted the swashbuckling image. Rosko had only spent a short period with Radio Caroline and was better known for his work with French Radio Luxembourg. He continued to present his programmes from Paris once he had joined Radio One. Mike Ahern and Rick Dane, despite having been very popular presenters on Caroline, were woefully miscast in Radio One's schedules. Both lasted only a short time, in Ahern's case, precisely one programme, despite having been voted the third most popular DJ in Britain in a *News of the World* poll carried out on the eve of Radio One's opening.

In the initial Radio One line-up of 33 presenters only two other disc jockeys were hired from offshore radio. Stuart Henry, regarded by BBC management as the only potential talent to emerge from Radio Scotland, had an Equity card, and an agent, Bunny Lewis, who also looked after Simon Dee's interests. Mike Raven, formerly of Radios Atlanta, KING, and 390 had, like

Henry, been out of the pirate business for over a year, and had a successful rhythm and blues show on Radio Luxembourg. BBC recruiters recognized his authoritative knowledge of a specialist area and hired him as 'an expert in the field'. The remaining pirates were ignored in the first roster of Radio One DJs.

No one involved in offshore radio management was taken on by the BBC. After the pirates closed down Ted Allbeury and Philip Birch went briefly into radio consultancy, and made programmes for the North American market. The Radio London programme manager, Alan Keen, continued in music publishing before joining Radio Luxembourg as General Manager in 1970. Birch became prominent again in commercial radio when the first ILR stations were licensed in 1973. Having built up and maintained Radio London as a consistent market leader for three and a half years, Birch and Keen suddenly found there would be no place for them under the new regime. However, the BBC did retain London's image of professionalism. The popular press began referring to 'Wonderful Radio One', and 'Radio Wonderful', and the new network even began to use station identification jingles from the same PAMS series introduced to British listeners by Radio London. The call sign 'Wonderful Radio One' was substituted for 'KLIF Dallas', and the BBC package matched its American equivalent word for word, harmony for harmony. When the first schedules were announced it became clear that several of the key daytime and weekend slots were to be occupied by ex-London staff. The station's primary purpose had been to bring commercial radio to Britain, and being legitimized by a public broadcasting monopoly was a convenient, albeit slightly ironic way of moving nearer to this objective. As subsequent events showed Radio One provided a convenient half-way house for those who were prepared to wait another political term for independent local commercial radio to come about.

Pirate recruitment overshadowed the extent to which the BBC was prepared to retain established broadcasters. Former Light Programme and Luxembourg staff such as Jimmy Young, Keith Fordyce, Jack Jackson, Don Moss, and Alan Freeman were hired to work alongside the ex-pirates; the decision to allocate the prime morning show to Jimmy Young was controversial. There was also considerable horizontal movement and several announcers were brought in from the World and Overseas Services to host evening and late night shows. Some of those chosen to present programmes on Radio Two, such as Pete Murray, and the former *Much Binding in the Marsh* star Sam Costa were publicly hostile to the aims of their pop competitor. Equally significant was the policy adopted towards the recruitment of production staff.

From having an occasional pop music programme they suddenly needed 12 or 14 new producers. As far as I remember, almost all of them except me were in-house appointments. I think this was a mistake and it set the seeds for a lot of the problems and the attitude towards Radio One that subsequently developed, because all they took on was the people they knew, namely young guys who were good engineers, and people who had worked a lot with Ted Heath and his boys and the Acker Bilk band ... instead of saying, 'Actually you're the kind of guys we don't want – we want to get something like the pirates, something that's totally separate. This has got to be a new view of radio.' Instead of that it just became the Light Programme part two, in the sense that a lot of the guys who had been working with Light Programme for years doing 'Marching and Waltzing' and the NDO were still there.

(John Walters)[9]

Despite being the only external appointment on the production side, Walters himself was typical of a certain type of creative talent which could be accommodated within the BBC. At the time of his recruitment he had a Top Ten record, a successful musical career playing trumpet with the Alan Price Set, and was clearly regarded by his employers as someone with an insider's understanding of the pop scene. Several of the Corporation's existing production staff, many of whom were to play an integral role in shaping the new pop channel, had similar musical backgrounds. Bill Bebb and Roger Eames, for example, had both been jazz musicians. Bev Phillips and Paul Williams were former music teachers. Backgrounds in jazz, the RAF, and variety seemed to be common denominators. Ron Belchier and Ted Beston had worked in variety and light entertainment, Belchier on *The Goon Show* and *Beyond our Ken*, Beston on *Round the Horne*. The senior producer Derek Chinnery had come straight from school in 1941, and after spending his National Service as a trainee pilot in Rhodesia immediately rejoined the BBC. Bryant Marriot's background was public school, Oxford, and the Suffolk Regiment, where he was a Second Lieutenant. For the BBC Light Entertainment department he had produced jazz shows, and documentaries for both the Light and Third Programmes. Johnny Beerling had come from Forces Radio, Stuart Grundy from BFN and Luxembourg. The ex-Radio 390 man Peter James was the sole production recruit from the pirates.

Radio One also recruited the producers Bernie Andrews and Aiden Day who were used to working at the 'sharp end' of station output. Tim Blackmore, Malcolm Brown, and Jeff Griffin had all joined the BBC in the early 1960s and represented the first generation of recruits who were able to nurture their empathy with pop music, rather than develop an inherent institutional animosity towards it. Griffin was yet another blues and jazz fan who had produced specials for the Third Programme. These were the kind of producers with known innovative track records who in theory were hired to enhance rather than counteract the natural unorthodoxy and iconoclasm of the DJs they worked with.

The curriculum vitae of Radio One's first Programme Controller Robin Scott read 'Bryanston, the Sorbonne, Jesus College, Cambridge', 'distinction in the field' with the BBC French Service in 1942, the first postwar jazz programmes on the BBC, commentaries on state visits, funerals, and coronations, Eurovision television, and BBC 2's *Jazz 625*. Perhaps less incongruously than it seemed at the time, he also devised the Eurovision inter-regional game show *It's a Knockout*. Adopting a high media profile in the run-up to the launch of Radio One, Scott came across as both genial and persuasive, with little of the traditional Corporation defensiveness or stuffiness of earlier years. He was frank about the BBC's previous failings and about the limitations imposed upon the new network but was confident in pre-launch interviews, promising self-op DJs, over seven hours of needle-time, and considerable exposure for new groups and artists.

Despite this optimism there were still formidable obstacles to overcome. The disc jockey David Symonds reflects on Radio One's initial problems:

> I don't think Radio One ever had a pirate image. I think if anything it's been unable to shake off the establishment image. But as far as music goes it's more fundamental than that because the processes of the establishment don't let them get close enough to the street. I'm sure those people were terrific when they were producing *Worker's Playtime* and *Variety Bandbox*, and then overnight somebody said, 'You are now a Radio One producer', and they didn't know where to begin ... If you look at the staff structure of the BBC it's like the Civil Service. You get some guy who's on the books, it's a pensionable position, he's there till he's 60, and then there's a change, either dictated by a trend, or internal reorganization or whatever. So an administrator who is in the business of putting names against assignments takes this 50-year-old person and says, 'You are now a Radio One producer'. I mean Jesus, what do they do? They buy the *NME* and *Melody Maker* I guess, and they see what's selling, and you end up with this very tame programming.
>
> (David Symonds)[10]

Wonderful Radio One

After a largely favourable media buildup, aided by considerable self-promotion by the BBC, Radio One began broadcasting on Saturday 30 September at 7.00 a.m. Initial programming was a patchwork of the innovative, the familiar, and the incongruous.

The Tony Blackburn Show   (7.00–8.30 a.m., Mondays to Saturdays)

I took the play-list idea one step further and created a format for the breakfast show. We worked on what was an adaptation of the original Radio London format, which was in turn pinched from the standard American format. Nobody ever spotted it. I say nobody – actually one guy in the music business said to me, 'Every half hour of your programme is the same isn't it?' He was the only person in two and a half years who recognized that every half hour in that show was identical.

(Tim Blackmore)[11]

Radio One programmes commenced each day with pirate radio's most popular presenter continuing to promote his cheery pirate persona with wisecracks, inane quips, and Tamla Motown. Blackburn managed to epitomize the BBC's new style while simultaneously promoting the values of commercial radio. The breakfast show was the flagship for the new network, with an audience reach of 13 per cent of listeners, or six to seven million people, in the late 1960s. What those listeners were getting, complete with authentic jingles, was a blend of Radio London and KLIF Dallas minus the advertisements. The competitions and promotions were also largely the product of American commercial radio. Blackburn's 'tie-swap' promotion (a chance for listeners to exchange one awful tie for a similar one from a complete stranger) had first been aired on WINS New York – in 1957!

Junior Choice   (8.30–10.00 a.m., Saturdays and Sundays)

The revamped *Children's Favourites* was hosted by the *Crackerjack* presenter Leslie Crowther to ensure that the Uncle Mac legacy wasn't entirely forgotten, but the approach now tended very definitely towards 'Yippee kids!' rather than 'Settle down, children'. Nellie the Elephant and Paddy McGinty's goat learned to co-exist with Gerry Anderson's Thunderbirds and Batman.

Saturday Club   (10.00 a.m.–midday, Saturdays)

The show Radio One chiefs said would never be axed, *Saturday Club* survived in its new incarnation for a matter of months.

While maintaining the policy of using BBC house bands to perform cover versions of the hits of the day, the show continued to break new ground and ensured exposure for new and unknown acts.

Midday Spin   (midday–1.00 p.m., Mondays to Saturdays)

Described in the *Radio Times* as a 'programme of gramophone records', it was hosted by various DJs during the week. The show became a separate entity at weekends and was presented by Michael Pasternak, son of the American film producer Joe Pasternak, and better known to his audience as Emperor Rosko. Apart from being known to those who had heard him during his brief spell with Radio Caroline, Rosko was new to English listeners. He already had an international reputation as 'Le President Rosko', who presented syndicated shows for Barclay Records in France, broadcast nightly on RTF Europe One, Radio Monte Carlo, Radio Benelux, and on the pop services of Spanish and Italian radio. Rosko gained considerable press attention with his extrovert image and frenetic radio style. In fact this style (and indeed the title) was a highly derivative amalgam of KYA San Francisco's Emperor Hudson, the original KBLA Los Angeles Rosko, and the verbal repertoire of legendary night-time presenter Wolfman Jack. On the BBC Rosko championed what he called 'rock and soul music', an innovative subcultural fusion of west coast rock, and Stax and Atlantic Memphis soul, but his first programme on Radio One was memorable for an incident which has entered pop radio folklore. Halfway through the cacophony of bells, whistles, shouts, and psychedelic soul, listeners heard the impeccable clipped tones of a BBC announcer commence the 12.30 bulletin with a slow and deliberate 'And now the news – in English'. DJ patter continued to be brought back to earth every hour on the half hour by Received Pronounciation.

Midday Spin, one of only two all-disc programmes in the weekday schedules, (the other being the *Tony Blackburn Show*) showed Radio One's formative programming policy at its most schismatic. Having a different presenter and production team each day meant there was little musical cohesion. Simon Dee played material from the classier end of quality pop (Scott

Walker, Jack Jones, Barbara Streisand) while the following day Stuart Henry might promote the discothèque sound of the Four Tops or Otis Redding. The programme continually veered from mainstream pop to experimental rock depending on the host.

The Jack Jackson Show   (1.00–2.00 p.m., Saturdays)

Referred to by the popular press as 'the 61-year-old self-styled grandaddy of them all', Jackson had been a top bandleader and trumpet player. In the early 1960s he had retired to Tenerife for tax reasons but continued to tape programmes for the BBC. His approach, novel at the time, was to blend music and comedy extracts. Jackson's show, a mixture of big band, light orchestral music, and novelty items, was more suited in tone and temperament to Radio Two (as, arguably, was 50 per cent of Radio One's initial output).

Where It's At   (2.00–3.00 p.m., Saturdays)

One of three magazine programmes for the weekend schedules of news, reviews, and new releases, *Where It's At*, hosted by Chris Denning, had begun life on the Light Programme. It was the programme in which, in May 1967, Kenny Everett interviewed the Beatles for a Sgt. Pepper special in May 1967. From innovative origins *Where It's At* rapidly became a hostage to trendiness and was soon replaced in the schedules. The show revealed what was to become a familiar stylistic trapping on Radio One, a contrived pacey approach with a host desperately trying to sound 'with it' (broadly synonymous with shouting a lot). In the words of one reviewer, the show 'sounded decidedly without it'.

The Best of Newly Pressed   (3.00–4.00 p.m., Saturdays)

Presented by Pete Murray (who had already expressed dismissive views of the new station), the programme, later retitled *What's New*, had previously been the daily late-afternoon new

238

releases show on the Light Programme. New record releases were exempt from the existing needle-time ruling and *What's New* owed its continuation almost entirely to Radio One's limited needle-time quota. More by accident than design this became a genuinely innovative area of programming, subject to the whims of its varied rota of presenters and producers. Qualitative considerations were overridden by quantitive ones to the point where it scarcely mattered whether there were 30 new releases in any one week or 90. During slack periods for new product (for example, the height of summer or the weeks either side of Christmas) it was not unusual for programmes to be padded out with 'B' sides and LP tracks. This emphasis on bureaucratic rather than cultural criteria led to some interesting juxtapositions. In the late 1960s, for instance, it was not uncommon to hear experimental underground groups like Tyrannosaurus Rex and the Nice gaining exposure alongside the new Cliff Richard or Tom Jones single at peak late afternoon listening time.

Pete Brady (4.00–5.00 p.m., Saturdays, 2.00–4.00 p.m., weekdays)

One of the station's early pivotal figures, the ex-Radio London DJ Brady, presented both the peak-time weekday afternoon show and the Saturday show. But the practice of continuing the weekday strip shows into the weekend schedules with the same presenter was dropped within a few months. The Saturday slot became a blatant administrative dumping ground where 'the best of the weekday sessions' were repeated. Radio One listeners could tune in, turn on, and drop off to sleep to the likes of the Bert Weedon Quartet, Stan Reynolds and his Music, and Spencer's Washboard Kings.

Country Meets Folk (5.30–6.30 p.m., Saturdays)

Presented by Wally Whyton, *Country Meets Folk* honoured the BBC's continued obligation to specialist programming. It was informed and uncontrived, and swiftly despatched to a later evening slot.

Scene and Heard   (6.30–7.30 p.m., Saturdays)

The last item on the Radio One schedule before it amalgamated with Radio Two's output for the rest of the evening (unkind critics suggested it had hardly been separated all day), *Scene and Heard* was another topical magazine programme. Burdened by the same pacey style and forced delivery as *Where It's At* the programme's individual components were put together with stop-watch precision. Heavily scripted down to the last ad lib and adopting what John Walters described as a 'colour me' approach to scheduling, its format was rigidly adhered to. In the same way that *What's New* was guided by quantitive criteria, a series of vacant slots had to be filled irrespective of what was available to fill them. There had to be an LP of the week, for example, regardless of whether the production team thought there had been ten great LPs released that week or none.

Initially the BBC didn't know how to present intelligent pop programming that was neither pompous nor patronizing, which led to some very stilted early shows. Despite this *Scene and Heard* evolved into an informative critical mouthpiece for a rapidly changing pop scene, in a sense an audio adjunct to *Melody Maker*, similarly analytical in tone, adopting a forthright editorial stance and treating its subject matter seriously without being over-reverential.

For the remainder of a Saturday night listeners could hear *Caterina Valente Sings*, *Pete's People* (Pete Murray, with studio sessions from Manfred Mann and Geno Washington, and live performances relayed from the Grosvenor House Hotel by Cleo Laine, Acker Bilk, and the Royal Philharmonic Orchestra), and *Night Ride* (more film sound-tracks and light orchestral sessions in what was later to become another genuinely innovative area of programming – thanks to the initiatives of various individual producers). Pete Murray later claimed that his show, retained from the Light Programme, was intended to be transformed by Radio One into a more radical mix of modern groups and sessions.[12] Murray and his producer resisted this and the show soon reverted to its original Light Programme brief, illustrating the extent to which autonomy was negotiable at the outset of Radio One.

On Sundays scheduling juxtapositions were equally pronounced. The bulk of the morning output was familiar Light
Programme fare such as *Children's Favourites, Easybeat,* and
Two Way Family Favourites (or *Junior Choice, Happening Sunday,*
and *World Wide Family Favourites,* as they were now respectively known). In the afternoon these gave way to specialist
shows such as *Top Gear* (initially just another magazine programme), *Pick of the Pops* (expanded to two hours to cover more
new releases), and Mike Raven's rhythm and blues show (an
invaluable outlet for authentic blues and soul, but recognizably
Reithian in its scholarly style of presentation). The rest of
the evening was simulcast on Radio Two and taken up with
Humphrey Lyttleton's comparatively radical *Jazz Scene,* and the
indisputably mainstream David Jacobs's show, featuring in its
first airing the Radio Orchestra, the Mike Sammes Singers, and
interviews with Julie Andrews, Clement Freud, Twiggy, and
Donald Pleasance.

Weekday transmissions began with Radio One relaying Radio
Two's *Breakfast Special,* a light music programme hosted by Paul
Hollingdale (who as a presenter with the short-lived CNBC in
1962 could claim to have been the first British pirate disc
jockey). After the Tony Blackburn show the pop network linked
up again with Radio Two for the revamped *Housewives' Choice,*
now known as *Family Choice.* On what was ostensibly a pop
music channel listeners were invited to sit down each morning
with Joe 'Piano' Henderson, Geoffrey 'Top of the Form' Wheeler,
or Sam 'Much Binding in the Marsh' Costa, for an hour of
what the *Radio Times* called 'toe-tapping morning melodies'. At
10.00 a.m., still simulcasting with Radio Two, came *The Jimmy
Young Show,* one of Radio One's more controversial scheduling
choices. Young had gained most of his experience on Radio
Luxembourg, after enjoying some success as a singer in the
1950s. On Radio One he continued to serenade from a daily
selection of needle-time free favourites, interspersed between
reading recipes for housewives and introducing regular sessions from resident outfits such as the Acker Bilk and Terry
Lightfoot trad bands.

Media response to Radio One's initial programming was
mixed. On the whole the popular press gushed uncritically,
while the quality papers talked of 'sycophantic celebrations of

young men whose talent lies in peddling adolescent dreams'.[13] The more astute commentators picked up on the contrived paciness of most programmes, the unforeseen extent to which Radios One and Two were broadcasting the same material, the constant rotation of chart records, and the preponderance of nervous DJs trying to establish themselves within the confines of six-week contracts. 'Modernity' was stressed with 'snappy' show titles such as *Happening Sunday* and *Where It's At*; it was recognizably the same network that had offered younger listeners programmes titled *Get with it* and *On the Scene* back in the 'youth club of the airwaves' days of Light Programme pop provision. The exaggerated extent to which Radio One screamed '*This is the place*' was undermined by what the *News of the World* critic Weston Taylor called 'ridiculous plugs for square programmes'[14] by Light Programme stalwarts such as Max Jaffa and Sandy McPherson. Other devices, the playing of station identification jingles for example, appeared ironic given the BBC's renewed monopoly function. The claim 'we play more music than any other station', in particular, had a slightly hollow ring to it now that the 'other stations' had been outlawed.

It was all go at Auntie's first freakout. The solemnity with which the conventions evolved by the pirates have been plagiarised is almost Germanic in its thoroughness . . . and yet somehow the effect is of a waxwork, absolutely lifelike but clearly lifeless.

(George Melly)[15]

'First get your anchor band'

I remember saying to a senior producer that I'd be doing the new afternoon programme, and she said, 'First get your anchor band. Book your anchor band.' Which simply meant, get your Johnny Howard, or your Johnny Arthey and his boys – they were all called Johnny. And it was the *same* band. The same ten guys in either band. They were the session musicians who answered the phone and who practically lived at the BBC.

(John Walters)[16]

A letter appeared, I think in *Melody Maker*, that read some-thing like 'The Harry Stoneham Trio? The Joe Loss Orchestra? Ray McVay and his Button Down Brass? Who says Radio One doesn't cater for minorities?' And that letter was typical of a lot of the criticism we were getting at the time. Having come from a situation where the listeners were able to receive non-stop pop records 24 hours a day they had had to put up with a situation where quite seriously they would perhaps on a Friday lunch-time hear the Joe Loss orchestra doing their version of 'Have you seen your mother baby standing in the shadows?'

(Tim Blackmore)[17]

In 1967 the BBC still had separate departments for live music (the popular music department) and recorded music (the gramo-phone department). The values upon which these were founded (authenticity versus mechanical reproduction) remained en-shrined within BBC policy at the start of Radio One. The continued use of live musicians was necessitated partly by restrictive needle-time agreements and gave an audible indi-cation of the extent to which Radio One was obliged to retain the Light Programme's work practices. The decision to con-tinue live lunch-time shows meant that each day listeners could hear an entire programme of BBC house bands play-ing their versions of the hit parade. The legacy of *Workers' Playtime*, *Go Man Go*, and *Parade of the Pops*, lived on in such shows as *Monday Monday*, *Pop North*, *The Joe Loss Show*, and *Pop Inn*, which were all retained from the Light Pro-gramme schedules. *Pop North* announced itself with theme music more appropriate to encouraging the listener to subscribe to a course of twisting lessons. During its first Radio One airing on 2 October 1967 *Monday Monday* featured exactly the same line-up of session bands and singers as it had the previous week on the Light Programme, while *The Pete Brady Show*, the prime afternoon slot, featured a session from the Edmundo Ros Orchestra.

This continued dependence upon session bands hindered those working for Radio One who wanted to create a plausible successor to the pirates. The revivalist sound of trad bands and house orchestras – Terry Lightfoot, Alex Welsh, George

Chisholm, Bernard Herman and the NDO etc. – dominated those early peak-time strip shows. Outfits normally used to performing 'evergreens', 'standards', and 'jaunty toe-tappers in the modern idiom', were hired at scale rates from a permanent pool of available musicians to interpret the latest hit by everyone from the Jimi Hendrix Experience to Petula Clark. Sheet music was still common currency and these workmanlike versions of Top 20 tunes epitomized the cultural and administrative shortcomings of the BBC's pop network. The Corporation was anchored to the past.

> You suddenly got a show and you were *the* anchor band. In other words when Jimmy Young came on Johnny Arthey and his boys would do three or four numbers, perhaps the latest hit from the Supremes or whoever. Peel claims to have heard Bernard Herman and the NDO do 'Purple Haze', and I've no reason to disbelieve him because the band looked down the charts at the new entries. They'd then get the sheet music which would exist somewhere, because in those days everything was published and the sheet music would be whizzed off to some arranger who would actually write it out for brass.
>
> (John Walters)[18]

By the time Radio One began broadcasting in 1967 studio technology had become more sophisticated, as had many of the musicians and producers exploring its uses. A 'Good vibrations' or a 'Strawberry fields forever' could not necessarily be reproduced by a session band – although many tried. All bands who performed live on the radio were required to be members of the Musicians' Union; this contractual obligation gave endless potential for experimentation, and certainly the more adventurous producers began to use more new groups to fill their quota of sessions, indicating that interpretation of the hits didn't necessarily have to be the domain of Joe Loss or the Northern Dance Orchestra. It was not live music *per se* that was problematic, it was the particular way in which the BBC chose to interpret what was required.

They could have had who they liked. The Musicians' Union weren't counting. It was the bums on seats agreement. They just wanted a certain number of musicians to be employed. It was that tradition. Obviously you didn't get orchestras on the pirates but you got them on the BBC. Nobody wanted them except the musicians. The Peel show largely changed all that, in that the live music wasn't simply a substitute for records.

(John Walters)[19]

Despite its vague production brief Peel's *Top Gear* was to make innovative use of live sessions. Initially the Sunday afternoon show had dual presentation. The anchor DJ position was allocated to Pete Drummond, who was to be joined each week by a guest announcer. The rota included John Peel, Tommy Vance, Rick Dane, and Mike Ahern.

There were five of us on *Top Gear* competing in theory for two positions as regular presenters. They thought that no single person could handle a three-hour pop programme and it was seen as a great feat to be able to produce a show of this length. The people who were responsible for programming were trying to create something out of nothing really and they had no idea of what it was I wanted to do or had been doing. The original brief of the programme was something along the lines of 'looking over the horizons of pop', which as they understood it, meant going to the London Palladium to interview Lulu about her forthcoming LP. In fact we had a session from Lulu on the first programme. But the original producer Bernie Andrews liked the idea of new music, and he really stuck his neck out and did a kind of three card trick with the BBC and gave them the impression that something else was what they were going to get. They just expected a straight pop magazine programme.

(John Peel)[20]

If *Top Gear* had adhered to its original 'looking over the horizons of pop' brief then the DJs Mike Ahern and Rick Dane would have made ideal presenters. Ahern was a former morning show host on Radio Caroline and some argued that

245

he should have been given the weekday slot allotted to Jimmy Young. He would have relished the opportunity to talk to Lulu at the Palladium. Dane had done similar mainstream work with Radio Caroline, interviewing film and theatre stars. But *Top Gear* quickly became a showcase for the underground and both presenters found themselves in an alien environment and were dropped after one show each. Pete Drummond was also dropped after the first rota of dual presentation, and for the next three months John Peel and Tommy Vance co-hosted the show. It was an uneasy alliance, with the two presenters nervously swapping quips and anecdotes and the almost audible sound of non-renewable contracts being rustled in the background. Peel eventually shook off the stylistic trappings of the show and made the slot indisputably his own.

Once rid of its dual presentation and showbusiness ethos, *Top Gear* rapidly became a focal point for esoteric and experimental music. Peel continued to explore the territory opened up by *The Perfumed Garden* on Radio London, although *Top Gear* was probably less of a bulletin board for underground causes and was curbed of its former freeform indulgence. It relied more on drawing listeners' attention to music not receiving exposure elsewhere. During its first two to three years *Top Gear*'s output read like a who's who of rock's avant garde.

If Peel provided a weekly inventory of rock's radical fringe, David Symonds's weekday programme was an equally exploratory piece of scheduling. His show, (from 5.30 to 7.30 p.m., Mondays to Fridays) also broke from the tradition which equated live performance with duplicating recorded performance. Symonds gained his initial broadcasting experience in commercial radio in New Zealand and brought many of its production values with him when he joined the BBC in 1965. He introduced the first jingles ever played on the Light Programme, and working on the Sunday morning *Easybeat* in early 1967 with the producer Ron Belchier he altered the show's established format, replacing a live audience with an all studio presentation. Belchier became the senior producer to *The David Symonds' Show* on Radio One. The production team also included Keith Bateson, who had been responsible for introducing ex-pirates such as Tony Blackburn, Dave Cash, and Ed Stewart to the Light Programme, prior to Radio One going on air; and Jeff Griffin, who frequently deputized as *Top Gear* producer when Bernie Andrews was on leave, and others similarly inclined towards the 'sharp end' of station output like Malcolm Brown, Bev Phillips, and John Walters. As well as promoting the well-known exponents of psychedelia and west coast rock Symonds's programme also regularly aired the less acknowledged undercurrent of English 'paisley pop'. During its first year Symonds's show featured the first live radio performances of groups such as Grapefruit, Honeybus, Orange Bicycle, the Equals, Love Affair, and Kaleidoscope, a band later to be managed by Symonds. He also developed a close working relationship with the Moody Blues, and appeared as a narrator on their 'Threshold of a Dream' LP. Like John Peel, Symonds had an empathy with many of his musician colleagues which went beyond merely endorsing their product as a public relations man. His show illustrated what could be done with peak-time mainstream obligations, given a sympathetic team, and creative production values.

> There was always a compromise area. Our needle-time quota was something like 40 per cent but the majority had to come from sessions. So we would talk about it. We all listened. We all went to clubs, we tried to make it our business to know what was going on. And so sessions were a challenge. If you have to lay off so much of the music in a non needle-time area the challenge when you're doing that is not to find someone who can cover a current hit adequately but to think of non-needle-time music as alternative programming.
>
> (David Symonds)[21]

During the early days of the new network alternatives were still being defined. A gradual process of demarcation was slowly beginning to manifest itself in Radio One programming, reflecting wider demarcations in pop music and popular culture generally, and giving rise to occasional contradictions. Leading agencies at the time still devised package tours of seemingly uncomplementary groups. In 1967 audiences could still see the Jimi Hendrix Experience, the Walker Brothers, Cat Stevens, and Engelbert Humperdinck on the same bill at their local Odeon or ABC. In its recruitment of live acts *Saturday Club* continued to reflect similar thinking right up until it was axed. Ken Dodd was still as likely to appear on *Saturday Club* alongside the Troggs as he was on the Jimmy Young show. The Spencer David Group, in its brief post-Stevie-Winwood-psychedelic incarnation, was equally as likely to get an airing on the *Pete Brady Show* alongside Edmundo Ros, as on Symonds's programme. The lunch-time pop audience was still liable to be treated to the glory that was Ray McVay and his Button Down Brass performing an abridged rendition of 'Mac Arthur Park'. By the end of the 1960s the BBC dance orchestras and revivalist trad bands were slowly being phased out or moved to Radio Two along with some of the DJs less suited to pop presentation. But change only came gradually and a new regime of more pop-oriented session outfits ensured that 'anchor bands' continued to dominate the schedules.

Misfits (production values and the politics of assimilation)

> The tradition in the pre-Radio One days was; a studio would be booked. The presenter would sit at a table with a microphone and a script and his own stop-watch. There would be a producer and his secretary, both of whom had stop-watches going, timing down to the exact minute and second, making sure things went in and out as on the script. Nothing would be left to chance. Nothing was ever dropped or changed unless of course you ran out of time. Then the producer would say, 'Drop the Herman's Hermits' or whatever, and move straight on. There was also someone in the background playing the records, someone else playing the tapes. There seemed to be all these people waiting for hand cues or verbal cues which were worked out. You would go through the whole show all morning, 'topping and tailing', rehearsing in cues, out cues, break for lunch and then do the show live in the afternoon. There were all these instructions, all this watching the clock. One guy could have done it.
>
> (John Walters)[22]

The pirates had proved that previous broadcasting experience was not a prerequisite for running a radio station, but it now became clear what a unique working environment the offshore stations had provided. The entire output of Radios Caroline and London could be determined 24 hours a day, seven days a week, by a nucleus of no more than five or six people. This intensive small-scale method of operation was alien to the BBC's bureaucratic procedures and there was no guarantee that the atmosphere generated on a ship on the North Sea could continue to be disseminated via the administrative filter of Broadcasting House. Disc jockeys used to the cramped confines of a rusty vessel in a force nine storm were now introduced to the cavernous splendour of the Aeolian Hall, the imposing Civil Service ambience of Egton House, and the plush politeness of the Paris Theatre. Those who did try to recreate the pirate atmosphere wholesale on Radio One encountered problems.

> Most houses in England have seen 'The Laughing Cavalier' or 'The Duke of Wellington' or the 'Mona Lisa'. But they're all reprints, all copies. The original is sitting in a museum. Radio London and Caroline were the originals, but Radio One is a very bad copy. Nobody can imitate the original brush stroke, the original colour combination. Radio cannot be timed to 'we want you to be honest, happy, and ad lib – but for no more than seven seconds'. No one does this. It's impossible. But this is what they wanted at the BBC.
>
> (Mark Roman)[23]

Those who regarded working for the BBC as a natural career progression had fewer problems. Working for Radio One required a similar level of discipline, for example DJs were still salesmen, promoting their commercial wares even if they no longer used actual product commercials. The only thing Radio One seemed inclined to advertise was itself. In the clamour to condemn the BBC many disaffected disc jockeys idealized their previous situation to a ridiculous degree, but the shrewder announcers willingly complied with the new restrictions and tempered their acts accordingly. There was a tradition of self-imposed professional etiquette which worked regardless of whether its assumptions were emanating from the North Sea or Broadcasting House. What could not be assimilated so readily was the spontaneity of pirate radio's most pioneering moments. The difference was between philosophy and pragmatism, between libertarian gestures and boardroom planning, between anarchy and administration. The difference, in other words, between Radio Caroline and Radio London.

> The way that the BBC worked then was with a big staff, and you had to prepare everything well in advance. And there wasn't the energy there or the enthusiasm, there was just a lot of bureaucracy ... It was amazing how many people were involved at the BBC with the setting up of a half hour or hour show; secretaries and producers and what have you. I mean everything we had done on our own was suddenly done with all these people. Of course everybody has to justify their existence so suddenly you've got all this politics to deal with and you're not doing radio anymore, it's a whole different ballgame ... my view on Radio One was that it was a very poor substitute for the pirates and that was mainly because it was such a big bureaucracy. Naturally it couldn't have that flow and that instantaneous situation that had existed with the pirates. The fact [was] that you had to prepare your programme and all your records. It lacked the mechanism for spontaneity which was one of the powers of Radio Caroline.

> (Tom Lodge)[24]

DJs had become used to a high level of autonomy on the ships. Now every adlib was scripted, every announcement rehearsed, every action accounted for. The former exuberance of many ex-pirates turned into stilted *bonhomie* as they found their opportunities to improvise curtailed in the new environment. As Programme Director on Radio Caroline Tom Lodge had initiated some of the most genuinely spontaneous programming ever heard on offshore radio. By January 1968, as part of Radio One's second generation of recruitment, he found himself presenting a short series of one-hour shows on Monday lunch-times called 'Radio One o'Clock'.

The BBC had deliberately recruited a surfeit of disc jockeys, all on short-term contracts. The Programme Controller Robin Scott made it clear that there would be an inevitable 'sifting

out process'. Some 45 to 50 DJs, including existing Light Programme staff announcers, were initially offered six-week contracts. The standard contract had been 13-week, with renewal
often a formality. It was common procedure in the days of the
Light Programme for presenters from a constant staff pool to
rotate alternate seasons of 13 weeks each. The prospect of a
six-week contract with no guarantee of future employment
directly contributed to the nervous pace of early Radio One
transmissions. Pirate DJs who had been used to holding down
five or six hours of self-operated programming a day, now found
themselves trying to impress within the confines of one short
weekly show. At times the early programmes on Radio One
sounded like one mass audition, because effectively that is
what they were. An appraisal of Radio One in the magazine
New Society captured the pre-launch atmosphere of ex-pirates
jumping through hoops in order to impress.

> [Mike] Lennox was doing a dummy run of it on Friday,
> bouncing and swaying to the records he introduced while
> tweedy BBC traditionalists watched from a control room
> . . . a spoof phone call came from a Mr Williams who told
> Lennox, a Canadian from Radio London, that he was taking
> English people's jobs. 'There must be many people who like
> me' said Lennox blandly. 'Sticks and stones may break my
> bones but . . .' He added something about moving in the
> grooving here on Radio Wonderful. 'May I call you dear
> hearts and gentle people? I hope I'm not being too familiar,
> but I like to establish a mood between you and me' . . . [after-
> wards] Lennox stalked out of the studio, abruptly dropped
> the mid-Atlantic honey and the professional DJ manner and
> said worriedly that he thought it had gone badly.[25]

As its title ('The Phoney Revolution') denoted the *New Society*
piece conveyed a traditional Fabian Left wariness of mass
culture and commerce (DJs were described as 'quick witted,
ambitious, and cynical young men anxious, like the Snagge
and Michelmore generations, to secure themselves a decent
wage, a reasonably secure future and a little passing acclaim
by exploiting shifting public taste'), but unlike some of the less
analytical accounts published by the PR-minded popular press

the piece also acknowledged the Corporation's past 'reputation for eccentricity and iconoclasm' and the way in which this 'legacy of tolerance' would assimilate the pirates as it had done the 'fly boys' of the 1930s before them.

> Watching and hearing Lennox ... personable, thoughtful, quietly articulate, the kind of promising young man one might find in any profession, from hotel management to merchant banking – watching him in the BBC club one felt he could easily be absorbed into the BBC hierarchy.[26]

Lennox was one of those who did not outlast his first six-week contract; as if fulfilling the prophecy, he returned to Vancouver and became a stockbroker! But for those who passed the 'audition' national radio opened up new opportunities unfeasible on the pirates. Many of the early Radio One team were immediately invited to co-host *Top of the Pops* (then produced by BBC TV's Light Entertainment department) alongside the regulars, Alan Freeman, Jimmy Savile, Simon Dee, and Pete Murray. At the beginning of 1968 another short-lived marketing ploy, designed to turn pop presenters into pop stars, saw several disc jockeys releasing their own records. None sold spectacularly; their promotional prospects were hampered by the fact that they were largely individual or industry initiatives at a time when the BBC, although keen for the new pop network to establish an identity for itself, was wary of the more compromising aspects of self-promotion. Tony Blackburn was a notable exception to this, appearing regularly on Radio One's Joe Loss show as resident session singer.

Blackburn personified the new cheeky populist image actively cultivated by BBC pop radio. He enjoyed a high profile in the *Radio Times* and popular press, hosted his own television pop show, and along with other ex-Radio London colleagues, frequently appeared on BBC radio quiz programmes. On Radio Two's *Sounds Familiar*, an informal parlour game in the 'name that tune' mould Blackburn appeared with fellow ex-London DJs Keith Skues and Tony Brandon alongside the regular panelist Barry Cryer, the host Dennis Norden and other former Light Programme stalwarts. Tony Brandon could be effortlessly goaded into doing his impression of Jimmy Young, while Blackburn took regular gentle swipes at pillars of the DJ establishment such as Sam Costa. Barry Cryer, representing the old guard, obligingly played devil's advocate, mocking the new terminology of 'revived 45s' and 'blasts from the past'. There were aged variety jokes about Max Jaffa, Moira Anderson, and Sandy McPherson (acceptable lampooning targets also favoured by television performers such as Morecambe and Wise and Stanley Baxter); in the midst of all the cheery banter the DJs could be heard easing themselves into the light entertainment mainstream.

But the BBC had only a finite capacity for assimilation, and in the case of Radio One the limit of this assimilation often came arbitrarily. Some ex-pirates failed to secure a position at Radio One because they could not, or would not, adapt to the new situation. Some were ideologically opposed to being part of a monopoly broadcasting system, some resented their more successful colleagues, others were simply miscast in the schedules. Almost every member of the original Radio London team (although not its senior disc jockey or programme director) had been employed; just a handful of former Caroline DJs were among those receiving temporary contracts in the second batch of appointments towards the end of 1967. With only one exception (Dave Lee Travis) all the Caroline recruits were allocated 'sacrificial' slots on Saturday afternoons, where they were expected to select their programme material from the 'best' of the week's live sessions, on what the BBC, with characteristic modernity called its 'Saturday swingalong show'.

The BBC wanted pirate guys mainly because they wanted to buy the names. They didn't want to buy the experience . . . on Radio London you were part of a team but on Radio One you were just another guy running around for a job. They wanted the audience from the pirates but they didn't want half the guys who had built that audience.

(Mark Roman)[27]

After being dropped from *Top Gear*, Mike Ahern joined Brisbane's top commercial station, 4BC. Mark Roman also went to Australia, shortly after expressing his thoughts about

Radio One in an outspoken article in *Disc and Music Echo*. Tom Lodge returned to Ontario to work with kindred spirits, such as Buckminster Fuller and Marshall McLuhan. Others went into children's television, continuity work, advertising, public relations, and pop group management. Although job fluidity was less marked than on the pirates there was piecemeal work to be had at the BBC. Those who failed to obtain the more attractive peak-time shows could always pick up the occasional week on the rota of *Family Choice*, or reviewing the singles on *What's New*. Some found a more natural place (and pace) on Radio Two.

Working for the BBC didn't only help to integrate Radio One personalities into the wider world of showbusiness, it also consolidated processes of accommodation which paralleled those occurring in the pop music industry as a whole. This becomes more apparent when examining the ways in which Radio One coped with its rebels, the new generation of fly boys and dissenters. These rebels became the focus of new levels of conflict, signifiers of wider cultural tensions. Disc jockeys do not operate in a permanent state of compliance; as pirate radio showed, they can also operate at variance with the goals and policies of their employers. A significant minority of Radio One's original disc jockeys disregarded their initial guidelines in a similar way. A feature of Radio One's formative years was the extent to which experimentation occurred during daytime programming. Therefore Radio One's parameters of tolerance are best shown not by those working in recognizably iconoclastic territory but by assessing the contribution of those who, often unwittingly, defined what was permissible or forbidden during prime time.

Mavericks (the negotiation of policy and the limits of dissent)

I think the BBC is the most astonishingly accommodating organization anywhere in the world. It's the sort of organization that if somebody throws mud in its face it is quite happy to employ that person if he is good at his job. Kenny Everett would attack the BBC regularly but there were enough people in the organization that would recognize his ability and would want to use it, and urge for him to be returned when his name was hardly mentioned in the place. And these people won out and were re-employed, and in Everett's case re-employed again.

(Teddy Warwick)[28]

The word professionalism . . . is used in a variety of ways. Inside the BBC professionalism includes doing as you are told. Professionalism is also a way of describing the process of enforced intellectual obedience, or collective obedience, and because it is a way in which a hierarchical organization has to make the necessities of hierarchy seem the result of a collectivity it is called professionalism.[29]

Autonomy within pop music radio, negligible at the best of times, is frequently demonstrated by the indignation displayed at being denied the right to play a particular record; the conflict between individual initiatives and editorial directives is one of the ways in which pop radio's production values are clarified. Simon Dee, for example, was sacked from *Midday Spin* in January 1968 for putting principles before policy. He wanted to play Scott Walker's recording of Jacques Brel's 'Jackie', banned by the BBC because of its references to opium dens and bordellos. David Symonds confronted similar editorial restrictions on his early evening show.

I was always passionately keen on the sharp end of the spectrum but I would not like to emphasize the importance I had on the programme. Any BBC disc jockey only has limited influence. You can bring things to people's attention but you can't force their hand. Sometimes it worked, sometimes it didn't work, and sometimes there were unholy rows. But I guess there has to be a level of editorial control and that editorial control is not vested in the disc jockey. It's vested in the producer or higher up.

(David Symonds)[30]

On one occasion Symonds wanted to feature Judy Collins's 'Both Sides Now' as his single of the week. This slot (the

'Symonds diamond') had a high profile on the programme and the chosen disc was played every evening. Symonds trusted his judgement, claiming that both songwriter (Joni Mitchell) and performer had credibility as artists but he was 'advised' not to take a risk with such an unknown quantity. Even though the song is now acknowledged as a modern folk standard (indeed, classic easy listening Radio Two material) it was made clear at the time that an obscure Greenwich Village folk singer was unsuitable for early evening exposure on mainstream pop radio. Symonds decided that this was happening rather too often and clashed frequently with his producer. After a series of 'unholy rows' he was demoted, to the Sunday morning show, ironically to where he had first made an impression on the Light Programme with the revamped *Easybeat*. Again, thanks to sympathetic and creative production values, instigated by John Walters, experimentation thrived. Symonds's Sunday show immediately scooped Peel's *Top Gear* by securing the first live radio sessions by groups such as Blodwyn Pig and Thunderclap Newman, at a time when Peel and his producer Bernie Andrews had virtually established a monopoly on the hiring of progressive and underground musicians.

> We used the kind of groups that were in the clubs pulling in the kids, but weren't necessarily making popular records, like Geno Washington and Cliff Bennett. We used a lot of the new bands who were breaking at that time like Status Quo and Amen Corner. And a lot of strange things – like we even had the London cast of 'Hair' in: Marsha Hunt, Paul Nicholas, all those people just burst in and did it and it was very popular. A lot of people had seen the show, but couldn't see it on radio. It was a funny thing to do on radio, but we tried to say 'Let's do something you can't just buy on your records'. We won't just be second division records, which was already the Peel–Bernie Andrews philosophy of course, but I didn't take it from them. It was just a commonsense thing to do.
>
> (John Walters)[31]

On joining Radio One Stuart Henry's first noteworthy transgression was to display an apparently characteristic disregard for punctuality by missing both the press reception to launch the station and the much publicized posed photograph of the original DJ team on the steps of Broadcasting House. However, Henry immediately impressed the BBC hierarchy. His television debut on an otherwise lacklustre *Top of the Pops* was well received by the pop music press, and within months Henry had bridged the gulf between the underground and the mainstream pop played on daytime radio. During the first year of Radio One Henry was the only disc jockey to present both the Sunday staple *World Wide Family Favourites* and a progressive daily show. Adorned in kaftan and beads, he also had a higher profile in the first *Radio One Annual* than Tony Blackburn! Others wore their eccentricities as self-consciously as they wore their kaftans or afghans. Henry was unselfconscious, abrasive and outspoken and frequently challenged the limits of pop programming.

On his regular Saturday and Sunday morning shows Henry achieved a reputation for innovation and unpredictability. He ran a regular feature called 'She's leaving home', which acted as an information service for young runaways and anxious parents without exerting emotional pressure for reconciliation or exploiting the sentimentality and voyeurism generally latent within such human interest items. That Henry did this without sermonizing was in itself a radical departure from the norm. 'She's leaving home' acknowledged the shifting moral ground of the 1960s and Henry's approach was as much a subcultural indicator of its time, of youth seeking independence and self-discovery, as any rock song of the period.

Henry also initiated an ecology slot, advocating 'saving the whales' long before it was an accredited environmental issue. Radio One was initially cautious about introducing politics to pop music programming; illusory consensus and token outrage were permissible editorial devices, but a platform for individual campaigns, and investigative journalism to pinpoint causes were out. When Henry's ecology slot was introduced it was intended to occupy the safe middle ground of public concern guaranteed not to offend anyone. Such a brief permitted Henry to play Marvin Gaye's 'Mercy mercy me (The ecology)' after a suitably thought-provoking piece about pollution, but would not allow explicit connections to be developed. Henry, though, became impatient with such a narrow brief and the spectre of litigation began to hang over Broadcasting House.

> Stuart to me spelt trouble. He could be great fun and was very well intentioned, but you would agree to do an ecology slot with him on a Saturday morning and he would go beyond the brief that you'd worked out, so the next thing you knew you would have to be apologizing to the British Association of Detergent Manufacturers or something.
>
> (Tim Blackmore)[32]

Another DJ who demonstrated the limits of creative eccentricity at Radio One was Kenny Everett. He had produced the original promotional jingles for the new network, which were aired on the old Light Programme prior to Radio One's launch, but was not given a daily show in the original schedules. Although an integral part of the Radio One set-up from the start he was also its court jester and most persistent critic.

> it's mostly a filing system for human bodies ... really to be a good Beeb person you need to be a superb clerk, marvellous at filing, because for every programme that goes out on air, the BBC makes sure there's at least fifty volumes of type-written waddage about it filed and clerked. On Radio One there's only about fifty people who have anything to do with the actual programmes themselves. All the rest are people who write down how long the records lasted and whether the programmes got out on time. It's all run by Hitler.
>
> (Kenny Everett)[33]

Everett had first approached the Light Programme in 1964 with a home-made 'demo' recording. The BBC had recommended the pirates. The common theme of the programmes that had influenced Everett was fantasy, a love of radio for its creative and technical possibilities. He was inspired by *The Goons, Journey into Space,* and announcers such as Jack Jackson who linked records with comic sketches and sound effects. Unlike Jackson, who drew upon a recognizable British and American audio heritage (from Hancock to Stan Freberg) and just added wry and sardonic observations, most of Everett's characterizations were his own. Although they were recognizable English comic archetypes (a staid upper-class butler, an eccentric gran, etc.), they utilized pop music's growing sense of surrealism. All previous announcers of this kind were from the pre-pop era. Everett's reference points were contemporary and although often satirical in tone revealed a less dismissive notion of modernity than the stock-in-trade put-downs of the old school. His first assignment upon joining the Light Programme had been to interview the Beatles while they were making the Sgt. Pepper LP. The interview that was eventually aired was as immersed in psychedelic other-worldliness as the record itself. Everett had befriended the Beatles in 1966 while reporting on the group's USA tour for Radio London. He developed a close personal friendship with John Lennon, and was to produce and edit the 1968 and 1969 editions of the Beatles' own Christmas records, issued annually to members of their fan club.

The BBC's problem, and it was certainly perceived as such, was how to harness Everett's unpredictable approach. Initially he was unscripted, the BBC reasoning that a Kenny Everett *sans* spontaneity was not really Kenny Everett, although as a matter of scheduling convenience he was required to rehearse and time all taped inserts. During this period Everett produced some of the most imaginative pop radio ever heard in Britain, comparable in its field to Spike Milligan's intense period of creativity while solely responsible for *Goon Show* scripts in the late 1950s.

After several outspoken interviews Everett was forced to sign an agreement, promising not to criticize the BBC – an undertaking he was publicly to transgress within days, in the pages of both *Melody Maker* and the *Daily Mirror*. The BBC could shrug it off with well-honed diplomatic aplomb when Everett referred to Douglas Muggeridge (Controller of Radios One and Two from February 1969) as 'a pin-striped prune'. In a more serious outburst in *Melody Maker* Everett caused embarrassment by being outspoken about the Musicians' Union and the needle-time agreement. His eventual dismissal, though, was not due to another outspoken interview, but a seemingly innocuous on-air indiscretion which occurred on the Saturday morning of 18 July 1970.

At 10.30 the newsreader finished the summary by saying, 'the Minister of Transport's wife, Mrs Peyton has just passed her advanced driving test. More news at 11.30.' Everett said, 'Well we all know how you do that don't we? She just bunged the examiner a fiver', and off he went, punched up a jingle and into a record. And I thought to myself – being versed in the way the BBC worked – first of all the fact that Everett confused the advanced driving test with the ordinary driving test, that's just Everett, and that's a minor point – but the programme had only been on half an hour and I didn't want to start thumping the table and asking why he said it because he'd got one and a half hours still to do and he mustn't be brought down. But I strolled into the studio from the cubicle and said, 'Now Kenny, if that same news item appears at 11.30 you won't start saying anything like that again will you?' – as jovially as I could make it but still making the point. He didn't think there was anything wrong with what he had said but I knew how touchy people could get. I walked back into the cubicle and the studio manager said, 'The duty officer is on the phone for you.' The duty officer said, 'I've got the press on the phone, who wish to know did Kenny Everett make a remark about the Minister of Transport's wife, implying that she bribed a driving examiner?'

(Teddy Warrick)[34]

Despite the producer's initial refusal to confirm or deny the press allegation the press agencies soon realized they had a story. By the Saturday evening the episode was on the front pages of the London evening papers. On the Monday morning Kenny Everett was sacked. Political sensitivity about the issue had been heightened by the fact that Edward Heath's newly elected Conservative administration had just taken office with a pledge to introduce commercial radio, but there was no direct political motivation behind the sacking. It was made clear that this latest incident was the final one in a long line of intolerable burdens which Everett had placed upon the BBC. He was dismissed with a telephone call, a headmasterly 'this is going to hurt me far more than it is you' preamble, and the words 'I'm afraid the time has come for the parting of the ways, Kenny.' By commenting on the particular news item that he did, Everett had fallen foul of exactly the same values which had deemed the item to be newsworthy in the first place (passing an advanced driving test is not normally considered worthy of inclusion in news bulletins). By constantly attacking some of the BBC's most sacred cows (including the unwritten professional rule not to comment on news items) Everett had helped define the boundaries of tolerance within the BBC. It was a turning point for Radio One.

Everett was hastily replaced in the schedules by Noel Edmunds, formerly of Radio Luxembourg, and one of the first of the post-pirate generation to establish a new direction for Radio One. On his weekday show Johnnie Walker preceded a trailer for the new programme with mock funeral music, a gesture for which he was subsequently 'carpeted'. Many on the production side openly regretted that Everett's idiosyncratic gifts could not be nurtured more appropriately by the BBC. Walker himself maintained that it was short-sighted of Radio One to employ someone with Everett's unpredictable talent and then complain when he occasionally transgressed the ill-defined boundaries of proper conduct.

Having served a period of penance after his post-Marine-Offences-Act involvement with Radio Caroline, Walker was taken on by Radio One in May 1969. First he was allocated a Saturday afternoon programme, but was soon promoted to a weekday show. Here he was eased somewhat incongruously into the 9.00–10.00 a.m. slot, bridging the gap between the two figureheads of Radio One prime-time scheduling, Tony Blackburn and Jimmy Young.

I think the executive producer of those daytime programmes saw me as the cheeky milkman type image. This good looking guy who's a bit risqué sometimes, who would come round and knock at the door when the old man's gone to work and make slightly suggestive jokes for the housewives. But I think one of the problems I gave them was that I was never very comfortable doing an image.

(Johnnie Walker)[35]

261

In the late 1960s and early 1970s pop radio's demographic assumptions were still rooted in a stereotypical notion of 'the housewife'. But now Walker was expected to lay to rest the ghost of *Housewives' Choice*, mediating between Blackburn's corny wisecracks and getting the kids off to school and Young's recipes, crooning, and Acker Bilk sessions. It was customary for DJs to link their shows at the top of the hour with light-hearted banter, but there was often an audible tension in Walker's links with both Blackburn and Young.

By the end of the 1960s such oppositional tendencies were becoming more apparent within Radio One. Tribal demarcation between pop and rock was emerging and although the schism was greatly exaggerated in both marketing and cultural terms specific allegiances undoubtedly existed. What this led to in policy terms was a redefinition of the BBC's traditional conflict between populism and purism. The familiar Reithan triumvirate 'educate, inform, and entertain' re-emerged, to be debated in a new context. Plurality of intent had been evident throughout Radio One's schedules, and once again it became a device which allowed the BBC to reform its approach to popular culture in general. If the new network was to continue to be the provider of all things to all pop people then it resolved at least to provide all things to all people at different times of the day. The era of glorious juxtapositions, cultural contradictions, creative tensions, and subtle manœuvres within grey policy areas was drawing to a close. The new situation required new processes of rationalization. Radio One began to streamline.

The new Reithians

I feel that all the fusions happening now will influence every field of art and society by demonstrating how barriers can be broken. The BBC's main problem is that it has to experiment in public.

(John Peel)[36]

Polydor Records is the next call. [Tony] Hall drives with his right hand, flips through radio channels with the left; 'It's

useful to get records on the French stations now; the kids
may start listening now the pirates have gone.'[37]

The re-establishing of a sound broadcasting monopoly in Britain
in 1967 immediately brought about a narrowing of promotional
opportunities for record companies and artists. As a result it
became important to get exposure of new product on the BBC.
By the late 1960s the words 'Radio One type material', in a
review in the pop press, was an accolade most pluggers and
promoters aspired to. Apart from the underground groups
who transcended cult following, soul artists whose appeal
was consolidated in the clubs and discothèques rather than
through radio airplay, and established names like the Beatles
and the Rolling Stones, the UK pop charts of the late 1960s
bore the unmistakable imprint of Radio One's influence. Many
new groups made the kind of mainstream pop sound that
seemed to be a prerequisite for inclusion on the Radio One
play-list. Even performers who had built their success during the beat group era tailored their approach to suit the
formula.

The light entertainment legacy also endured. Singers who
enjoyed Top Ten success at the height of what was supposedly
the flower power era included Englebert Humperdinck, Vince
Hill, Anita Harris, and Des O'Connor. After three years of Radio
One little had changed. The Top Ten selling singles of 1969,
apart from one disc each by the Beatles and Rolling Stones, and
one banned by Radio One despite reaching number one (the
infamously erotic 'Je t'aime' by Serge Gainsborough and Jane
Birkin) also included ballads by Dean Martin, Donald Peers,
Karen Young, and Robin Gibb. The biggest selling single of
that year was 'My way' by Frank Sinatra. The last two British
number ones of the decade, which had supposedly signified a
pop music revolution, were 'Sugar sugar' by the Archies and
'Two little boys' by Rolf Harris.

The dominance of the ballad sound was complemented by
the television companies' continued packaging of singers into
all-round entertainers. Career crossover opportunities into the
variety mainstream meant that between 1967 and 1970 an
unprecedented number of performers (for example Cilla Black,
Lulu, Dusty Springfield, Scott Walker, Tom Jones) hosted their

own television shows. These stars were regularly guests on each other's programmes while three or four house orchestras monopolized the residencies. Pop continued to reflect this formidable heritage, as the orchestras and chorales of the backroom boys subliminally constructed the dominant beat ballad sound of the late 1960s. The most successful songwriter of the period, Les Reed, who wrote and scored hits for Engelbert Humperdinck and Tom Jones, was a former pianist with the former Light Programme resident session outfit Bob Millar and his Millarmen. The influence of the television duopoly (two employers sharing one light entertainment tradition) was echoed both in the gimmicky and anodyne sounds which dominated the simulcast daytime schedules of Radios One and Two, and in the promotion process that had ensured their success. By 1970 hit records by groups of ex-session musicians (such as Edison Lighthouse's 'Love grows (where my rosemary goes)' and Blue Mink's 'Melting pot') were on the increase.

During this period a series of controversial and well-publicized issues challenged the BBC's integrity and caused it to be wary of some of the less salubrious aspects of record industry promotion. One that confronted Radio One was the storm that broke over allegations of chart rigging. Procedures governing promotion were tightened to clamp down on the kind of inducements that, it was being hinted, were required for a record to gain airplay, and new restrictive policies were introduced to combat bribery and payola. In February 1969 the Radio One Top 40 was reduced to a computer-linked Top 30 compiled by the British Market Research Bureau. The daytime play-list was reduced accordingly.

There had always been an uneasy relationship between the record pluggers and the BBC, and the short-lived chart rigging scandal forced Radio One to review its procedures in an area where business ethics were often at their most flexible. By insti- gating a new code of conduct for pluggers all that Radio One effectively did was legitimize certain promotional strategies in preference to others. But in the space of ten years the BBC had moved from holding pop music in virtual contempt to utilizing Radio One as a mechanism for monitoring malpractice. The new network had envisaged having to fulfil many functions when it began broadcasting, but being moral guardian to the pop world was perhaps not one of them. The policing of the airwaves showed that 'Auntie BBC' had not entirely shaken off her more authoritarian persona.

Two other issues arising during Radio One's formative years indirectly influenced the station's programming policy. The inability of television pop producers to formulate a clear policy over the issue of 'miming', and the less than startling revelation that records by many chart topping acts were actually performed by session musicians, brought the question of authenticity to the fore again. Despite a unilateral ban on miming by all television companies *Top of the Pops* had its cover blown in May 1967. The host Pete Murray introduced the Jimi Hendrix Experience, a group eminently capable of live performance, who began a bemused rendition of 'Purple haze' to the strains of the backing track for the Alan Price Set's 'The House that Jack Built.' The guidelines regarding 'miming' on television had a multitude of interpretations, and included the vocalist singing live while the group mimed (either to the record or a pre-recorded backing track) or alternatively the singer 'lip synched' to the record or a pre-recorded backing track while the group played live. Sometimes everyone mimed. It was very rare that everyone played live. When the Love Affair's record 'Everlasting love' reached number one in February 1968 it became apparent that some people didn't play at all, not even on their own records. This brought a spate of similar admissions from groups such as Herman's Hermits and the Walker Brothers. It was an open secret that the Monkees did not perform in any of their early hits. Others posed the rhetorical question: How many Beatles, did people suppose, had played on 'Yesterday' or 'Eleanor Rigby'? The entire Stax, Atlantic, and Tamla soul repertoire relied on interchangeable 'families' of session musicians. After this there was a concerted attempt to demarcate between disposable pop and artistic integrity. Questions of craftsmanship and aesthetics were back on the agenda.

Radio One had been conceived at a time when pop music was undergoing radical changes and a fundamental media reappraisal. It was during 1967 that the quality press finally discovered that it could relate to pop music, not as working-class disposable commodity, but as art. During the same year *The Times* carried a full-page advertisement petitioning for changes in the marijuana laws, signed by leading academics, doctors, lawyers, artists, and all four Beatles. In 1963 in the same newspaper William Mann had compared Lennon and McCartney to Schubert and Beethoven, in *The Times*'s first review of a pop record. Now recognition was accorded to the 'Sgt. Pepper' LP, as high cultural criteria were applied to the kind of music which would previously have been reviled by the quality press. In this critical transformation serious artists were portrayed, not as purveyors of puffery and obsolescence, but as producers of thought-provoking statements. By shifting the emphasis from passive to creative consumption the cultural establishment had appropriated a significant area of popular music's traditional domain and had transformed it in their own highbrow image. Passive pop fans disappeared overnight and became serious intelligent appreciators of rock.

The music industry having already picked up on the terminological schism that existed between 'groups' and 'bands', and between 'pop' and 'rock' recognized that by the late 1960s LPs were not only accounting for a rapidly increasing proportion of all UK record sales, but were also an indicator of artistic legitimacy, and began to exploit both these quantitive and qualitative factors more fully. 'Rock', with its emphasis on musical progression and technical excellence lent itself to a traditional high cultural critique. The climate of experimentation and excess, much of which had been genuinely uncommercial, had been remarkably short-lived, and in the face of corporate interest the underground had shed its innocence very quickly. Even the concept of an underground was effectively pronounced dead in March 1967 by its house magazine *International Times*, who in a protest against the inevitable commercialization of the moment, held a mock funeral procession at the Cenotaph. The impetus for what the media interchangeably called flower power and psychedelia, the era of 'Be-ins', 'Love-ins', and 'Happenings', had lasted less than a year.

By the late 1960s the music was increasingly being referred to as progressive rock, a loaded term which further called into question the relative merits of pop and rock. Progressive rock received strong record industry patronage and was sold as the new orthodoxy. Every major record company launched a 'progressive' record label geared to promoting its product. EMI had Harvest, Decca had Nova, Philips had Vertigo, Pye had Dawn, RCA had Neon. CBS's 'Sound of the Seventies' campaign was built around budget-price sampler LPs such as 'Rock Machine I love you', 'The Rock Machine turns you on', and 'Rockbusters'. Lavish double-page advertisements were taken out in selected areas of the music and underground press where the discriminating target audience was to be found. Advertisements in *Melody Maker, Sounds, Rolling Stone,* and *Friends* pronounced 'The revolution is on CBS' without a trace of irony. The accompanying press release read 'Don't compromise, because the music doesn't'. Both trade advertisements and press package conveyed standard publicity information, such as band line-up, place of origin, latest merchandise available, and so on. Two additional categories were significant: 'type of music' reflected the increasing categorization and fragmentation of pop and rock forms as they transmuted into a variety of shrewdly marketed jazz, folk, and blues hybrids. 'Band philosophy' stressed the integrity of the artists, and cultivated a sense of communal fraternity between musicians and audience. The philosophy for the band Flock read, 'Music is for all the people. We're doing a thing with the people. When we're ready the people are ready because we're the people.'[38]

The campaign also promoted Santana, Janis Joplin, Bob Dylan, Laura Nyro, Spirit, Simon and Garfunkel, the Byrds, and Leonard Cohen. Another CBS act, Chicago, dedicated their first LP 'to the revolution'. For as surely as a Che Guevara poster could hang without irony on a Hampstead bedsitter wall, or a boutique could be named after Chairman Mao, or John Cotton cigarellos could market a 'smoking revolution' advertising campaign complete with stereotype Mexican bandits, then it was clear that pop's own cultural revolution could be packaged and sold retail.

Radio One gradually reflected those changes in its programming and in its paternal attitudes towards those who championed minority and specialist tastes. John Peel, although never feeling that he had job security, or even that the BBC particularly understood what he was trying to do, did find that the Corporation was always willing to defend him in situations of adversity. His sometimes candid comments on issues unrelated to pop music, such as Biafra, and the assassination of Bobby Kennedy, coupled with frank admissions on BBC 2's *Late Night Line-Up* about venereal disease, brought Radio One to the attention of moral campaigners such as Mary Whitehouse for the first time, and Radio One was added to the list of social institutions to be purged of indecency and permissiveness. Peel also wrote a regular column for underground newspapers such as *International Times* and *Gandalf's Garden*, where his liberalism contrasted noticeably with the call to arms constantly advocated elsewhere by hippie politicos.

In March 1968, in addition to the weekly *Top Gear*, Peel was given a short season of the after-midnight programme *Night Ride*. Pre-publicity for the show indicated little more than late night link-ups with the facilities of Scotland Yard and the Meteorological Office. The only musical directive was that the programme would feature no needle-time product. Drily promising 'a selection of your favourite motoring flashes' on the first show, Peel, as in the *Perfumed Garden* days, found his weekly chronicle of alternatives thriving within a slot that was conceived as little more than a scheduling afterthought. *Night Ride* was more esoteric than either *The Perfumed Garden* or *Top Gear*, pursuing themes that had not previously been editorially feasible on the pirates. Access to the BBC archives encouraged eclecticism and on any one night the selection might include Tolkien reading his own works, Indian ragas, baroque music, Vietnamese folk dances, or rural spirituals from the southern states of the USA. Typical guests on *Night Ride* included an Anglican monk who talked about the influence of Gregorian chant and plainsong on rock music, Liverpool poets, Adrian Henri and Brian Patten, and various other non-main-stream, non-pop artists. Mick Farren, the *International Times* journalist, and member of the Social Deviants politico-rock group, ponderously informed listeners on an early programme that 'pop music as such is ceasing to exist', that rock was making politics obsolete, and that Pete Townsend propelling his arms while playing his guitar had a definitive dialectical meaning which 'the kids' intuitively understood. In another programme Peel prophetically advocated that more artists, poets, and musicians should independently produce and distribute their work, without relying on the major conglomerates. Occasionally pompous, sometimes paradoxical, sporadically enlightening, and often all three, John Peel's *Night Ride* was unmistakably educative and constantly attacked assumptions about how pop culture should be treated by pop radio.

Like several other Radio One innovations Peel's *Top Gear* had arisen from an uncertain programming brief. By the late 1960s the producer Bernie Andrews, who had been largely responsible for turning the programme into a show-case for the best of the underground scene, had himself fallen foul of the very BBC bureaucracy he had so skilfully exploited to get the show established.

Bernie could be a very awkward guy and didn't like to be told what was what. He would do things like not go to his annual interview. They could never get him in. The secretary to the Head of Department would say, 'Can I make an appointment next week?' and he would say 'Very busy next week'. So they would say, 'OK, how about the following Monday morning then?' Bernie would say, 'I shall be busy Sunday night and won't be in until Monday lunchtime.' He would always make things less easy. He saw the Establishment as *them*. You talk to Bernie now and he would still be the same. And so he was ideal for Peel at the start. Whereas I would not have gone that far at all. But Bernie finally got too awkward for them. They told him he would have to take on something else, and couldn't just do this one programme, spending all his time listening to records. Bernie would not accept that he had to do something else. Finally they put him 'on standby' which simply meant that on a Friday morning or whatever he was on a rota and had to be available in case anyone called in sick. And then it was down to Aeolian Hall to do the NDO or whatever. But he still said, 'I don't accept this.' Then something did come up after a few weeks and they said 'can you come in and do Frank Chatsfield and his band at the Playhouse?' and he said, 'No I've always told you I'm not on standby and I'm not.' And that pushed them into making an example. They took him off his programme and shoved him off to the World Service or something. I inherited his office, his secretary, and a certain amount of ill feeling.

(John Walters)[39]

Producers have been 'pensioned off' or 'moved upstairs' for inefficiency or lack of ideas (and in one or two cases outrightly dismissed for soiling their hands on payola), but the Bernie Andrews case is atypical. He appears to have been one of the few people employed at production level to have been admonished simply for not conforming to the rota. When the new producer, John Walters, took over *Top Gear* he continued the experimental stance of the show but initiated a further set of unlikely cultural tensions.

I would never have thought of *Top Gear*. Once *Top Gear* was going I could have kept it going but I'd have made it my style of revolution and quality which would have been far more like *Symonds on Sunday*, with more of a soul input, and Tamla, which was my underground from being a musician. Because people forget Tamla was underground. So I would have pushed it into a more jazzy, bluesy thing because the hippy thing would not have been pleasing to me.

(John Walters)[40]

This was a period when it was obligatory for musicians to apply Bert Weedon's 'Play in a day' method to the sitar, while absorbing Eastern philosophy in about the same amount of time. The same beat groups whose pop press interviews two years previously had been full of breathless accounts of being chased down the Edgware Road by screaming typists now expounded to the readers of *New Musical Express* or *Melody Maker* upon the problems of the world and the potential within their music to heal all suffering. By 1967 Eric Burdon of the Animals could state in all seriousness, in the promotion for his new single 'San Franciscan nights', 'my friends and I want you to enjoy and perhaps *learn* from our sounds.' Such pseudo-profundity readily found an environment in which to flourish as the high art principle of 'appreciation' over 'enjoyment' resurfaced in a fresh cultural context. Walters was responsible for tempering a little of *Top Gear*'s self-indulgence and complacency, editorially sifting the genuinely innovative from the derivative. Such judgement was valued within the BBC even if Radio One initially did not know how to promote it. *Top Gear* generated its own prestige, relying on contact with a scene which the BBC knew little about, even though it would have found its guiding aesthetic familiar.

> The criterion for David Symonds's show was whether it was good or bad music. When I worked with Savile it was whether it was popular or unpopular. But with John it was a moral decision. It was a right or wrong.
>
> (John Walters)[41]

1968 was a minor landmark in the annual music polls. The readers of *Melody Maker* chose John Peel as DJ of the year, an event which effectively signalled the end of the ten-year domination of 'the big four' of Murray, Jacobs, Savile, and Freeman. At the presentation ceremony, in a shrewdly stage-managed gesture, the deposed poll winner of the previous five years, Jimmy Savile, made a humorous and captivating speech before suddenly handing over the award so swiftly that it was only afterwards that the press realized they hadn't got one photograph with both Savile's and Peel's hands on the trophy. It was the meeting of two worlds, the era of pragmatic professionalism handing over the trinkets and totems of cultural power to the idealists. But Peel never felt fully comfortable with his newly assigned role; the thinking behind 'progressive rock', for instance, was anathema to him.

> The word people always used to use at the time was alternative, but I was never entirely happy with that. I saw it as being an addition. The thinking such as it is – and I've never really articulated around the area of policy – has always been: well this stuff you're listening to may be fine but this also exists. Consider this if you will.
>
> (John Peel)[42]

On Radio London Peel had been disparaging about the efforts of those who desired to package 'love and peace', but the disapproving letters from a significant minority of the *Perfumed*

Garden listenership (centring mainly on the regularity with which he featured authentic blues material) was early indication of the progressive rock audience in gestation. However, Peel had no editorial control over the ghettoization of the music he favoured, its compartmentalizing into convenient programmable categories. But Radio One did, and heralded the new decade by announcing the start of a series co-incidentally bearing the same name as the CBS campaign to market the exponents of progressive rock, *Sounds of the Seventies*. It was aired every weekday evening between 6.00 and 7.00 p.m., and a different DJ hosted each show. John Peel was allocated one slot (a repeat of the live *In concert* programme) and the others went to Alan Black, Mike Harding, Stuart Henry, and Bob Harris.

What was significant about *Sounds of the Seventies* was not the fact that the BBC had recognized progressive rock but that the way which it promoted it effectively excluded all other notions of an underground. The programme therefore indicated future possibilities for the selective packaging of 'alternatives'. Progressive rock was a recognizable part of the BBC middle-class cultural and intellectual milieu in a way that, say, soul or reggae could never have been, and enjoyed a monopoly on promotion that was denied to most forms of black music. (One BBC maverick recalls a departmental meeting in the early 1970s with a former Radio One controller who couldn't pronounce 'reggae'.) After 50 years the BBC was still distinctly ill at ease when venturing into the arenas of Afro-Caribbean dance culture.

The lineage that could be traced through calypso, ska, bluebeat, rock steady, and reggae, made little impression at all on Radio One. In the 1950s the linking of Teddy boys, razor gangs, cinema riots, and rock and roll contributed to keeping the music off the airwaves. In the late 1960s, similarly embroiled in moral panic, the undesirable subcultural presence of the skinheads was seen by Radio One producers as justification enough to avoid reggae. All forms of dance music were denied merit in this new era of artistic profundity and cerebral deities. With its more progressive strands ignored by mainstream pop radio, soul continued to rely on the clubs for sustenance. There were frequent indications of this in the pop charts of the late 1960s, with Tamla re-issues by Martha and the Vandellas, Marv

Johnson, Edwin Starr, Junior Walker, R. Dean Taylor, and the Isley Brothers, all owing their success second time around to the club scene rather than radio airplay, as did other products of the soul underground such as Bob and Earl's 'Harlem Shuffle', and the Showstoppers 'Ain't nothing but a houseparty'.

When the BBC, an organization versed in cultural hierarchy, first entered into discourse with pop culture's diversity of forms its first significant act, not surprisingly, was to incorporate those aspects which offered themselves most readily to traditional high culture criteria. Considering the swiftness with which BBC pop radio appropriated the territory of artistic experimentation in the late 1960s it is ironic that Afro-Caribbean musical forms throughout the twentieth century have often had little choice, because of the kind of cultural and political exclusion which the BBC has at times practised, but to locate themselves in the underground. The BBC's part in this process of exclusion has ranged from banning 'scat singing', and hot jazz in the 1930s, to emphasizing 'appreciation' over 'enjoyment' through the socio-anthropological documentary approach utilized by the Third Programme in the postwar years. When confronted with such dynamic and participatory genre in the late 1960s, the BBC, as in the 1930s and 1940s, perceived dance music to be superficial and transient. The rock audience, meanwhile, was depicted as united by a spirit of community and integrity which had somehow eluded pop consumers all along.

Such cultural priorities were enshrined in the editorial stance adopted by *Sounds of the Seventies*. Thus renewed, they indicated Radio One's programming policy for years to come. The new orthodoxy of progressive rock was echoed in the breathy tones and quasi-reverence adopted by several of the show's hosts, which both paralleled a similarly mellow approach to presentation that was developing in American FM radio (although *Sounds of the Seventies* was not broadcast on FM until 1972), and unintentionally parodied John Peel's natural broadcasting style. Mike Harding had a slot in his programme where listeners could request a favourite solo. These extracts were presented as examples of the virtuoso at work in a style familiar to the Radio Three audience. The quasi-classical leanings of the new music gained approval from

Radio Three itself, which began to run occasional features on the pioneers of progressive rock.

Promotional trailers for *Sounds of the Seventies* aired on Radio One throughout daytime programming were announced by Michael Wale in earnest tones which distinctly echoed the earlier CBS campaign. Wale later hosted the equally portentous *Rockspeak*, successor to *Scene and Heard*, the 'colour me' magazine programme which did not survive the streamlining of the early 1970s. Despite its ultimately distracting attempts to convey 'with-it-ness' and pace, which ran counter to its recognizably informative and educative function, *Scene and Heard* had offered a serious analysis of pop-related issues that went beyond simple promotional hard sell, and the kind of public relations plugs which masqueraded as features in the less discriminating pop music press. But the programme's demographic targeting and editorial rationale were becoming increasingly anachronistic by 1970. By this time it was becoming clear to Radio One producers that the people who wanted to hear a Neil Diamond interview were probably not the same people who wanted a preview of the new Led Zeppelin LP, who in turn were not the same people who wanted non-stop reggae. It was the growing awareness of this market fragmentation that finally killed *Scene and Heard*. Similar rationalization also brought *What's New* to an end in 1971. Its shop window function was taken over by *Rosko's Roundtable*, where each week a panel of DJs and pop personalities passed judgement on the new releases. *Roundtable* continued to reflect pop radio's friction and diversity. The appearance of John Peel and Noel Edmonds together on the programme was consciously promoted as the meeting of two worlds. In fact all that happened was that Edmonds contrived a few controversial observations while Peel refused to rise to the bait, finding merit in everything and offering a tolerant counterpoint to the mock provocation which was positively encouraged by *Roundtable*'s format.

Weeks later the seemingly innocuous pairing of Stuart Henry and Tony Brandon ended in acrimony as the editorial consensus of mild controversy was broken and the programme degenerated into a stormy argument about the relative merits of rock and pop. The incident was nervously alluded to through a smokescreen of jokey references for weeks afterwards, and

Henry never appeared on the programme again. Although the new found spirit of pop pluralism theoretically allowed the two worlds of pop and rock to exist in positive juxtaposition rather than cultural attrition, mutual hostility continued to break out. Though maligned for what was perceived as his reactionary viewpoint Tony Blackburn frequently mocked the earnest *Sounds of the Seventies* trailers whenever they were aired on his breakfast programme. In particular he questioned progressive rock's rights to the title of 'Sounds of the Seventies', claiming that the Four Tops and the Supremes were more suitable heirs. Blackburn also voiced the opinion that the genre was more suited to Radio Three.

John Peel consistently criticized the assumption that music labelled as alternative deserved no more than a slot reserved for miscellany. He saw no reason why, say, Fairport Convention or Kevin Ayers could not be played during the day alongside pop. However, Peel was also shrewd enough to realize that if he didn't promote the fringe areas few others would. Radio One's blinkered perception of new pop phenomena has, more often than not, vindicated his view. Peel's role therefore remains crucial to an understanding of how the BBC mediates pop culture.

I've always been more of a functionary in the BBC than Everett or any of them ever were, because I was a kind of safety valve, rather like Tariq Ali in his day, where the Establishment could point to him and say, 'His existence, his voice, is a demonstration that we are a liberal regime after all.' So in a way you become part of a – not repressive system, that's quite hysterical – but a conservative system certainly, because you are a kind of token figure.

(John Peel)[43]

In the late 1960s the BBC was once again confronting the problems implicit in operating public service ideals within the market-place. What was interesting about Radio One's venture into the populist terrain was precisely what had been most interesting in the past: the tensions and inconsistencies displayed. The birth of Radio One did more to make such tensions explicit than any other single factor during the BBC's history.

275

Maverick broadcasters such as Kenny Everett, producers like Bernie Andrews, and others who fell foul of protocol, helped to define the limits of autonomy within pop radio. By the early 1970s Radio One was beginning to get a clearer understanding of the pop process, providing its production staff with a sense of context and prescribing carefully formulated limits for the token outrageousness of its personality disc jockeys. This did not offer a radical break with past practices; indeed the appeal to a sense of corporate duty showed that certain institutional imperatives had remained undiminished since the days of John Reith. During the early 1970s Radio One continued to show variants on a conflict between entertainment and instruction which had first been revealed 50 years previously.

Radio One, like its parent organization, has proved itself capable of assimilating some of the most gifted and idiosyncratic cultural commentators of the times, whilst also holding court to successive regimes of reactionary advocates of the cultural status quo. Pop radio's evolution continues to be informed by the complex relationship that exists between ethical integrity and commercial pragmatism.

> The BBC is a very strange phenomenon to try and get a grasp of and understand, because it's this big umbrella underneath which there are all manner of people, a lot of them really creative and talented, but a bit sort of whacko – often the types who couldn't survive under more commercial pressures in ratings situations. The BBC likes to be bigger than its broadcasters. It was a great turning point for them to have a pop programme using someone's name, they had never done it before. The BBC would have *Midday Spin* or *Housewives' Choice* with so and so presenting. So there had always been a situation where if anyone was a nuisance they could get rid of them and put somebody else in, and the essence of the programme would remain exactly the same. To have *The Tony Blackburn Show* or *The Jimmy Young Show* ran at odds with what they were used to. They always wanted to maintain that control and that reminding of people that they are the BBC and they could manage very nicely without you, thank you very much.
>
> (Johnnie Walker)[44]

The manner in which the pragmatists deal with the structure of BBC bureaucracy makes a mockery of the stereotypes of automatons spewing forth mindless pap. They have a professional intuition which recognizes that conformity will be nurtured within the bosom of the BBC every bit as comfortably as innovation. Many abide by these unwritten guidelines to such an extent that they need not be imposed as matter of policy; the very fact that they are uncritically adhered to in itself constructs pop radio's group norms. However, because many of the BBC's public service obligations were self-imposed they remain malleable. Those working at the sharp end of pop output have certainly not hesitated to cite Reithian principles when they wished to force the Corporation's hand. This partly explains the endurance and integrity of certain mavericks, and the temporary initiatives and dismissal of others.

A theory widely subscribed to among producers and DJs alike, regarding the early days of Radio One, holds that if inappropriate work practices and personnel were initially the problem then future recruitment procedures inevitably provided the long-term answer. This familiar rationalization of options too readily assumes that such tensions can be eradicated by natural wastage. No doubt the more anachronistic aspects of Radio One's light entertainment inheritance were eroded as much by time as any other factor, but their lingering demise was in the final analysis only a grudging acknowledgement of more rapid transitions operative within pop culture in general and did not indicate any wholesale shift in policy. Because commercial radio in the UK passed from illegality to legality through the filter of a broadcasting monopoly the early years of Radio One remain crucial to an understanding of the pop process. The end of the 1960s marks off a particular stage in this process and to extend the debate further to take account of the start of independent local radio in 1973–4 would necessitate opening up new avenues of inquiry. What remains pertinent is that after half a century of broadcasting there is still no recognizably cohesive tradition of opposition working within popular music radio; there are only individual initiatives. But these initiatives remain valuable indicators of cultural tensions, tensions which continue to emerge whenever the constricting orthodoxies of pop radio confront pop culture's multiplicity of forms. Pirate radio showed that the process cannot simply be reduced to the crude 'us and them' dynamics of rebellion which continue to inform the 1960s myth. As Radio One's formative period showed, the process is also more complex than the mere allocation of monopoly resources would suggest, and while the ability of pop's administrators to swallow up alternatives and churn out legitimacy should never be underestimated, neither should the opposition.

Notes

Chapter One

1 Briggs, A. 1968 *The History of Broadcasting in the United Kingdom*, Vol. IV: *Sound and Vision*. Oxford University Press, p. 762.
2 Sykes Committee Report 1923, (cmnd. 1951) para. 41.
3 Briggs, A. 1965 *The History of Broadcasting in the United Kingdom*, Vol. II: *The Golden Age of Wireless*. Oxford University Press, p. 189.
4 Barnouw, E. 1966. *A History of Broadcasting in the United States*, Vol. I: *A Tower in Babel*. Oxford University Press, p. 133.
5 Barnouw 1966, p. 158.
6 McPhee, W., Ennis, P., and Meyersohn, R. 1953. *The Disc Jockey*. Unpublished paper, Bureau of Applied Social Research, Columbia University, p. 5.
7 Barnouw 1966, p. 179.
8 Barbrook, R. 1985. Entertainment as work: The mass media as a capitalist labour process. *Ideas and Production* 3, pp. 44–60.
9 Briggs, A. 1961. *The History of Broadcasting in the United Kingdom*, Vol. I: *The Birth of Broadcasting*. Oxford University Press, p. 63.
10 See Head, M. 1980. *The Beginning of Radio Luxembourg, 1930–1939*. Unpublished BA dissertation, Polytechnic of Central London.
11 Head 1980, p. 33.
12 Ibid., p. 67.
13 Briggs 1961, p. 361.
14 Briggs 1965, p. 364.
15 Ibid., p. 366.
16 Head 1980, p. 67.
17 Ibid.
18 Eckersley, R. 1946. *The BBC and All That*. Low & Masters, pp. 163–4.
19 Scannell, P. 1981. Music for the multitude? The dilemmas of the BBC's music policy, 1923–1946. *Culture, Media and Society* 3, pp. 243–60.
20 'The Year in Entertainment', in *BBC Yearbook 1947*. Uncredited. BBC.
21 McPhee, Ennis and Meyersohn 1953, p. 8.
22 Ibid.

23 For a more comprehensive account see George, N. 1988. *The Death of Rhythm and Blues*. Pantheon.
24 Barnouw, E. 1968. *A History of Broadcasting in the United States*, Vol. II: *The Golden Web*. Oxford University Press, p. 220.
25 Hall, C. and Hall, B. 1978. *This Business of Radio Programming*. Billboard, New York, p. 328.
26 Lazarsfeld, P. and Stanton, F. 1949. *Radio Research*. Harper & Bros.
27 Briggs 1965, p. 111.
28 Hall and Hall 1978, p. 180.
29 Ibid., p. 169.
30 Ibid., p. 181.
31 KLIF Dallas, 19 September 1986, *Tribute to Gordon McLendon*.
32 Hall and Hall 1978, pp. 180–1.
33 Ibid.
34 Briggs 1968, p. 1018.
35 Head 1981, p. 48.
36 Gifford, D. 1985. *The Golden Age of Radio*. Batsford, pp. 226–35.
37 Briggs 1968, p. 755.
38 Ibid., p. 346.
39 Scannell 1981, p. 248.
40 *BBC Yearbook 1952*. BBC.
41 *Radio Times*, various issues, 1947.
42 Personal interview, 1987.
43 Ibid.
44 Green, J. 1988. *Days in the Life: Voices from the English Underground, 1961–1971*. Heinemann, pp. 28–9.
45 *Disc*, 20 January 1962.
46 Ibid.
47 *Record Retailer and Music Industry News*, 21 December 1961.

Chapter Two

1 *Television Mail*, 29 May 1964.
2 *The Times*, 26 May 1964.
3 *Tribune*, 5 June 1964.
4 *The Observer*, 31 May 1964.
5 *New Society*, 21 October 1965.
6 Hansard, Oral Answers, 27 October 1965.
7 Benn, T. 1987. *Out of the Wilderness: Diaries 1963–1967*. Hutchinson, p. 440.
8 Ibid., p. 226.
9 Ibid., p. 353.
10 Ibid., p. 379.
11 Ibid., p. 394 and *passim*.

12 Granada Television *World in Action*, May 1965.
13 See for example Eckersley, P. P. 1942. *The Power behind the Microphone*. Cape.
14 Personal interview, 1987.
15 Ibid.
16 Murray, P. 1975. *One Day I'll Forget My Trousers*. Everest, pp. 207–8.
17 Personal interview, 1987.
18 Ibid.
19 *The Sunday Times*, 31 May 1964.
20 Personal interview, 1987.
21 Bishop, G. 1975. *Offshore Radio*. Iceni, p. 29.
22 BBC Audience Research Report, March 1965. BBC internal report.
23 Ibid.
24 Ibid.
25 K. W. Electronics Ltd., Audience Survey, July 1965.
26 Radio Caroline Press Release, October 1964.
27 *The Times*, leader, 2 April 1964.
28 *Guardian*, leader, 2 June 1964.
29 *New Statesman*, 28 February 1964.
30 Scannell, P. 1981. Music for the multitude? The dilemma of the BBC's music policy, 1923–1946. *Culture, Media and Society* 3, p. 258.
31 Hoggart, R. 1957. *The Uses of Literacy*. Penguin, p. 341.
32 e.g. Clive Donner's 'Some People' (1962), Gordon Flemyng's 'Just for Fun' (1963) Lance Comfort's 'Live It Up' (1963).
33 Whitehead, F. 1964. In D. Thompson (ed.) *Discrimination and Popular Culture*. Penguin, p. 23.
34 Ibid., p. 46.
35 e.g. Kaldor, N. 1975. In M. Barnes (ed.) *The Three Faces of Advertising*. The Advertising Association, pp. 103–45 and Simon, J. L. in ibid., pp. 147–70.

Chapter Three

1 Channel 4 Television, 13 July 1987, *The Black and White Pirate Show*.
2 Shapiro, H. 1986. *Waiting for the Man*. Quartet. pp. 110–11.
3 Personal interview, 1988.
4 Coleridge, N. and Quinn, S. (eds.) 1987. *The Sixties in Queen*. Ebury Press. See in particular Jocelyn Stevens's introduction.
5 Personal interview, 1987.
6 *The Daily Telegraph*, 1 June 1964.
7 Interviewed by PAMS Productions (UK), May 1984.
8 For a fuller appraisal of this whole area see: Evans, R. and

Novak, K. 1966. *Lyndon B. Johnson: The Exercise of Power*. New American Library and Caro, R. 1990. *The Years of Lyndon Johnson*. Bodley Head.

9 Interviewed on BBC Radio Medway, 15 February 1971.
10 Ibid.
11 Internal memo, October 1964.
12 BBC Radio Medway, 15 February 1971.
13 Broadcast transcript, January 1965.
14 Ibid.
15 *Advertising Weekly*, 8 May 1965.
16 BBC Radio Medway, 15 February 1971.
17 Radio London Memo, 2 December 1965.
18 Personal interview, 1987.
19 *Advertising Weekly*, 23 October 1965.
20 *Advertising Weekly*, 18 July 1964.
21 Personal interview, 1987.
22 Radio Caroline. Internal memo, Michael Parkin to Ronan O'Rahilly and Allan Crawford, 10 March 1965.
23 Personal interview, 1988.
24 Ibid.
25 Ibid.
26 Personal interview, 1988.
27 Personal interview, 1987.
28 *New Society*, 21 October 1965.
29 Venmore-Rowland, J. 1967. *Radio Caroline*. Landmark Press, p. 143.
30 Personal interview, 1987.
31 Original transcript of interview included in edited form in Pearson, R. (ed.) 1984. *Happy Birthday Radio Caroline*. Monitor, p. 28.
32 Personal interview, 1987.
33 Ibid.
34 Ibid.
35 Ibid.
36 Ibid.
37 Venmore-Rowland, 1967, p. 65.
38 Magarshack, D. (trans.) 1960. *Stanislavsky on the Art of the Stage*. Faber, p. 140.
39 Personal interview, 1987.
40 Henry, S. and Von Joel, M. 1984. *Pirate Radio: Then and Now*. Blandford Press, pp. 27–8.
41 Personal interview, 1988.
42 Ibid.
43 Memo, 15 September 1965.
44 Should the reader find this description unnecessarily coy he or she is directed to Everett's own autobiographical account for a more frank appraisal: Everett, K. 1982. *The Custard Stops at Hatfield*. Willow.
45 Personal interview, 1987.
46 Ibid.

47 Broadcast transcript, 19 July 1967.
48 Ibid.
49 For an extensive account of The Firm's seminal influence on rock and roll marketing (and their other activities) see Green, J. 1988. *Days in the Life: Voices from the English Underground, 1961–1971.* Heinemann.

Chapter Four

1 Broadcast transcript, August 1964.
2 See Downing, J. 1984. *The Political Experience of Alternative Communication.* Southend Press.
3 Michaels, J. Patrick. 1968. Pirates of the Airwaves: British Offshore Commercial Radio 1964–1968. MA thesis, Annenberg School of Communication, University of Pennsylvania, pp. 22, 32.
4 Personal interview, 1988.
5 Ibid.
6 Woodforde, J., *Sunday Telegraph*, 17 October 1965.
7 Personal interview, 1988.
8 Personal interview, 1987.
9 See Sklar, R. 1966. *Rocking America.* St Martin's Press, New York.
10 *Evening Standard*, London, 4 March 1966.
11 Personal interview, 1987.
12 *London Weekly Advertiser*, Radio News Supplement, 28 February 1967.
13 Ibid.
14 Personal interview, 1987.
15 Ibid.
16 Ibid.
17 Broadcast transcript, July 1966.
18 Rogan, J. 1988. *Starmakers and Svengalis.* MacDonald. pp. 76–115.

Chapter Five

1 Michaels, J. Patrick 1968. Pirates of the Airwaves: British Offshore Commercial Radio 1964–1968. MA thesis, Annenberg School of Communication, University of Pennsylvania, pp. 22, 32.
2 *The Sunday Times*, 26 June 1966.
3 Ibid.
4 Pearson, J. 1973. *The Profession of Violence.* Panther pp. 241–9.
5 Benn, T. 1987. *Out of the Wilderness: Diaries 1963–1967.* Hutchinson, p. 437.

6 Rogan, J. 1988. *Starmakers and Svengalis*. MacDonald, pp. 76–115.
7 Ibid., p. 113.
8 Hansard, 15 February 1967.
9 Personal interview, 1987.
10 *The Economist*, 1 October 1966.
11 Personal interview, 1988.
12 Hansard, 13 July 1966.
13 Hansard, 26 October 1966.
14 Ibid.
15 Hansard, 5 April 1967.
16 Hansard, 15 February 1967.
17 Hansard, 5 April 1967.
18 Hansard, 15 February 1967.
19 Ibid.
20 Hansard, 5 April 1987.
21 Hansard, 15 February 1967.
22 Ibid.
23 Ibid.
24 Hansard, 15 February 1967.
25 *The Economist*, 5 November 1966.
26 Hansard, 15 February 1967.
27 Hansard, 5 April 1967.
28 Personal interview, 1987.
29 Personal interview, 1988.
30 Personal interview, 1987.
31 *Disc and Music Echo*, 12 August 1967.
32 News, BBC Home Service, 14 August 1967.

Chapter Six

1 *Advertising Weekly*, 28 January 1966.
2 Adams, James R. 1971. *Media Planning*. Hutchinson, p. 19.
3 Personal interview, 1987.
4 Ibid.
5 Personal interview, 1988.
6 Personal interview, 1987.
7 See Rogan, J. 1988. *Starmakers and Svengalis*. MacDonald, pp. 54–81.
8 Personal interview, 1987.
9 Personal interview, 1987.
10 Ibid.
11 Ibid.
12 Personal interview, 1987.
13 Personal interview, 1987.
14 Personal interview, 1987.

15 Ibid.
16 Ibid.
17 Ibid.

Chapter Seven

1 Hansard, 12 May 1965.
2 Personal interview, 1987.
3 Hansard, 30 June 1967.
4 Personal interview, 1988.
5 Broadcast transcript, January 1967.
6 Hansard, 15 February 1967.
7 Personal interview, 1987.
8 Ibid.
9 Personal interview, 1988.
10 Personal interview, 1988.
11 Personal interview, 1988.
12 Murray, P. 1975. *One Day I'll Forget My Trousers*. Everest, p. 251.
13 *Guardian*, 2 October 1967.
14 *News of the World*, 1 October 1967.
15 *The Observer*, 1 January 1967.
16 Personal interview, 1988.
17 Personal interview, 1988.
18 Ibid.
19 Ibid.
20 Personal interview, 1987.
21 Personal interview, 1988.
22 Personal interview, 1988.
23 Interview in 1970, source unknown.
24 Personal interview, 1987.
25 *New Society*, 5 October 1967.
26 Ibid.
27 Interview in 1970, source unknown.
28 Personal interview, 1987.
29 Unidentified speaker. Fourth Symposium on Broadcasting Policy. University of Manchester Department of Extra-Mural Studies, February 1972. Transcript offprint, p. 167.
30 Personal interview, 1988.
31 Personal interview, 1988.
32 Personal interview, 1987.
33 Bill Williamson (ed.) *The Dee-Jay Book*. 1969. Purnell, p. 108.
34 Personal interview, 1987.
35 Personal interview, 1987.
36 *The Observer*, 3 December 1967.
37 Ibid., 'Promotion and two per cent'.
38 *Friends*, 31 January 1970.

39 Personal interview, 1987.
40 Ibid.
41 Ibid.
42 Personal interview, 1987.
43 Ibid.
44 Personal interview, 1987.

Index